The Little Girl That Could

A Memoir

Marianne Tong

authorHOUSE®

AuthorHouse™
1663 Liberty Drive
Bloomington, IN 47403
www.authorhouse.com
Phone: 1-800-839-8640

First published by AuthorHouse 12/23/2009

ISBN: 978-1-4490-4679-8 (e)
ISBN: 978-1-4490-4677-4 (sc)
ISBN: 978-1-4490-4678-1 (hc)

Library of Congress Control Number: 2009913714

Printed in the United States of America
Bloomington, Indiana

This book is printed on acid-free paper.

THE LITTLE GIRL THAT COULD

Little Marianne. Little Leighton. These two children, one born and raised in pre-World War II in Koblenz, Germany and the other in Inner-city Los Angeles, California, would one day meet and marry.

In 1955, Marianne, having just graduated from a Bermuda high school took a job in the Base Exchange on Kindley Air Force Base. Leighton, serving a tour of duty with the U.S. Air Force, sought to augment his salary by working part-time in the same store.

Marianne fell in love with Leighton at first sight and proceeded to enchant him. He proposed marriage on Christmas Eve that year. She accepted, and he gave her an engagement ring on Valentine's Day. After overcoming agonizing resistance from many sources, they married in Los Angeles late 1956.

Earning college degrees while raising a family of four children who now have children of their own, both have been living a happy, adventurous and prosperous life. This is their story.

MEMORIES

Dedicated to my dear soul mate Leighton

Be kind, O spirits, as the soul explores
The Caverns haunted by its familiars.
It is the time. Marianne must speak.
Grant her the strength to bring this opus to fruition.
Guide the eye through the terrible light
And let it not be blinded by the awesome dark.
As memories crowd memories, and visions blur the sight,
One shape appears to take control of life: Leighton.
Under the Oleander tree, Love grows.
There is no Triangle over Bermuda when
War-weary meets Street-wise. Nothing had prepared them
For the filmy, incredibly soft, Absolute.
Airplanes with bombs disappeared.
Crowds of skeletons disappeared.
All threats were obliterated and replaced
With the petals of Easter lilies and sweet odors
Of Hibiscus, Herculean muscles, and Heaven on Earth!
Inevitably, bliss is not blessed by all.
Prejudice, jealousy, prejudice, hate, prejudice, despair...
At every turn, the fragile embryo of new love meets
Opposition!
Has not one soul compassion for two young lovers?
Stolen moments on pink beaches; a shy hand held
In the enveloping charm of a movie theater;
Brief floating on a dance floor before the parting.
As the great machine lifts off, a final tear
Dissolves their gaze. Each is alone and vulnerable
Again.
Above the clouds, Love is propelled toward the West.
On the ground, Love slouches toward a sleepless night.
The world rejoices. Miscegenation has been thwarted
At the expense of two young hearts.
Yet love does not die. As with the wings of angels,

The great machines made by man float daily missives
Between Marianne and Leighton.

A new wonder appears: the magic of words.
Songs of longing and verses of desire make daily
Voyages across the continent.
Each soothing line erases another tear.
Each written thought strengthens their resolve:
No power on Earth would destroy their precious hope.
Time, space, and opposition would be vanquished.
Had not the world failed to dampen their childhood?
Had not two broken children grown to meet and love?
Has not the human spirit strength to transcend the wall?
There will be music; there will be light; there will be
Living Love!

KNÖPPELEE

Before the bombs destroyed it, our apartment house was one of several on the Löhrrondell, a large traffic circle at one end of the Löhrstraße, the commercial center of Koblenz. Among many large and small establishments loomed Lütke's, my mother's favorite department store.

My mother had grown up in Koblenz and learned her seamstress craft there. She had many friends who had also become her clientele after her training. One "auntie" worked at Lütke's, a Department store in the center of town, so we frequently stopped by to visit and shop. Tante Annemie would let me play with the loose button box kept on a counter in the notions department while my mother shopped. As a cute little two or three-year-old, I entertained the salesgirls and even the customers until my mother had made her purchases. Buttons are "Knöpfe" in German, so they soon gave me the nickname Knöppelee.

"Knöppelee, where is your mother?" I had appeared one day at the counter, holding a bolt of a dark red print with tiny white flowers.

"At home," sent Tante Annemie into a tizzy. I didn't know that little girls weren't supposed to go shopping by themselves. Everyone in this familiar store had always been so friendly, but now they were all excited. I was puzzled. Who, at four, realizes the dangers of independent exploration?

Friendly hands promptly plopped me on the counter to play with the button box while someone went to get my mother. She had apparently noticed that I was no longer in my room playing quietly with my dolls. The police had already been alerted, so there was much commotion when she arrived.

My simple explanation, "My doll needs a new dress," brought forth relieved laughter.

After a spanking and some crying in my room, I was allowed to watch my mother make a dress for my doll. Unfortunately, the doll, the dress, in fact, the entire apartment block bit the dust two years later.

1940 Marianne in Bedding

Marianne with Oma and Opa

THE SOUL SURVIVOR

In 1943, I was a robust six-year-old German girl looking forward to starting school. Despite the war raging in Europe, I was snug in my grandparents' care. The still-standing apartment house that my grandparents lived in had already withstood the ravages of World War I, the great Depressions, and Inflations of previous decades and seemed a fortress against all that could possibly spoil the tender blossom growing in the midst of chaos. My mother was a young woman with a husband in the German army. She diligently worked at her learned trade (a seamstress) and doggedly kept her dream of educating me alive. I had already learned to read and was filled with aspirations of going to school in September of that year.

One day before I was to start school, I became feverish. To this day I don't know whether I was simply overexcited about my impending adventure or whether one of the many germs released over Europe by its enemies caused me to get ill and panic my mother, but that doesn't matter now, anyway. At any rate, a doctor was called, and the diagnosis was clear. I had "Scharlach Fieber" (scarlet fever), an ambulance was called, I was admitted to a hospital, and my nightmare began.

The first thing that I remember about the hospital is a series of injections which I was given to "prevent" diphtheria and cure what was troubling me. I must have indicated that I wanted to know why I had to get these shots because the strangers in white explained everything to me. I drifted in and out of consciousness for an indefinite time. I was in a bed with tall rails in an enormous room which contained many other similar beds. As my perceptions cleared, I became aware that all the other beds were occupied by children. There must have been twenty or thirty of us in that ward. From the talk among the nurses I gathered that it was an "Isolation Ward" meaning that we were isolated from our parents and other members of the healthy population but not from each other. All types of diseases were represented, measles, polio, scarlet fever, and who knows what else. Somehow, I had entered the world of children who had no hope, no future, and no contact with loving relatives.

It became my sole purpose to get out of that awful place and go to school. Though I had never been in a hospital before, I sensed that this was not the place to spend the rest of my life. I wanted to see my mother, my grandmother, and anyone else who was familiar, but I was told that no one was allowed to come visit me. This seemed fair to me; after all, I had been led to believe in the adult world of authority, rules, and regulations. I was sure that adults only had my best interests at heart and believed that my protection and defense was the main point of the war raging outside. Nevertheless, there had to be a way I could get out of the extremely unpleasant situation of the hospital, and I was going to find it. At age six, I was forced to plot my escape from an unsurvivable situation. My mind reeled with impossible schemes. For six weeks I was "treated".

There were lots of injections, bad dreams, terrifying screams (perhaps my own) and waves and waves of pain. My ears throbbed. I couldn't move my legs. I was not touched by loving hands but by rough pulling and tugging which left me weak and unable to breathe. The food I received was often inedible. I had been accustomed to decent food at my grandparents' home, and now I was forced to look at a bowl of grayish oatmeal or some other concoction which was simply not acceptable to a child in my condition. I couldn't force my throat to swallow the goop which was stuffed into my mouth and usually let it drop back out. I was punished for this behavior because it messed up the bed linens and made more work for the staff.

The main staple on the menu for midday and evening meals was a combination of potatoes and apples. These two were cut into bite size pieces and boiled in water, making a sort of whitish hash that was then served in enamel bowls. Even though I had liked boiled potatoes, and was especially fond of applesauce, my overworked system recoiled at the taste of the two cooked together in this unseasoned witches' brew and yearned for a change of diet. Worse yet, the same portion in progressively deteriorating condition was served several times in a row as punishment for my stubborn refusal to eat. I often received the same bowl of "Himmel und Erde" (heaven and earth) along with lectures about the shortage of food, ungrateful children, and other unkind words

The symptoms which had delivered me into the hands of these demons were gradually replaced by behavior problems. I was convinced that I had become ill on purpose and was now behaving badly just to make the lives of the nurses more difficult. Their attitudes did nothing to make me think otherwise. They grudgingly responded to my plaintive requests and often ignored me when I had to go the bathroom. If I soiled the bed I would get punished with scolding or the subtle agony of being threatened with death.

One day, after I had contacted a virulent case of measles and become deaf as a result, I was taken into a laboratory. I remember being held in a seated position on the lap of a nurse, and a young man in a white coat approached us. I was absolutely terror-stricken and for good reason. Long needles were pushed into both my ears and the pain made me faint. When I awoke, I was on a different ward and my head was bandaged. The subsequent treatment was worse than anything that I have ever endured before or since then. The bandages were removed regularly and some gauze or whatever was pulled from my ears. Then something was stuffed back into them, and the throbbing would begin all over again.

Part of my treatment included periodic visits to the air-raid shelter in the basement of the hospital while the rest of the world played war. The atmosphere of total terror among the adults in the shelters did little to speed the healing process. Sitting in the dark silence, I had no idea what was happening outside of my painful presence, nor did I care. I became completely internal. Later in life I learned the term "autistic" which probably describes me during that time. No one and nothing existed for me except my own six-year-old person. I forgot my former life and only occasionally thought coherently. The word "Schule" (school) drifted in and out of my mind as did other isolated words that had no relationship to my conscious state. I no longer had an appetite, and began to deteriorate. My arms and legs became very thin, and food that was forced into me usually came out in spasmodic bursts of vomit or diarrheal discharge. I was, I'm sure now, dying.

The incident which finally forced the staff to release me back to my family occurred as a result of my soiling the bed.

I remember having terrific stomach cramps and being roughly lifted out of the mess. For some reason I understood, despite my bandaged ears that were supposed to be deaf, one nurse telling the one that was carrying me, "Why don't you wash her over here in the sink, at least it has hot water?" But the offer was refused and I was told that I didn't deserve to be washed in warm water and that I needed to be taught a lesson because I had been a bad girl. The nurse, a rough giant of a woman, filled a tub with ice cold water and immersed me, scrubbed me, and threw me shivering back into bed. I must have gone into shock because a doctor was called and I was declared beyond help. Not too long after that, I was dressed in my street clothes and half-carried-half-walked out to the main lobby by two nurses. They had called my mother who was waiting for me there.

I still remember the expression of horror on my mother's face when she saw me. Again I was terror-stricken and whispered, or perhaps only thought, "Don't you remember me?"

She took me home to my grandparents. There was nothing left of the robust six-year-old girl they had left behind six weeks earlier. I had become a totally deaf and partially blind skeleton, but there was enough of me left to sense the warmth and unconditional tenderness of my mother and my grandparents. The entire population of the apartment house made it its business to nurse me back to health. Warm smiles appeared in front of my eyes again. People who had practically no food for their own families brought me appetizing morsels in the hope that I would be tempted into eating. I ate. Little by little I regained my trust in people. Little by little I regained my hearing and my sight. I laughed. I made people forget that bombs were falling all around them.

PERFECT CIRCLES

How could anyone expect a little girl who had just started school after surviving six weeks in a hospital and three months in convalescence at home to draw perfect circles in order to produce a slateful of cursive *a*'s? Apparently I expected this. I was crying, and my mother was trying to soothe me.

"Come here Marianne, let me help you," my mother said as she reached for the slate. "Give me your Griffel. I'll write them for you." A griffel is like a pencil, except that it is made out of slate and sometimes screeches as it is drawn across the framed slate writing surface. We had no paper and pencils during the war and had to practice our alphabets on wooden-framed slates.

"But, Mutti, I'm supposed to do this homework myself!" I protested. "The other children have already been in school a few weeks. I'll never learn to write like they do. I hate writing!"

"Marianne, you're only six years old. You already know how to read. In time, you'll learn how to write," Mutti tried to be patient with me, but I was crying harder than before.

"I can't! I just can't!" I yelled as I ran into my room and threw myself on the bed.

Our Löhrrondell apartment in Koblenz was still intact. My room was full of toys. It was my comfort zone. The air raids had already inflicted a great deal of damage on our city, but we had been spared. The entire population still believed that normal life, including going to school, would go on. Children were still expected to learn reading, writing and arithmetic.

Only three weeks later the schools closed. By that autumn in 1943 the air raids had become too intense, and many people had left the city to escape to safer country villages. Koblenz, our home town, was effectively shutting down. My father, like all the other young men was in the military. We hadn't heard from him since his last furlough, so my mother and I spent a lot of time in the cozy apartment of my grandparents. Oma and Opa lived about a half hour's walk away from the center of town, but their street was no safer than ours. We could see a railroad station from the living room window, and train tracks, especially depots, were prime bombing targets.

"Listen, I think I hear an airplane," my mother's ears had perked up.

"No, if that were an airplane, the sirens would go off," my grandmother argued.

Moments later we heard a loud boom. "What was that?" my grandfather came into the kitchen where we were staring at each other in fear instead of enjoying the cake and coffee my grandmother had just served.

"I don't know, but now it's quiet again. If it was an airplane it was only one, not like the squadrons that usually …" my mother was interrupted by the scream of sirens. Oma, Mutti and I immediately grabbed the already packed bags and headed for the cellar that served as a makeshift bomb shelter. Every apartment house basement had been converted into a bomb shelter, but many people were killed when the entire apartment house collapsed on top of them. Yet, it seemed safer than remaining in a second or third floor apartment with windows that could send shards into a room. My grandfather had grabbed his volunteer fireman equipment and headed outside to participate in the civil patrol.

An hour later we wearily and warily climbed the stairs back to the cake and coffee still waiting on the kitchen table.

"I'm so tired of this constant back and forth," Oma declared. "I'm not going into a shelter anymore! From now on I'll stay right here," and she pointed at her pride and joy, the sparkling kitchen stove. "If a bomb drops on me, it'll be a quick death, and if no bomb drops on me, you'll have something good to eat when you return from the bomb shelter."

My mother shook her head, "You're crazy! What would I do without you? I don't want you to die," she had started to cry. I ran over to her and tried to wipe her tears away.

"Mutti, don't cry. Let's go home. I want to play with my dolls in my room," I was asking selfishly.

"Marianne, as soon as Opa comes back he'll tell us how the city looks after today's air raid. Then we'll go back to our Löhrrondell apartment, and you can play with your dolls." Mutti assured me.

A couple of hours later, my grandfather reappeared. His face was grim. "Tilly," he said to my mother, "I have some bad news for you."

"What happened? How bad is it?" I could feel my mother trembling. "Marianne and I were planning to go home and spend the night there."

"Don't take Marianne. Your apartment building is gone. The single airplane that flew over just before the air raid apparently released a couple of air mines over the Löhrrondell. The whole block is totally destroyed. The air raid kept us from getting close, but I saw it with my own eyes. It's nothing but a pile of smoking rubble now. Opa was trying to illustrate the destruction with gestures while my grandmother was slamming pots and pans around.

"I am so disgusted with this damned war! When is it going to stop! I've survived a war that was supposed to stop all wars when my children were babies! I've survived the ridiculous Inflation when money was worth nothing! I've kept my family alive through thick and thin, and I'm tired of this whole political crap that destroys more and more!" I had never seen my Oma so animated and so strong.

"Vatter, do you think there's anything left to salvage?" my mother interrupted their loud voices to ask her father.

"There's no use. The whole block is completely destroyed. It's a good thing that you already took a truckload of your best furniture to your friends in Müden," he replied. Müden was a small village on the Mosel river about twenty-five kilometers away from the city of Koblenz. Against my father's wishes, my mother had transported her most valuable possessions to Müden for safe-keeping. My father had argued that the German government's promised insurance program would replace any losses sustained by the civilian population after the victorious end of the war. My mother was skeptical. She wasn't so sure that Germany would win the war, so she had arranged to move her stuff. Now the rest was gone!

I never got to see my dolls again.

"I simply can't stay here anymore," my mother wailed not too long after that fateful day. "Have you ever heard of St. Wolfgang, a resort village in Austria?" Oma nodded. "The Allies have taken over all the hotels in St. Wolfgang for wounded British, American, French and Russian soldiers, so there's no bombing there. But no Germans are allowed into the village unless they have a local sponsor. Yesterday Lotte got a letter from her distant relatives who live in St. Wolfgang that they would sponsor us. So I'm taking Marianne, and we'll be leaving soon. She'll be able to go to school and learn how to write."

My grandmother was speechless. She had no idea that my mother and her friend had been planning to escape. My mother was resolute; she was not staying in Koblenz even if she had to walk away. Meanwhile I looked forward to going back to school

We endured a few more air raids, including one while we were standing on the platform waiting for a train to stop at the train station. As we clambered into a freight train wagon, we waved toward the apartment building where my grandparents promised to wait for our return.

ST. WOLFGANG

Shivering from cold and terror, I sat on one of our fourteen suitcases. We were escaping. The air-raids upon our city of Koblenz had become unbearable to my mother, so she and her girlfriend, Tante (aunt) Lotte decided to move to safer ground. Our little group included the two fearful young women and their two vulnerable daughters ages seven and five. I was the older one. My experience in the hospital had also made me terribly mature. Despite my own discomfort, I tried to calm my mother who was fretting about the train arriving before the next air raid on this dark night.

The platform at the train station was crowded with other people just like us. Surrounded by their bagged-up worldly goods, they were hoping to find a place to survive the war. It was late October 1944, and the city had already sustained enough damage to convince the people that Germany would not be victorious. Even as a seven-year-old, I vaguely understood the concept that simple personal survival had become more important than national pride.

Just when the sirens screamed their terrifying warning that more bombs were headed our way, a freight train pulled into the station. All the waiting people clambered on. Children and baggage were handed up. Some people were lucky enough to find an open car where they could share space with some cattle. Some of us had to climb onto the tops of the coal cars. Gratefully we rested on the black lumps as the train carried us out of the city as the bombs started to fall.

Throughout the night we traveled on. No lights anywhere. Occasionally the train stopped to avoid an air-raid. At each stop more people climbed on to head south. Our goal was Austria where the Alps would afford some shelter. Getting there was fraught with great danger.

When the train made one of its frequent stops, my mother and I jumped off to relieve ourselves under some nearby trees. Suddenly someone yelled, "Mach schnell!" (Hurry up!) We got back on just in time. What a panic!

One of the cities we passed through in the night was Würzburg. There were many fires. I was very scared. My mother told me that the air-raid was over now. As long as the train tracks weren't damaged, we could keep on moving. For three days and nights, we traveled south. My little person staunchly endured the stinging eyes from the coal dust and the discomfort from hunger, thirst and exhaustion. I lived on the promise of better days.

"We are here. This is St. Wolfgang," my mother announced one afternoon. I looked around. Snow, great mountains and a huge lake made the world seem very bright. I was reminded of scenes described in the book, <u>Heidi.</u> The cold had become more insistent. The train left without us, so there we stood. Where was the town? My mother explained that we would have to get on the ferry and cross the lake to get to the town. I was sure I didn't want to make that trip, but to please my mother, I bravely joined the crowd boarding the rickety craft. There was no motor. A couple of strong men rowed while the rest of us remained as quiet as possible.

Once we felt the solid ground of the village under our feet, I regained my senses and chattered incessantly. I wanted to know where we were going to sleep, what we were going to eat and whether I would be able to go to school. My mother explained that we would be staying with a (distantly related to Tante Lotte) family that had sponsored us. When we arrived at their small home, this family gave us some food. They were not very friendly. My mother explained that they did not want us to live with them and that we would soon have to find another place to live.

St. Wolfgang had been a resort town during better times. There were fifteen fancy hotels, numerous restaurants and a number of "Pensions" which are bed and breakfast boarding houses. In the winter, vacationers had enjoyed skiing; in the summer, water sports. Traces of the happy years were everywhere; however World War II had changed the character of this place.

Now St. Wolfgang had become a sanctuary. The fifteen hotels served as field hospitals for the Allies. The wounded military being cared for included Americans, English, French soldiers as well as some German prisoners of war. A general agreement among the Allies had made the airspace above St. Wolfgang a no-fly zone. No bombs would be dropped there. Entry into this town was strictly controlled, and only those who were sponsored by local people were allowed to come in. We had to consider ourselves lucky, but we certainly didn't feel lucky. We felt unwelcome and lost.

Finally my mother and Tante Lotte found a couple of rooms in a summer boarding house. The windows were single panes, and one free-standing coal heater was expected to provide comfort on cooler summer nights. Unfortunately, the building had not been built for family occupancy during the harsh Alpine winters. There was no kitchen, no running water, and no bathroom. A common necessary facility was located down the hall and halfway down the stairwell. My mother's resourceful talents soon transformed this temporary shelter into a home.

My mother offered her expertise in dress-making during a time when store-bought clothes were unavailable. The owner of a restaurant hired her to do all the sewing for her family in exchange for daily meals for the four of us. This arrangement proved to be very satisfactory. After months of hunger, we were eating a hot meal every day. Best of all, we didn't have to worry about bombs dropping into our soup!

It was difficult to overcome old habits. One time, when taking a Sunday afternoon stroll, we heard some airplanes approaching. We dived under a sturdy park bench to avoid being strafed. Onlookers laughed at us. They tried to assure us that no harm would come to us here. It took a while for us to accept a normal routine.

TWO WEEKS OF SCHOOL

"Mutti, I want to go back to Oma's house," I said one morning after a particularly difficult night of fearful dreams.

"Marianne, Koblenz has become too dangerous. The air raids and bombings are going on all day and night. We can't go back. We have to stay in St. Wolfgang until the war is over, and guess what! You'll be able to go to school soon," my mother's voice soothed me.

"Will I learn to write?" I wanted to master those abominable perfect circles of the cursive *a*'s. "Do you think my circles will be good enough for the teacher?"

Once we had settled into a regular routine, my mother enrolled me in school. It was a dark fearsome place for me. By age I was in the second grade, by reading skills I could have been in the fourth grade, but by my writing skills I was nowhere. What would the teacher think? How would the other students treat me? School was nothing like I had dreamed about.

"You'll start tomorrow morning," my mother explained. "First I have to buy you a new slate, a couple of Griffels and a sponge for erasing, then I'll take you to school."

"I'm scared, Mutti, can't you stay there with me?" I wasn't at all sure I wanted to go to school after being introduced. "Maybe I don't have to go."

"You were always begging me to let you go to school. What happened?" My mother was puzzled about me new attitude.

"It's so dark and cold in that classroom. And I don't know anybody. And the teacher looks scary. And…"

"Stop! You're going and that's that!" my mother ended the discussion.

For two weeks I sat miserably in the cold light- and lifeless classroom, not understanding what was going on. No one paid particular attention to me, so I did the best I could copying things from the blackboard and generally making a mess out of my slate. My handwriting did not improve, and I had to make frequent use of the grubby little sponge that had taken on an unpleasant odor in its moist canister.

"Well, Marianne, you are getting your wish. You don't have to go to school anymore." My mother announced one day.

I was puzzled. "She usually doesn't give in to me. I wonder what happened." I thought to myself as I asked, "Do you mean it?"

"Yes, your teacher and several others have been arrested. Nobody is sure what they did, but I think it has something do with being Nazis," my mother explained. "Maybe he was a spy, or whatever. I'm not even sure who arrested him, the Allies or the Nazis. All I know that the second grade does not have a teacher anymore. There are only a few teachers left for some of the older students. The rest of the younger kids have to stay home."

"Yay! I get to play with Helga all day," I was elated. 'I don't have to sit in that horrible room anymore!"

"Yes, but there better not be a lot fighting. Tante Lotte and I are nervous enough without you two little devils screaming at each other," my mother's face was stern. She had a lot to worry about, and her nerves were already at a breaking point without Helga and me arguing about the most insignificant things.

"We'll be good," I promised, but I was already looking at Helga with a satisfied smirk, "I'm older and bigger. Helga will have to do what I want," I thought as I scampered away.

SMILE, THE WORST IS YET TO COME

As the winter grew more severe, new problems entered our lives. Food was scarce, and the water pump in the front yard was frozen solid. Fuel for our heater was rationed. One cord of firewood per household was supposed to last for a whole month. It got so cold that the pillows on our beds had thin layers of ice: the moisture from our breath had remained in the cloth and frozen during the day. Despite the hardships, my mother was concerned with making Christmas a happy time for us two little girls.

From a local carpenter, she purchased several turned dowels. She made a number of cute doll dresses, and presto! we had Christmas presents. A little tree decorated with homemade hang-ups and cookies completed our festivities. The cookies tasted a little funny, but I didn't mind. I knew that despite the rancid butter, my mother had provided the most important ingredient: Love. We somehow huddled together and celebrated Christmas with sounds of "Stille Nacht." (Silent Night) I was conscious of my mother's tears and felt her sadness. That night I prayed and prayed that my mother would be happy in the future.

In reality the future held more terrors for me. In the poverty, Tante Lotte did what she could by working as a cleaning woman to earn rent money. My mother was desperate to provide food and winter clothing for us. When news of a supply of sugar and other staples available in a neighboring town reached her ears, she determined to go there. I begged her not to leave because I was terrified of her passage across the lake, but she felt she had to try.

I cried myself to sleep when my mother had not yet returned by midnight. I was sure she was dead. Early in the morning she did return, nearly frozen to death. She had quite a story to tell.

She had made her purchases at Bad Ischl. The train back to St. Wolfgang was delayed, but she decided to brave the late night return trip. When she and one other lone passenger got off the train, they realized that the ferry could not cross the lake. The lake had frozen solid while she was gone! The other person was a young man in uniform. Perhaps he was a soldier on furlough or a deserter. Who knows? In any case, he set out across the frozen lake on foot. Afraid to be left alone at the train station, my mother followed him. She was loaded down with supplies and trudged along slowly. She begged him to walk a little slower, but he headed faster and faster toward the tiny lights shining through swirls of snow. However cold and poor the village was, it would be infinitely more comforting than the icy water under their feet. For more than an hour, my mother pressed on. Now and then the ice was covered with pools of water several inches high. One particular indentation allowed water to spill over the tops of her boots. Her feet were cold and wet. The icy fear that gripped her heart rivaled the ice below her feet.

For the next few weeks, we nursed my mother back to health. She was strong. Soon she was back at the sewing machine inspiring us toward better times with stories of personal triumph over impossible situations.

One such triumph arose out of a crime of desperation. The new ration of firewood had been stacked in the market place. Each household was assigned one cord of firewood in logs one meter long and about six inches in diameter. Hoping to increase their resources, my mother and Tante Lotte stealthily dragged several logs home in the dark of night. The next day when they went to pick up their legally allotted portion, they were told that someone had stolen their cord of wood. Despite a guilty conscience, my mother was able to make such a scene that the people felt sorry for her. She was given another cord of wood, all cut to the proper size for the stove. Her ill-gotten logs were never discovered, although it was extremely difficult to make use of them. The logs were too big for our stove. With a tiny kitchen knife, she had to carve slivers that could be used as kindling, but at least she wasn't arrested for theft!

With love and a sense of humor we somehow survived this winter, and enjoyed the warming spring. News of the war brought new hopes and fears. We heard of the Russians advancing towards us, raping every female in sight and killing anyone who offered the slightest resistance. We heard of the Americans advancing towards us, taking only young women for sex and giving chocolate and cigarettes to anyone else. We didn't know which army would reach us first. My mother prepared to escape within a moment's notice. We were all packed for days, ready to move out. One sunny afternoon a Jeep passed by our boarding house. It was American! We breathed a sigh of relief. Soon a parade of tanks, jeeps and large trucks with noisy waving Americans who tossed chewing gum and Hershey chocolate bars to the children moved past our house toward the town. The worst appeared to be over. We could go home soon.

Going back to Koblenz proved to be as difficult as getting to St. Wolfgang. In the general hubbub of the American take-over and the warming season of spring, my mother became very ill. She had large boils in her mouth and was unable to eat. She grew weaker with each passing day. Once again I was afraid for her life. Just when all hope was gone, two men came to our rescue. Tante Lotte's husband and my mother's brother, Onkel Jupp, arrived to take us back to Koblenz. Despite my mother's ill health, we boarded a train.

Again, we traveled for three days and nights. In horror we saw the devastated cities and crossed make-shift bridges which creaked under the weight of the train. Now and then we had to walk transfer to another train where the tracks had been destroyed.

When our miserable little group arrived in Koblenz, we shocked all the friends and neighbors who had remained behind. My mother, whose body was racked with an unidentified infection, was barely able to stand up. I was fairly robust except for my eyes. The coal dust and other pollutants had caused them to generate a discharge which glued my eyelids shut. I had to use my fingers to open my eyes. Tante Lotte and her little girl were also emaciated and sick. We needed fresh water, food, and medicine. Unfortunately, all of these were scarce in Koblenz. Even though my grandparents' apartment house was still standing, the city we loved had been eighty percent destroyed, and we had to find another place to live.

Though the bombing had stopped, many homeless people were looking for shelter. The authorities forced anyone who still had an apartment to share rooms. My grandmother's pride and joy, her kitchen, was now occupied by another unfriendly family. The room my mother and her sister had shared while they were growing up was occupied by a stranger, and only the former master bedroom remained ours. With broken hearts, my grandparents had left their beloved home and moved to Macken, my grandmother's birthplace. My uncle and a German girl he had met in Paris lived in the one remaining room, so there was not enough room for my mother and me to move in with him. Though we were home, we had not yet come home.

My mother took me to live with my grandparents while she would regain her health and travel from friend to friend earning a living with her ability to sew clothes.

The following year my father, who had been taken prisoner of war, also returned to Koblenz. He was a broken man, unable to assume the duties of a husband and father.

Against all odds, we had managed to return to our destroyed city. Would we be able to pull our family together and strive toward a better future?

1945 Jakob Simon is tired of war

Ein Bild der Verwüstung. So bot sich am 18. März 1945 das Lährrondell einem amerikanischen Stoßtrupp. Heu
tummelt sich hier die Jugend an einem der lebhaftesten Verkehrsknotenpunkte der Stadt.

1945, This picture of our destoyed home
was taken by American soldier.

RETURNING VISION

I was only eight years old when I moved to the country village, but I was already a seasoned veteran. My sense of self- preservation had been honed to the fine point by the droning of the B-17's, whistling incendiary bombs, medical experimentation during a six-week hospital stay, air-raid sirens, and other fun events. Who knows what other unknown matters had entered my being throughout the previous four years or so. The child I should have been had mutated into a war-weary survivor.

In Macken, a village in the Hunsrück mountains, I found a safe, colorful, warm and friendly world that I hadn't even dared to imagine. My grandmother made it her business to heal me. First she got to work on my eyes which had been crusted shut by the coal dust. It had taken us three days and nights on freight trains to return from Austria under difficult and unsanitary conditions. It would be a challenge for my grandparents 'to give me my childhood back.

Both my grandparents were determined to reopen my eyes and make me happy about what I saw. With help of steaming chamomile tea, the pus around my eyelids disappeared. Little by little, things came into focus. It was summer, and there were flowers and grass and little bugs that seemed unaware of the war and its aftermath. Watching a ladybug crawl up and down my fingers and having the time to let a butterfly buzz around my nose were sheer luxury.

The little girl, who had become accustomed to running blindly for dear life at a moment's notice, began to relax and see.

THE HEALING VILLAGE

In Macken, after all the terrible experiences of air-raids, illnesses, cold and hunger, I found a new world which seemed like heaven on Earth. My mother and I arrived at my grandmother's house in Macken in late July 1945.

The house was the one my grandmother was born in. It had remained essentially the same since she left it as a fourteen-year-old girl in 1902.

It was an old two-story homestead, but it had remained intact despite the two world wars. My grandmother's older sister Katherine was still living there with her husband Nikola. The part of the ground floor which had been a small "Gasthaus" (restaurant) in better times was rented to strangers, but the kitchen and the upstairs rooms were still available for the family. There was no indoor plumbing except for one seldom-functioning sink in a common room downstairs. Primitive electric wiring had been installed, but electricity only flowed sporadically during the post-war years. My mother hated this place, but the warmth of loving arms and appetizing food which welcomed me won my heart forever.

My grandparents, Oma and Opa, had somehow transformed the upstairs rooms into a clean, cheerful apartment. When they moved from Koblenz, they had brought some furniture with them. I immediately recognized Oma's pride and joy--her kitchen stove. It was a white enamel monster with shiny chrome legs and handles, a well-scrubbed cooking surface, and a black pipe which conducted the smoke up a chimney. Smoke? Yes. The stove was a coal-or-wood burner, but it was a modern one which had a side panel with knobs for natural gas, but there were no gas pipes in the house to be connected to. Oma had to fire up the stove with wood before she could do any cooking. A few other familiar things had also been carted to Macken. The kitchen was furnished with the table and chairs which matched the precious "Schrank." (A schrank is a free-standing kitchen cupboard with decorative glass panels in the doors.)

There were some other necessary items which had been rescued from the city apartment that Oma and Opa had been forced to abandon. A couch, some books, a bed, a large framed picture, a few tools, some kitchen utensils, and some clothes and linens all had been trucked to Macken by a friend. During those post-war days everything was so complicated. No one had private transportation. There were no cars, and people had to travel by trains which were crowded and slow. A friend, Pitt, from Koblenz who owned a truck he was allowed to keep because he had also transported people and equipment for the government, had helped to move my grandparents to Macken. Whenever he had some time, he helped his friends. My grandparents were grateful that he was able to move their possessions, and to this day I have a few of the rescued things in my home.

So there I was with my beloved Oma and Opa who had seen me through troubled times before. My mother only stayed a few days before heading back to Koblenz where she would be able to earn money with her sewing skills. She knew that I would be well taken care of. Most importantly, there would be enough food for me in this country village where the people lived off the land.

1947 Marianne with grandparents Maria and Hans Küppers

Macken only had two streets laid out in a T-shape. The steep road approaching Macken passed the town's cemetery. There were about six or eight small farm houses on that road before it ended at the street that ran smack through the middle of the village. This main street branched off to the left and the right with approximately half of the eighty farm houses in the "Unterdorf" and half in the "Oberdorf" (the lower and upper village). There was a village square where the villagers met on Sundays after church. The church with its rectory was adjacent to the square, and on the other side stood the community "Backes" (a shed with two giant wood-fired ovens where the villagers took turns baking their bread). This area was the hub of town activities.

One of the most pleasant things I remember about life in the village was the way bread was baked--it was a social event! I'm not just talking about the recipe that was a sourdough work of art in itself, but the entire process from the decision to bake bread until it emerged as a fragrant, steaming loaf from the oven.

Since there were only two large ovens in the community Backes (the bakehouse), there had to be a system of time-sharing that everyone could adhere to. A tradition of drawing lots had evolved over the years that served the purpose of choosing who went first, second, and so on the next morning.

Every day at noon, those women who wished to use the oven on the following day would gather in front of the Backus. Each would bring a twig and a sharp knife. While chatting, they would then cut an inch-long piece off the twig and carve a special design into the bark. When everyone was satisfied with her token, they tossed into the upturned apron of one of the women. Another woman then reached into the apron and drew the lots out, one at a time. The order of the draw determined the order of the starting times of the following day's baking.

After chatting for a few more minutes, the women went home to prepare the dough. In a wooden trough, specially reserved for bread-making, a large amount of flour was heaped high and shaped into a crater. A sourdough leavening saved from the previous week's baking would be mixed with liquid and poured into the hollowed-out spot. Some of the flour was mixed with it and then left to rise. Later, the kneading would begin. The dough had to be kneaded several times and left to rise. That evening, the house always smelled promising. By the next day, the dough would be ready to be shaped into loaves.

The dough, along with enough wood to bake it, was taken in bulk to the Backus. Anywhere from six to ten loaves would be shaped out of the amorphous mass and baked at once in the fired up oven. Great paddles were used to remove the cinders and then push the loaves far back into the hot chamber. Sometimes there would be a little lump of dough left over; not enough for another loaf of bread but just enough for an apple cake!

A couple of apples were peeled and diced and kneaded into the dough. A bit of sugar (if somebody had remembered to bring it, or a kid would be sent home for it) was sprinkled on top of the scored round form before it was placed just inside the oven. There were always plenty of children around to wait for this special treat.

Two important public buildings: the school and the forest ranger's residence, stood at the upper end of the town. Two tiny general stores where one could purchase such items as sugar or shoelaces, a shoe repair shop, a smithy, a public telephone at the makeshift Post Office, a shepherd and perhaps a few other services were dispersed throughout the town and privately maintained. Because my grandfather had been a railroad engineer in his youth and owned a few tools, he became the handiman everyone depended on to repair broken things and sharpen knives and scissors.

The farms were tiny self-sustaining estates consisting of a residence, a barn, a stall for the livestock, a yard for the chickens and a small garden for growing vegetables. Some had a few fruit trees growing in a backyard. Only three buildings in this town had indoor plumbing: the rectory, the school and the forest ranger's home. All the farms had outhouses next to a manure pile. The manure piles were carefully tended because they were used as compost during the planting season. The homes were usually two-story houses with no running water. Each yard had its own well with a bucket on a rope suspended from a hand-cranked pulley. The water in the wells came from frequent rains which kept the water table high. There was, of course, no way to keep the seepage from the manure piles out of the water source, so all water for human consumption had to be boiled. This was one of the reasons my mother hated Macken and, in fact, all country villages. On the other hand, as a child, I was oblivious to such matters. To me, the entire village was simply Mother Nature which nurtured me.

Soon after my arrival my health, especially my eyes, improved. There was talk of school. I could hardly wait. School would start as soon as a teacher was found. Finally, an elderly man was hired by the mayor of the town. He didn't last long. All he tried to teach us was some music. We children were hungry for REAL learning, like math and language; we didn't want to sing. Good teachers were difficult to find, however. We had to wait some more. The Priest, Herr Otto Andreas, tried to fill in with weekly Catechism lessons, but we were getting very impatient. The whole town was excited when Herr Zensen, an educated man, moved into the school's upstairs apartment with his wife. His wife, Frau Zensen, was very ill, so she seldom came out of the apartment. Herr Zensen proved to be an excellent teacher.

There were around sixty students ages six through fourteen. Herr Zensen kept all of us under control in one large classroom. Sometimes he let one or two of the older students work with the little ones. He never lost his temper, but he was a strong disciplinarian. At first we behaved because we were grateful to have a good teacher. Later we behaved because he had taught us exactly how he expected us to act. Two times

1939 Marliselti with friend Martha

a week, Herr Andreas came to school to teach Catechism. On Saturday mornings, a woman from another village came to teach us girls handicrafts while Herr Zensen took the boys to the school garden to teach them horticulture. I took to this routine like a duck takes to water. I had found a comfort zone at last!

I even found friends! There was one family which had six children. I loved visiting them because they treated me as a sister. The oldest, Martha, was two years ahead of me in school. She was the one who became my best friend. We spent hours reading or doing needlework. Next was Gerhard who I had a secret crush on. Next was a set of twins,

Phillip and Elfriede, who were my age. Then came Annemarie, and the youngest was Manfred. I also befriended a couple of other families.

Our neighbors had a daughter named Hiltrud who was a little younger than I. We invented a game that kept us amused for hours and hours. We called this game "Hannele" (short for handeln, meaning trade). Each of us kept a folder with all kinds of paper scraps, such as stickers, old bills, pictures, and anything that had some print on it. We spread our folders on a table and traded. We didn't have any fancy Pokemon cards, but we took our trading game just as seriously as traders of any generation.

There were so many wonderful things to keep us entertained in village life that no one was ever bored. We seldom had electricity, so we did not depend on the radio. Television had been invented but not yet developed for public use. Personal computers did not exist. In fact, anything electronic was still far into the future. For now, we amused ourselves with the natural resources on the land. We climbed trees especially during the time when fresh ripe fruit could be eaten directly off the branches. We found nooks and crannies to play "hide and seek" in. The dusk hour was our favorite time to run around and play "catch." "Helping" the farmers at harvest time was another favorite. We didn't do much work in the fields, but the ride home on top of a hay wagon pulled by two cows over rough country roads was always an adventure.

Another pastime was watching the annual slaughters in October and November. This was almost as exciting as watching a cartoon. One of the farmers in Macken was also a butcher. He had the skills and equipment to provide slaughtering services to all the other farmers. Each family needed the meat from one large pig every year.

The slaughter started early in the morning and took nearly all day. The pig had to be "bled" by hanging it up for several hours. Certain parts, such as the feet, had to be submersed in a tub of boiling water for sanitary handling. Some of the meat was salted, smoked or canned. Sausages which would keep for several weeks were cooked and preserved. All of this took place in the front yard in full view of anyone. Groups of children gathered around to watch. Now and then a naughty boy picked up the cut-off tail and ran away with it. One time a boy wrapped a tail up and took it to my old aunt, Tante Katt. He pretended that it was a sausage sent as a present from a neighbor. She discovered the trick immediately and-took off after him with a broom, but he was too fast for her. I felt bad for her even though I laughed along with the other children. My grandmother got mad at me for laughing and punished me.

A group of us especially enjoyed playing in the small woods behind the schoolhouse. There was a fire look-out which had a platform. We climbed up and played "house" for hours. We had gathered a variety of broken dishes and other utensils as our furnishings. Peacefully, we pretended to be families living a normal life visiting each other. When we got tired of playing house, we went on outings in the woods. It was a small forest of about a square mile. There were no wild animals and no dangerous plants. In the fall, we could pick blueberries right off the forest floor. Close to the road a small building intrigued us. It was apparently the town's water pump which did not work. We could climb up on it and yell down a large vent pipe. Strange echoes from within the building added to our delight as we told scary stories.

Several other forests which were not so child-friendly, offered resources to the villagers. In late fall groups of adults went into the woods to harvest beechnuts. These tiny triangular nuts were difficult to harvest. My grandfather had fashioned a large sieve to separate the leaves and other debris from the actual nuts. The nuts were then put in large burlap sacks and carted home. At home we spent the evenings sorting them. No pebbles or twigs were allowed. When we had several bags of well-sorted beech-nuts, we carted them to the oil mill a couple of miles down the hill. For every "Zentner" (100 kilograms) of beechnuts, we received one liter of oil directly pressed while we waited. The miller kept the remainder of oil as well as the husks which were pressed into fuel for use in the winter. This was a very satisfactory trade for everyone involved. No money was needed for this deal. This oil mill had the necessary machines which ran on energy produced on the premises by a giant waterwheel in the creek. There were other mills in the area.

One mill was in a village about a mile north of Macken. This is where we took the grain, usually rye, to be milled into flour. This mill was very primitive. Giant stone wheels ground the grain. The flour thus produced was quite unrefined, but the bread baked with this flour was delicious as well as nutritious. Another mill was three or four miles south of Macken. This was where we took the wheat to be ground into finer flour. I don't remember what type of equipment was used in this mill, but their machines must have been more modern. The villages in these mountains were truly self-sufficient.

The annually-grown produce included potatoes, cabbage, turnips, beans, peas, apples, and beets. Nearly every home had a garden for fresh green vegetables throughout the summer and fall. All the farmers preserved whatever wasn't eaten. The potatoes were kept in the cool root-cellars under the homes. The cabbages were pickled into sauerkraut which was kept in large stone crocks. Beans and peas were dried and kept in bags in the home. Fresh string beans were thinly sliced and pickled. Beets were pickled. Those turnips which were to be used as vegetables through the winter were kept in dug-out trenches in the backyards, while the rest of the turnips were boiled down into a thick syrup which could be used as a spread on bread or as a sweetener for baked goods. Apples were cut up and dried on strings. Other fruit and berries were canned or preserved in jams, jellies or juice concentrates.

Overripe fruit that had fallen on the ground was especially prized! Large crocks of rotting apples, pears, plums and cherries fermented in a shed next to our manure pile. My curiosity grew as I wondered whether I would have to eat the smelly stuff brewing in those barrels. Eventually, I found out what was happening: the ingredients for Moonshine.

Whenever my grandfather decided that the fruit had fermented enough (usually once a month), he brought a large kettle with copper tubing into my grandmother's precious kitchen, and the party began. Opa and a couple of his card-playing friends distilled the fermented brew into a very potent schnapps. One time he let me take a drop on my tongue. The stuff was so strong, I could barely breathe. Opa and his friends, however, loved sipping on this brew. Naturally, they always became quite intoxicated by the end of the day. They saved the rest in bottles which would come out on weekends. There was always a battle when he got drunk. Oma and I sometimes had to sleep at her friend's house when he got too wild.

Opa was a lamb when he was sober. He spent hours in his make-shift workshop repairing broken farm equipment and making toys or other useful items. We always had plenty of food because the farmers paid in goods for his services. He loved making toys for me and my friends. Nearly every child in the village had stilts made by him. Then he suddenly came up with a design for little chairs for dolls of every size. The boys especially like the trains he made from simple leftover pieces of wood. They even had metal-trimmed wheels!

My Opa's resourcefulness even included musical talent. He owned a small "Ziehharmonika" which is a type of accordion (or concertina) with buttons for both hands. Whenever the weather was balmy, he sat near an open window after the evening meal and played folk songs for the neighborhood. When I received a 12-bass accordion for Christmas 1947, he taught me to play a few songs and paid for lessons from a regular music teacher in town.

Macken was a magic place in winter. Shiny icicles draped from the eaves and trees and bushes were frosted in intricate patterns. Snow and ice often covered the street in the upper village. We children rode our wooden sleds with shiny metal runners down the middle of town. It was difficult to stay warm enough, but the homemade sweaters and mittens helped a lot. Oma spent a lot of time knitting. I loved most of the things she made for me, but I couldn't stand one sweater she knitted with wool from a local sheep. I suspect the raw fleece had not been properly purged of the sheep's "dinkleberries" before it was spun into yarn.

Every fall the town shepherd sold fleece of raw wool directly off the shorn sheep. First the hanks had to be washed and bleached. Once the wool was dry it could be spun. Almost all the elderly women in town owned spinning wheels. In the evenings, after the day's work was done, they loved sitting around, spinning the wool into thin strands of yarn while making small-talk. Sometimes I got to help wind the yarn into balls. Often the pungent smell of the natural sheep's wool was not washed out adequately. Consequently, the garments knitted from this wool had the same pungent aroma. Even though I appreciated my grandmother's effort, I hated to wear the smelly monster she had created just for me.

Among the most pleasant things I discovered in Macken was a cemetery. A cemetery pleasant? Yes. Just outside the village, this very special fenced-in garden welcomed me whenever I wanted to be truly alone and safe. The villagers customarily planted lots of flowers on all the graves. There was a special corner for children who had died before they turned six. Their headstones were decorated with angels of white marble. The inscriptions on the graves simply declared the existence of a person from one date to another, but I walked among the graves, reading and thinking of the people under the ground. At other times I thought long and hard about Jesus in the Garden of Gethsemane, trying to imagine what it must have been like for him. I often stopped to pray by the particularly large headstone of a village priest from long ago.

Sometimes I took a couple of friends with me to visit the "souls" in the graveyard. We sang and walked around happily, but we never disrespected the spirit of the place. We talked about the things that might have killed the people buried there. It never occurred to me be afraid. It was a place of eternal peace.

Whenever I think of Macken, a warm fuzzy feeling envelops me. Memories blend into a great satisfying, healing whole. The unconditional love of my grandparents, the resourceful locals, the mischievous children, the seasonal changes of the land and its rich harvests have given me a lasting respect for life on Earth. In 1945 I had arrived as a broken little girl. By 1950 I was ready to take on the challenges of a future in a completely different world.

THE JOURNEY BEGINS

The devastation that followed the war included the broken marriage of my parents. Neither one was able to mend the other's broken heart, and their no-fault divorce with joint custody of their only child, Marianne, became final in 1947.

My mother had married an American Air Force Sergeant and emigrated in 1949. She had left me in Macken with my grandparents in the hope that I would join her in Iowa after certain documentary procedures were fulfilled. My father was not so eager to let me leave Germany and bargained with my mother for my future.

Eventually the arrangements were finalized, and I was told of the opportunity to travel to America. Since I was only thirteen years old at the time, I was going to be accompanied by a German couple who was also emigrating.

I felt quite confident that I was equal to the adventure and eagerly counted the days until I could join my mother in America.

My grandparents and friends were not quite so eager. I remember that the last few weeks in Germany became quite tense. I had constant arguments with my grandmother. We were both on edge. There were several villagers who told me in plain language that I would never be happy or that my mother wasn't really planning to take me to America, anyway. I was going on simple faith. I knew that my mother was already in America, that my father was finally willing to let me go, too, and that was that! My mind was made up, and mentally I was already on my way.

The day I left the village, a very large group of people came to the bus station to see me off. The priest, who had been my moral support and beloved mentor, was there offering me his blessing and confirming my faith in myself. My teacher had given me lots of advice. My school friends hollered encouragements as my grandparents and I boarded the bus. As we rumbled through the countryside I felt tremendously important. Somehow I sensed how much hope was pinned on me. I had been a child of the war. The villagers had nurtured me knowing that I was not one of theirs and that I would leave again one day. They had known, so they filled me with the wisdom that comes from living within the earth. I had been an alien accepted with love, educated in their ways, and sent on my way into the greater universe to vaguely familiar places. The names of my destinations were the same names of old enemies. Would this child become one of them? My heart sensed my destiny. I was young, but I had read numerous books and was awed by the role I was chosen to play in the human drama.

As the bus rumbled through the beautiful forests of the Hunsrück, I waved Macken good-bye and neared Burgen by the Mosel River where we would catch the train to Koblenz.

We spent a few days in Koblenz saying goodbye to various friends and relatives. My father and my uncle were to accompany me to Frankfurt where I would board the train to Genoa, Italy. From there I would travel alone. The couple who had been assigned as my travel chaperones had been denied a passport at the last moment. Apparently, they had not been properly denazified after the hostilities, and their travel plans had been delayed. I was asked whether I was willing to travel unaccompanied and given the choice of waiting for the paperwork to be straightened out. Being more afraid of my own documents expiring and perhaps never getting to America than of making the trip to America without direct adult supervision, I insisted on leaving. Secretly, I was glad that I would not have to answer to strangers for my every move and welcomed the opportunity to assert my own maturity. How many children get the chance to step into adulthood in such a gloriously independent and unmistakable manner?

The moment of truth had arrived. We stood around in the train station awkwardly trying to make sense out of the situation. My grandfather was offering last minute tips on how to deal with strangers. My grandmother gruffly tried to shut him up while my uncle and my father took care of the tickets and the luggage. I remember trying to convince everybody that I would be just fine. Their fears made me strangely nervous, and I had moments of wanting to throw myself against them and beg them to keep me there. Visions of my mother and a future stepfather confused me further, and I was grateful for the matter-of-fact voice that announced the departure of our train. The world apparently cared little about my confusion and was willing to accept me as a full-fledged traveler

With Koblenz fast disappearing and Frankfurt materializing as my next goal, I became clear-headed again and busied myself with the immediate details of the impending journey. I still had the two strong men at my side. Although my father and my uncle were supportive, they were subdued. They listened in awe while I chattered on about all the things I would see and experience between Frankfurt and New York. They had never sailed the oceans themselves and couldn't deny my childish dreams. They must have sensed their parts in a greater drama. Looking back through the misty light of memory, I can understand the worried expressions on their faces. They were sending a thirteen-year-old girl into the world alone!

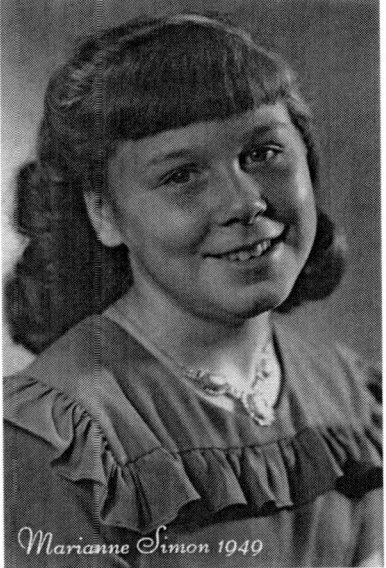

Marianne Simon 1949

BOUND FOR GENOA

Our arrival in Frankfurt was relatively uneventful. We stopped to eat a Bratwurst and play the "Groschenmaschinen" which were the popular slot machines of Germany. I was, of course, quite excited and eager to get on with my adventure, and had little time for caring about the feelings of my uncle and my father. They seemed part of another world which I was rapidly leaving behind, and I was barely conscious of their existence. Finally it was time for me to board the train which would take me to Genoa, Italy for the next leg of my journey.

After all kinds of last minute instructions, including my father's short lesson on bartering with souvenir vendors instead of paying their marked prices, I climbed into the waiting train. I double-checked my belongings. I had taken everyone's warning that people would try to steal my things very seriously, but my grandmother knew just how to fortify me with the knowledge that no one could get at my treasures without my consent. Sewn into my underwear, a little pocket hid what little money I had from the ever-grasping world. Two suitcases packed with clothes and a few presents for my mother from well-wishers, and the accordion case carrying my most precious possession, a 12-bass Hohner accordion, made up the bulk of my baggage. I also carried a small back pack containing my passport, my ticket and a roll of cookies from a friend. As I clutched all my earthly goods and took inventory over and over again, I sensed the great upheaval of whistles, loud voices, and conductors slamming the compartments shut. I was off. A quick look out of the window confirmed my departure from familiar faces. Soon my heart beat in unison with the clickety-clack of the moving train.

This was not the first time I had been on a train. As we rolled along, I reflected on some of my other train rides.

My mind went back to a cold October night in 1944. The bombings had become so intense over Koblenz that the greater part of the city was destroyed. Our apartment building had become a casualty while my mother and I were visiting my grandparents. We were now living between air-raids in a crowded apartment near a railroad station that seemed a likely target for future bombings. Escape from the terror became my mother's only desire, so she made arrangements to go with a girlfriend to a sanctuary in St. Wolfgang, Austria. "Go" sounds so easy! As we waited for the train on the drafty platform in the dark, an air-raid siren sounded in the vicinity warning of yet another bombing. We, two terror-struck young women and two little girls, stood shivering and silent amid our fourteen pieces of luggage, not knowing whether one of those chunks of exploding metal would come our way. A freight train finally arrived to carry us away on top of a full coal car.

Compared to that horrible ride, my present appointments seemed the lap of luxury!

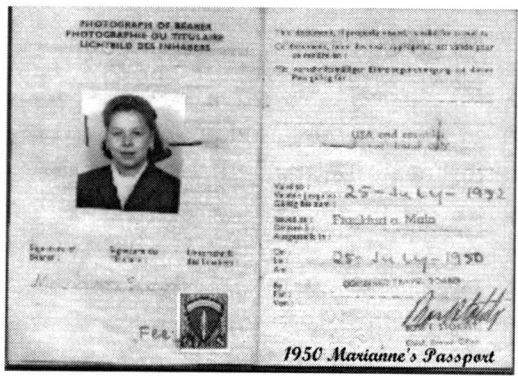

1950 Marianne's Passport

As the train rolled comfortably through Switzerland toward my destination in Italy, that other trip faded into a dream and my immediate needs demanded my attention. I began to get hungry and nibbled on the delicious cookies. I knew that my meal in the dining car had been paid in advance, but my fear of leaving my baggage unattended caused me to remain steadfastly in my seat. A kindly-looking conductor tried to assure me that my things would be safe, but I didn't trust him. I had been warned about kindly-looking people who cheat travelers and had no intention of being duped. I quieted my rumbling stomach with another cookie which didn't taste quite as good as before. The importance of keeping my possessions safe, made my hunger a trivial nuisance, and I thought no more about it.

Toward nightfall, the conductor reminded me that I was entitled to sleep in a berth. This was welcome news. I could take my suitcases into the compartment and lock the door to keep would-be thieves out. Ticket and passport checks behind me, I retired for the night.

The next morning, I awoke with a terrible taste in my mouth. Eating only a few miserable cookies the previous day had done nothing for my breath, so I eagerly began to wash up. My morning toilette was nearly complete when I discovered that I had neither hairbrush nor comb. I searched in vain. A young woman on an international voyage couldn't be seen in public with disheveled hair, could she? I thought about my problem for a while and came up with the brilliant idea of using my toothbrush to do my hair. I was quite pleased with the result and smugly stepped into the crowded passenger compartment, confident about my appearance.

Had I only been that confident about going to the dining car! It became more and more difficult to ignore the pleading of my stomach, but I was not yet ready to yield. I forced down a disgusting cookie.

Soon my attention was distracted again, however. Two ladies, speaking Italian, seemed very curious about me. They started to talk to me. Speaking only German, I couldn't engage in a lengthy conversation, but we did find a few common interests. With much hand-waving, pointing at signs and reading tickets, we suddenly discovered that I was on the wrong train!

The panic that welled up inside me became a monster. The conductor did his best to reassure me that it was not too late for me to get to Genoa. We were going to make a stop in Milano. If I was lucky the train to Genoa would still be in the station, and I could board it. I dared not think about what would happen if the train had already left.

As we pulled into the train station, the conductor showed me a train on the next platform. He and the two women were almost as relieved as I was. Hurriedly, my suitcases were placed on a porter's cart. A few Italian words were exchanged, and I trotted off towards the other train. The porter managed to get my luggage aboard, but refused to let me follow. He held his hand out. I was confused for a moment but soon realized he wanted money. I had no Lira and only a few dollars with me. Rather than let a little girl go, this man made me go to a money exchange window for his tip! I was stunned. What if the train left with my luggage but without me? Rushing around in a panic, I somehow managed to pay him and board the train just as it began to pull away.

I fell into an empty seat next to an elderly man. As soon as I said the first word, he identified himself as a German. He calmly assured me that we were indeed going to Genoa. He was astounded at my undertaking and wished me lots of luck. I would need it.

After about two hours the conductor yelled, "Genoa." My heart jumped. I dragged my luggage onto the platform and just stood there for a moment. I was looking for a man from the Red Cross. Arrangements had been made for such a person to take me to a hotel on the day of arrival and then take me to the ship the next day.

Suddenly, I felt someone grab one of my suitcases. I yelled, "Nein!" (No!) It was a porter trying to help me with my luggage. No way. I remembered the incident in Milano. I had been strong enough to carry my stuff before, and I was not going to spend any more money on unfriendly porters. We were still struggling over my things when the Red Cross guy arrived. Impatiently, he listened to my story. Then he grabbed one suitcase and told me to follow him.

We drove for a while in a taxi through some dirty streets. We stopped in front of a small hotel, Ristorante Firenze. In the lobby, I had to surrender my passport before being escorted to my upstairs room.

"What!?! Am I supposed to sleep in here? It's a bathroom!" I yelled as the door opened.

"This is the only room we have left, young lady. You can lock it from the inside, and no one will bother you." The manager assured me.

RISTORANTE FIRENZE

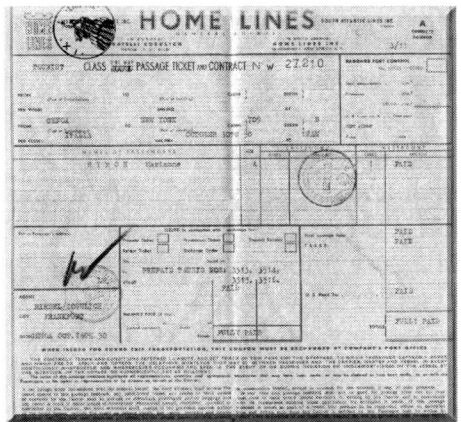

So, here I was, a world traveler and adventuress extra-ordinaire, expected to sleep in a bathroom in a dingy hotel in Italy! I knew I could manage for one night, so I accepted the key and decided to settle down. My immediate need for food urged me to go back downstairs to the dining room and try to talk to someone.

They understood. The meal, though served courteously, was not exactly my taste, but it filled a void. The next problem I had to solve was a little more difficult. My grooming the next morning would suffer greatly unless I acquired a comb and a new toothbrush. I convinced a fellow guest to walk with me to a flea market I had noticed on my taxi ride from the depot. The brisk walk in the balmy Italian evening completely revived my sagging spirits. After purchasing a few necessities, I regained the confidence to go on with my fantasy.

Back at the hotel I was not so sure. I looked the bathroom over very carefully. There seemed to be no rats, and it smelled pleasant. Sleep was unlikely that night, however. Being used to an outhouse on a farm, I was terribly afraid of indoor plumbing. The environment nearly overwhelmed me, but a kindred soul in another building across the alley kept me sane by serenading the world and me with heart-searing renditions of "O Sole Mio" until three o'clock in the morning. I finally dozed off and awoke to a bright new day.

Joyfully I got myself ready for breakfast. This was the day! The food was nice, but the bill was not. My family had assured me that all my expenses on the train and at the hotel were prepaid. The effect of seeing a bill for first-class accommodations next to my eating utensils was immediate.

The cute little thirteen-year-old German girl was suddenly transformed into a raging lioness. How dare they charge me for something that had already been paid for and was a miserable mess, besides! I stormed to the manager's desk and threatened to call the police. He tried to calm me down but insisted that I pay him the money or I wouldn't get my passport back. By the time the man from the Red Cross came to escort me to the harbor, the situation had deteriorated to loud name-calling, and a crowd had gathered to watch the melee.

Knowing that there was still plenty of time before my ship was to heave anchor, I insisted that we clear up this misunder-standing at the American Consulate. A puzzled taxi-driver took our angry threesome straight to the Consulate where the matter was quickly resolved. I did not have to pay, and furthermore, the manager was to return my passport to me, so that I could get on with my trip. I was beginning to sense that all three of them would be glad to get me out of Italy.

After picking up my things at the hotel, the man from the Red Cross, who had by now acquired a noticeably respectful posture toward me, accompanied me to the harbor. He dropped me off with profuse good wishes and a sigh of relief.

It wasn't long before I met several other Germans who would also be traveling on the SS Italia. In 1950, Germany had no shipping, so passengers had to sail via Italian liners. Waiting for our call to board ship, we solidified into a lively little group. I was certainly happy to hear German spoken even though I was presently talked out of some of my money.

One of the ladies seemed quite distraught. She felt it absolutely necessary to send a telegram which would cost ten dollars that she allegedly didn't have. Her story sounded so sincere that I was willing to part with half my pocket money in order to abate her distress. For the rest of the trip, she was eternally grateful to me and missed no opportunity to praise me and do things for me. She was sure that because of me, her American husband would be waiting in New York and ready to welcome all of us into the promised land.

Without any guarantees that the world was round, we embarked upon the open sea. I had read stories about Christopher Columbus being born in Genoa and eventually discovering America, and now I was ready to follow in his wake, so to speak.

I'LL GET BY

Without a word of German, a steward welcomed me aboard the ship. After careful examination of all my paperwork, he escorted me to my cabin. Down, down into the ship we went. Steep metal stairs. No windows. The resemblance to some of the bomb shelters I had experienced only a few years earlier weakened my knees. "I'm going to America. I'll soon be with my mother." The steward was amused at the chatter I used to comfort myself. He was just doing his job; I was risking my life!

My cabin was just large enough for four bunks with a narrow passage between them. One lady in the cabin told me in German that the top right bunk was for me. The two bottom bunks had already been taken by our two other roommates. I was surprised that no one was making a big deal out of my being a kid. After letting me get a quick look around the cabin, the steward matter-of-factly showed me the showers. He pointed to a sign which indicated in several languages, including German, that the water in this facility was saltwater and not drinkable. After leaving this pleasurable little place, we continued our tour of the ship. I followed him like a lamb being led to the slaughter although I felt an excitement welling up inside of me. This was not the dream of going to America; this was the real thing!

Chattering continuously and without being understood, I followed the steward across decks and up and down hallways. I was getting into the swing of the ocean voyage until I got to an opening from which emanated loud metallic clatter. Through the opening, I saw a catwalk, a very narrow hanging bridge above a non-passable space. It immediately became clear to me that this was only the way to the dining room. The space below was an engine room! From the years of thunderous air-raids and cage-like bomb shelters, I had become fearful of all metal things that made noise and avoided them despite their peaceful purposes. My heart stopped at the sight and sound of the loud machinery just below me. I imagined it grinding me to bits if I lost my footing or if the catwalk should suddenly collapse. The thought of having to walk back and forth across this abyss for every meal made me lose my appetite. I looked helplessly at the steward and hesitated setting foot on my lifeline to food for the next two weeks.

The steward smiled and held my hand as he led the way over the danger. Another door or two and the scene changed again. Now I was in an elegant dining room with tablecloths and flowers. Some people were already sitting at tables engaged in pleasant conversations. These people appeared unconcerned, so the memory of my fearful experience quickly faded. I heard happy voices and smelled food. The steward showed me to a table and then excused himself. Soon I was nibbling on my first shipboard meal. There was no German bread or potatoes, but for a hungry girl there was enough to live on. I would deal with getting back to my cabin later.

When I got back on deck, I realized that the ship had begun its voyage. We were sailing on the Mediterranean Sea, and Genoa was slowly fading into the distance. I looked around at the other people on the deck. Even though I didn't see a single familiar soul, I felt quite comfortable among my fellow human beings. We were all on a common adventure! Come what may, for the next two weeks, all we had was the ship to carry us to the promised land. Most of the people were speaking Italian or English, but that didn't worry me. I had a place to sleep, eat and get cleaned up. I had my suitcases with my clothes, a few toys, my paperwork and, most importantly, my accordion. Even without talking, I would make it through the next two weeks and meet my mother.

Suddenly I saw the lady who had borrowed ten dollars from me on the pier in Genoa. She was speaking German to another young woman. Nonchalantly, I joined them. From them I heard that there were about a dozen other Germans aboard the ship. This was good news! Some of them even spoke a little Italian or English to help translate, if necessary. This trip would be fun, after all.

"Waldeslust" had always been one of my grandfather's favorite songs, and he had taught me to play it on the accordion. Now I had the opportunity to break up the boredom of water, water everywhere with my music. My new-found friends liked watching me make a fool of myself, and I didn't mind playing the two or three songs I knew over and over again. It certainly helped to pass the time until we got to Naples, Italy.

A scheduled stop at Naples for several hours was too good to waste on a ship. My friends were making plans to tour the city and invited me to join them. I asked, "It this going to cost any money?" We were all quite poor.

"Let's just walk around and see what there is," said Annie Koch.

As the seven of us debarked, we saw posters next to taxi drivers offering rides around town for "one American Dollar, that's all." One of the taxi drivers gestured that he would let all seven of us ride for only six dollars. We looked at each other and decided to take a chance. With great courage, I pointed at the sign and shook my head vigorously and tried to make him understand that we wanted a bigger discount for the seven of us in one taxi. He smiled and wrote a big five on a piece of paper. I grabbed the pencil out of his hand, crossed out the five and wrote a four. He threw his hands in the air and then with a big grin let us climb into his cab.

One of the stops on this one-hour tour of Naples provided us with a view of Mt. Vesuvius, an active volcano. A street photographer took our picture. Here was another opportunity to haggle for a bargain! Again, I proved that my father's advice not to pay the full asking price to street vendors in Italy was true. The other ladies just let me take charge, and I was gaining confidence by leaps and bounds. I had left my sheltered life in Germany only three days earlier, and already I felt like a seasoned world traveler. Shortly after returning to the ship, we set sail for tomorrow's stop, Rome.

It was announced that we would not have much time in Rome, so no plans to go sight-seeing were made. The ship appeared to become more crowded. None of the people who boarded in Naples and Rome were German. An American family with children came aboard, and I noticed that several boys and girls my age came to the dining room that evening.

The next day the ship made a short stop at Palermo, Sicily. I went on the dock briefly to look what the vendors had to offer. I bought a white pearl rosary in a little metal box shaped like a bible. My money was dwindling, but there would be no need for money once we began the actual crossing of the Atlantic Ocean. As of this moment, we had not yet left the sight of land. We had been traveling down the length of Italy, and now we were about to pass through the straits of Gibraltar, familiar to me from an old Atlas.

Throughout the years with my grandparents, I had spent countless hours studying the few books they owned. There was a Holy Bible, a beautifully illustrated, leather-bound version of **Arabian Nights**, a set of out-dated almanacs, and a world atlas. A few children's books and some movie magazines completed the collection. For years I had memorized exotic names and geographic outlines and imagined myself traveling the world a thousand times. Now I would actually see the Rock of Gibraltar.

It was twilight. The sea welled up higher and higher as we left the calm Mediterranean Sea and approached the Atlantic. Nothing deterred me. Along with a dozen or so other brave (or foolish) souls, I stood awed in the bow of the ship. At our right, Gibraltar rose out of the water like a mighty fortress as we passed into the Atlantic ocean night.

For an hour or so, I could not tear myself away. A salty wind whipped my hair and tore at my clothes, but I didn't care. I was involved in a more important experience. There it was, no longer a flat outline on a paper map; I was looking at the real thing! Gradually, another thing that was real caught my attention. I became aware of a yucky cold feeling creeping over me. I needed to take a warm shower and get the salt out of my hair.

It's a good thing that I was still thrilled about seeing Gibraltar because the shower proved to be a big disappointment. There was no hot water, so I had to shower in the cold saltwater. Fortunately, the sink had fresh water to rinse my hair. A couple of ladies took this opportunity to yell at me about wasting the fresh water meant for brushing their teeth. Feeling guilty as well as salty, I crawled out of the bathroom like a whipped puppy and curled up on my bunk for a couple of hours.

A strange sensation in the pit of my stomach suddenly entered my life. At first I didn't understand it. When I mentioned it to Annie, she explained, "We're sailing on the Atlantic Ocean now, and this is November. The ocean is not as calm as the Mediterranean Sea. The ship is moving up and down and you are getting sea-sick." She was right. I was able to nibble on an orange or a hard dinner roll, but anything else came right back up.

As we approached Lisbon, Portugal, people cheered at the chance to walk on solid land again. We would have nearly six hours before we would have to get back on the ship. Our little German group decided to walk around the city and look for some souvenirs. It was a beautiful sunny day, and the city was very clean. On the pier, I was pleased to see vendors, offering items for sale. By this time, I looked forward to the challenge of bartering for a "bargain." I saw a straw hat costing ten American dollars which I bought for three. I also bought a pair of little handmade dolls in Portuguese costumes after haggling for a lower price. My friends just shook their heads and smiled.

Back on the ship, I was getting quite comfortable as we settled in for the uninterrupted ocean crossing. I had discovered a game room where I occasionally saw the American boys and girls play cards. One day, I tentatively approached them and heard them speak English as they played their game. With gestures and a few words, they invited me to play. I loved to play cards, and my grandfather had taught me many games, but I didn't know the game they were playing. After they let me know that this game was called Canasta, they started teaching me. It was the first time I realized that learning something had nothing to do with the different languages people use. We were able to communicate very well, and we met several times throughout the trip to spend an afternoon playing Canasta. The one thing that I regretted was that I could not afford to buy a drink while the other kids had money for a soda.

One of the attractions on deck was the sighting of whole schools of dolphins. Within picture-taking range of the ship, about twenty or thirty big creatures would arch out of the water gracefully and dive in again. People on deck went, "Oooh! Aaah!" at the sight. Of course, I had no camera, but my mind's eye can recall the thrilling sight. Several times the dolphins put on the show as we passed through their domain.

Another show I enjoyed aboard the S.S.Italia was the movie, *I'll Get By*. It was the first American movie I had ever seen, and I especially loved the music. To this day I have fond memories of Ann Blythe and Dennis Day.

Gradually, I became accustomed to the heaving and rolling of the ship. In the daytime I walked with confidence on the deck and was able to tolerate the strange Italian food even though my entire being craved the familiar taste of German bread. Even though I was looking forward to my new life in America, I began to miss the life I had so eagerly left behind. Visions of my grandmother crying for me and my grandfather making toys for somebody else made my heart ache. After a good cry, I played the accordion or took out my doll to comfort me. The nights seemed interminable. In the tiny cabin with three other people, I couldn't do anything but be quiet. Doubts began to creep into my thoughts of the past and the future, "Did my family in Germany stop loving me when I left? Will my mother really be waiting for me when I get to New York?" Sleep salted with tears brought some relief until the light of day invigorated me once again.

The landing in New York was scheduled for November 14. We would be passing the statue of Liberty at five o'clock in the morning. I had every intention of getting up early enough to witness the dramatic entry into the New World, but by the time I got on deck, the ship had already passed the landmark. It was a very foggy morning, and my friends assured me that the statue was very difficult to see, anyway. As the sky-line of New York City grew more distinct, my heart wanted to jump out of my body.

"Mutti, Mutti!" I screamed as I saw my mother's beautiful face in the crowd on the covered pier. There she was, awaiting our arrival. We waved vigorously to each other. I knew it would still be an hour or so before I could get off the ship and then I still had to go through customs. Now that the ship was docked, and I was looking directly at America and my mother, I could wait. Nothing mattered, I thought. Nothing mattered, except my accordion.

After walking off the ship with all my belongings, I had to place everything on a long table for the customs inspection. A mean-looking man ordered me to open my suitcases. He barely gave me time to hug my mother. I was afraid without knowing why and clung to my mother. After looking through all my stuff, the man yelled something in English at my mother. She explained to me that he would have to take away my accordion. "Why?" I screamed.

"The Hohner Company which made this accordion had also been involved in building weapons for Hitler's army," she explained. "Now the American government won't let any of this company's products into the country. You'll have to give up this accordion."

Now the screaming started in earnest. At first I yelled all kinds of German at him. When he didn't understand, I lost all control. I grabbed the accordion and put up such a ruckus that people started gathering around us. Finally, the customs agent relented, "Okay, let me have this crystal butter dish, and you can keep your accordion."

The butter dish in my suitcase was a gift to my mother from my grandmother. We were reluctant to let it go to this brutish man, but he was adamant. Either the butter dish or the accordion had to be sacrificed to the U.S. government.

Just then the lady who had borrowed ten dollars from me in Genoa came running toward us. "Here's your money. Thank you so much for helping me. Because of your kindness, my husband was able to come pick me up here in New York." My mother looked puzzled. After I explained the story to her, she took a long look at me, "You are really something. I'm going to enjoy getting to know you as a mother should know her daughter. Welcome to America."

THE LANGUAGE OF THE ANGELS

After I arrived from Germany, I became a different person. I realized at once that I would have to change completely from that bold and adventurous young lady who had talked her way across an ocean into a submissive child who had to obey her mother.

I don't quite know how this change came about, or why, or who was the most instrumental in bringing it about. I only know that I no longer had the chance to fight it out with hotel managers, customs officers, or men from the Red Cross. Now I know, of course, that I should have asserted myself a lot more to the right people, such as teachers, doctors and others in authority.

At the time, however, my mother did not want me to bother other people with our problems and I was persuaded to blend into the mass of teenagers as soon as possible. A face in the crowd, so to speak. Not making waves.

Somehow I managed to accomplish this. Now I can see that my accomplishment was actually the destruction of a very important part of me. I became withdrawn and antisocial. It took years for me to overcome the culture shock.

The age of puberty is difficult enough with the generation of hormones and the recognition of the opposite sex. The additional responsibility of having to forget one's customary way of thinking can, and did for me, cause irreparable damage. Because of my extreme self-consciousness about the words that came out of my mouth, I spoke very little for nearly a year.

My school work was, as a result, excellent. That sounds strange, but it was true. I spent hours memorizing spelling words. At test time, I nearly always got 100%. My math was already very good because mathematical symbols are identical, and all my homework was on time, neat, and correct. Other subjects, such as art and science also required more written work than social skills. There too, I got good grades. Teachers praised me. I was learning **English.**

There was, however, the unhappy fact that it was terribly important for me to forget all that I had learned in Germany. Not only were my German **language** skills useless in school but also my memories.... Hitler and World War II were expected to disappear in the joyful abandon of the American way. Unfortunately, they didn't.

They were merely suppressed and surfaced to haunt me again much later.

STUDY ONE LANGUAGE,
WRITE ANOTHER

My mother and father's 1947 divorce was "No Fault—Joint Custody." Sounds good, except that it wasn't as easy and pleasant as it sounds. When my mother married my stepfather in 1949, she had to go to America without me. My father did not give his consent for me to leave Germany until nearly a year later. Eventually I was allowed to emigrate with the stipulation that I was to write a letter to my father at least once a month. Other promises had also been made about me but not by me. Almost none of them were kept.

"Speak English! You're in America now!" was my stepfather's reminder whenever my mother and I spoke in our familiar German. I was thirteen and a half when I arrived in America and had to work hard in school to catch up to the students who had been going to school uninterrupted from the time they were six years old. My schooling in Germany had been sporadic: three weeks of grade one, two weeks of grade two, and practically none in grade three. My grandparents had taught me as much as possible, and I had become an avid reader, but my formal education had not started until I entered the fourth grade. As a result, I was barely able to put a German sentence together. Although my individual progress at school was excellent, I was unable to compete with my American contemporaries on almost every academic and physical level.

"Marianne, you have to write your father a letter. This is part of the deal," my mother begged me again. She had shoved some stationery toward me.

"Mutti, the last time I wrote him a letter, he criticized almost every word in his reply. I can't stand to write German. I'm studying English to please my American Dad and writing German to please my German father. It's just too hard to make you all happy and it feels like my brain is cramping!" I yammered.

"Do what you want!" she got angry with me and grabbed the paper away from me, so I went to my room and pouted. I was in the ninth grade in a Cedar Rapids, Iowa public high school. As a typical ninth grade girl who dealing with hormonal changes, boys, grades and other things that come up, I had enough trouble without the added stress of not being allowed to think in my own language.

I escaped into a familiar realm: books, magazines and especially comic books. I spent hours reading, in English, of course. At school, I was going to speech therapy twice a week where I was reading about Squanto and Hiawatha. At home I had a stack of comic books that kept me company. For a few hours I remained in my own space until the pouting stopped and I got hungry. Then I rejoined the family. This argument about letter-writing became routine between my mother and me. My German was fading away.

As a result I achieved more competence in English, but I lost my German in a hazy past. Letters to my grandparents and to my father became rare. Eventually, I stopped writing letters to Germany altogether.

LOST IN THE HOOD

Between childhood and adulthood lies a Never-neverland. My childhood had been chaotic, but I had survived. Suddenly I discovered that survival might not have been worth the struggle. Life as an alien in Cedar Rapids was a losthood.

The trip from New York to Iowa had taken nearly as long as the trip from Genoa to New York: two weeks. My step-grandparents, Gottfried and Johanna Miller, had brought my mother to New York in their huge Packard to pick me up. They were very kind and tried to make me feel at home by speaking German to me and welcoming me, but I was not able to make a rapid transition. There was no way these strangers could replace the dear ones I had left behind in Germany. On the return trip to Iowa we traveled on the Pennsylvania Turnpike and made a stop in Canton, Ohio. For a few days we visited Johanna's sister where I was introduced to rootbeer and comic books. I hated rootbeer but loved Nancy and Sluggo.

In the soft backseat of the Packard on the way to Iowa my mother filled my ears with ideas. I would have my own room in their new apartment. I would go to school. I would love America. She told me that they were selling their trailer home because they felt that it would be too small for a family of three. She talked of her wonderful husband. She talked of her new friends. Glowing reports. I threw up. They let me sit in the front seat for a while.

Cedar Rapids smelled. The Quaker Oats processing plant was located smack downtown and provided the atmosphere for anyone who breathed. It took me a while to get used to this air. In fact, it took me a while to get used to everything in my new life. I spent a great of time in the bathroom crying.

I wasn't particularly thrilled with my "own" room. Everything was strange, including the square ceiling light that cast mysterious shadows across the magazine pages I was trying to decipher. Even Christmas didn't do much to make me feel at home. When my mother and "Dad" took me to see their "trailer for sale" on the dealer's lot, I finally brightened up. This small home had no stone-like walls. There were lots of shiny wooden cabinets and windows. Instead of wide open spaces, the trailer had nooks and crannies where my spirit could feel safe. My mother and I both talked "Daddy" into giving up the apartment and moving back into the trailer. A spot near my new grandparents' trailer in the Hiawatha Trailer Park in Marion was readied, and we moved in before the winter snows stopped.

School. Before I arrived my dad had gone to the public schools to inquire about my placement. When he told them that I was in the eighth grade but had no English skills at all, he was told that I would have to start in the first grade and work my way up. That would not do. He then went to St. Matthews parochial school where he discovered that the nuns were willing to give me a chance to prove myself in my appropriate age group. With my trusty English-German dictionary held tightly against my heart, I took my seat behind a girl named Dixie.

1951 Marianne, John, and Tilli in Cedar Rapids

In time, I became one of the better students. My math was good, I understood science concepts, spelling was easy for me, and religion was my strong suit. Civics, however, was a whole other ballgame. From experience I knew that the government of a country could wreak havoc upon the common people. In Civics, I was supposed to learn that government was an orderly set of rules of checks and balances that allowed people to participate and vote. Never mind all the difficult

English I had to translate; I had trouble believing the concepts of a constitutional government. My dictionary was not much help. My dad did his best to explain things to me on the way to school. He promised that the American Dream was real; after all, this country allowed individuals to make their own decisions. He promised!

Getting home in the afternoons was an adventure in itself. I had to catch a public bus at the school. Near the Post Office downtown, I had to get off and walk to the Recruiting Station where my dad worked. He had rejoined the Air Force and accepted an assignment as a Recruiter. For a couple of hours every afternoon, I would be able to sit behind one of the desks and do my homework. Three military guys were always willing to help me, so I learned English by leaps and bounds. It was quite a satisfactory arrangement for a couple of months. Then suddenly it was spring.

For the first time since my arrival I began to look for friends my own age. My school mates were friendly enough, but they all lived far away from our trailer park. I made tentative steps toward Janice Shoemaker, a sixth grader who lived a couple of trailers down the road. My mother and dad took us to a roller skating rink on Saturdays. We also enjoyed playing on the playground with the small kids in the trailer park.

By May my mother and I had become familiar enough to invite a few girls from my class to help me celebrate my fourteenth birthday. I was so nervous I could have jumped out of my skin. After school, my dad piled us all in the car and drove us to our trailer. It was obvious from their behavior that none of the girls had ever been in a trailer before.

Suddenly I was very much aware of the chasm that existed between these rich girls from good homes and me, a poor girl living in a trailer. Bravely, I remained calm and enjoyed the party as much as possible.

For the eighth grade graduation we were to wear pastel colored dresses. My mother made me a lovely dress in a soft yellow with navy blue trim. I wore a hat and carried a purse. I had grown up at last.

Franklin High School accepted me because I had obviously learned enough English to predict success in public schools. I was finally able to ride the school bus! Another ninth grader, Faye Renner, had moved into the trailer park. We became good friends immediately. She played the clarinet in the band, and I had a little experience on the accordion. We also discovered the joys of Monopoly and giggling about boys. At school we ate lunch together and bolstered each other's spirits in the presence of a huge student body that welcomed very few newcomers.

One of my biggest problems was my pronunciation of the language. Teachers had trouble understanding me, so I was placed with a very friendly and effective speech therapist. She taught me to roll my "r's," tongue my "th's," and differentiate between the German and English "w's" with the book about Squanto, the Iroquois Indian.

I did so well in General Math that year that the teacher placed me in Algebra A for the second semester. I was very proud of my accomplish-ments and looked forward to going to summer school to make up the Algebra B. Up to that time I had never shared a classroom with a "colored person"; after all, it was 1951. Summer school turned out quite differently from what I had imagined. I thought I would actually learn Algebra B, but....

For six weeks that summer, I suffered through a noisy class at McKinley High School, which was located in a part of town I had never seen. "Colored people" lived there. I was afraid. Nothing had prepared me for the gulf that existed between us. The black girls, giggling in small groups, stared at me. Black boys made remarks. I had no familiar person to make me feel safe. When I expressed my concerns to my dad, he dismissed "those people" as trash. "Just get your credit, and don't worry about them."

Somehow I got the credit for that class to make me eligible for Geometry in the tenth grade; however, I learned more than math. For the first time I learned about race relations in America. An uneasiness crept into my soul. Hadn't I already witnessed the unpleasant results of racial hatred?

The hectic life of a sophomore at Franklin High soon made me forget the other side of town. I continued to make academic progress, but I remained very shy in social contacts. I learned that I could ward off boys' friendly advances by averting my eyes. I averted my eyes a lot that year. I had plenty of priorities in my life before boys.

For one thing, my family was about to grow. I would have loved to have a sister or brother, but I had to settle for an aunt. My mother's sister had survived World War II in Berlin. She had been a master beautician, but under the current economic stresses, she was not happy. "Tante Leni" wanted to come to America, and my mother and dad wanted to make this possible. Where would she sleep?

In December 1952 we drove to Chicago to pick up my aunt at O'Hare airport. Right away there was an argument between my mother and my aunt about money. Apparently, my aunt had spent all the pocket money my mother had sent her. The way home in the car was not happy. I was not too happy about having to share my bed, and my dad tried to make light of having to "take care" of three women now. The tension level increased noticeably. My mother became especially sensitive and often expressed her desire for peace and quiet.

The four of us in that small trailer had practically no privacy. It became increasingly more difficult to find the time and space for my mother and my aunt to write letters home. Of course, I was happy not to write anything!

There was another stumbling block to my learning to write: Typing Class. As an elective in the first semester of the tenth grade, I chose Beginning Typing. I thought this would make writing easier since I had never developed good penmanship. I hoped that if I could see my words in typing, they would look better. I was mistaken. Typing class was sheer torture. The typewriters clattered noisily, and the teacher was difficult to understand. My fingers didn't want to cooperate, so the keys kept getting glommed up. Each key of a typewriter was attached to a lever with a raised letter that had to press against an ink-filled typewriter ribbon that then imprinted the letter on the paper. The levers got entangled in the center of the machine whenever the fingers accidentally pressed more than one key at a time. In the effort to keep up with the speed tests, my fingers often pressed more than one key. I then had to disentangle the levers. In the process I usually got some of the ink on my fingers and smudged my paper. As I said, it was sheer torture.

I developed a true antipathy against writing and only wrote enough to graduate from high school; however, I was eventually given an opportunity to change my attitude.

Four people in one thirty-foot house trailer were at least two too many. The three adults tried to improve their lives by spending a great deal of time at the VFW drinking their troubles away. I began to dread their noisy returns from partying on weekend nights, but I found an escape.

I loved the comic books and the radio shows of the time. The Lone Ranger was my favorite! I listened to the Green Hornet, the Shadow, Sky King, Hoppalong Cassidy and many others. A world of fantasy took me away from the harsh realities of the adult world.

The need for money pressed everyone into action. Exhorting me to do well in school, my mother and my aunt started to work at a molasses factory instead of going to adult school to learn English. When I asked why they didn't work at their learned trades as seamstress and beautician, I was told that they didn't know enough English to get their required business licenses or be hired anywhere. They would have to work in a factory because they needed money and didn't have time to go to school. Yet the reason they couldn't work at their learned trades was their incompetence in English. This seemed very unfair to me, but it appeared that they enjoyed their jobs. My mother was determined to get her citizenship papers. She studied privately without going to school, passed the test, and proudly received her Certificate of Citizenship just before we left Cedar Rapids.

My dad was notified that he had been transferred to George Air Force Base in Victorville, California. We wondered whether we were ready for the Wild West as we set out one February 1953 morning. Without packing we moved our entire home. My dad had bought a large Packard to pull the trailer. We would arrive in California like Gypsies; I was excited.

1952 Leni, Marianne and Tilly on the way to California

The Western states awed us with their wide open spaces. We loved the huge cacti in the deserts, and we admired the unusual architecture in the towns. It was a long, exciting trip. When a truck tapped the back of our trailer, my dad had all he could do to keep the car under control as it lurched from side to side. We all screamed as we pulled to a stop. The truck driver offered my dad a small sum of money for the dent. He begged us not to call the police because he would get in trouble with his company. For fifty dollars cash, my dad agreed to let it pass.

Another experience left the car damaged. In Arizona a sudden sandstorm hindered our progress. The interior of the car turned all yellow as the sand around us swirled mercilessly. We held cloths in front of our faces during the worst of it. When the storm was over we checked outside. Much of the paint had been stripped off the passenger side of the Packard. I could hardly wait to get off the road and start a normal life again.

A few days later we knew that we had only one more hurdle before arriving at Victorville. My dad was not sure whether the Packard was strong enough to pull the trailer over the El Cajon, only a two-lane pass in 1953. If we got stuck on this road, we would block traffic for miles. In order to avoid trouble, we hired a truck to pull us up the pass. I thought it was quite interesting to be hitched to a truck and get pulled up a mountain, but my dad grumbled about the extra money this was costing him.

That night we slept in a trailer park which was to be our home for only a few weeks.

It turned out that George Air Force Base had housing available. My folks decided to put the trailer up for sale and move into base housing. Even though we had enjoyed the trailer, we had to admit that it was no longer suitable for the four of us. The tension between my aunt and me was becoming intolerable. We needed more space.

My aunt searched seriously for meaningful work. Eventually she moved to Los Angeles where she worked as a housekeeper for a doctor whose wife was permanently disabled and confined to an iron lung. My mother went to work in a doll clothes factory near Victorville.

I attended Victor Valley High School. There were only a few months left of my tenth grade. I rode the school bus and became acquainted with a number of other teens from the base. I also relaxed a bit more around boys although I still wasn't interested in developing relationships with them. I made friends with Lynda Hampton and her two stepsisters. During summer vacation I discovered that life as a teenager was not as depressing as I had made it out to be, and my mother also found some happy times.

My mother's talents as a dressmaker were rediscovered. She made all our clothes and consequently bought lots of fabric from Pennington's, the little fabric shop in town. One day the owner offered my mother the back room as her workshop. She could make clothes for customers who purchased materials in the store. I've never seen my mother happier. Her heaven included a husband who loved and supported her, a meaningful occupation, and a daughter who had finally made a noticeable adjustment to American life. It was important to my mother that I had made lots of friends. She was happy! And I was happy!

Our little group included several guys. Together we went to dances at the Youth Center and joined the church choir. There was a great swimming pool at the Officer's Club. Lynda's dad was an officer, so we spent lots of time there. We went to at least one movie a week and listened to music at home. Lynda and I especially loved the Lawrence Welk Show on TV. When we wrote notes to each other, we sealed them with the motto, "Lawrence Welk for President." I gradually gained enough confidence to let a guy kiss me that year. Exactly three weeks after my sixteenth birthday, I got my first kiss!

I looked forward to my junior year, and started school with high hopes and a sense of continuity. I had already attended three different schools since my arrival in America and desperately needed to feel a sense of security. For a while Victor Valley Union High gave me that but not for long.

When my dad came home with orders for Bermuda, I cried and cried. I didn't want to leave Victorville. I had finally become a normal American teenager, and now I was going to leave again. My dad had to leave first. He would send for my mother and me after he found a suitable home for us. Besides, there was still a lot of paperwork to be taken care of before we could travel legally.

In order for me to reenter the United States after the four years in Bermuda, I would have to obtain the appropriate documents before leaving. Since my mother had already made her citizenship, I was eligible, as a minor, for the derivative certificate. I had to go to a court in San Bernardino to get sworn in. I was excited about my U.S. Citizenship becoming "official" but I was less enthusiastic about moving on to yet another world.

My dad sent letters with glowing reports about Bermuda. After reading about this tropical island, I started to look forward to the move, but I became apathetic about attending school. I stopped attending classes completely for nearly two months. I miserably felt that I was going to leave soon, anyway, so I just hung around with my mother instead of my friends. In early December we quietly left for Los Angeles where we bid good-bye to my aunt before boarding a plane for Bermuda.

Secretly, I promised myself not to be so stand-offish once I got to my new school. Now that I had experienced fun with friends my own age, I was ready to become more accepting. Instead of thinking that no one wanted to be with me, I would think that other kids my age would be glad to have me around. I would act friendly, and they would not know what a miserable person I had been.

Finally, my mother and I were ready to join my dad in Bermuda. Once again, I was traveling across an ocean into the unknown.

MOUNT SAINT AGNES

"God, I hate this typing stuff!" The small classroom was clattering with Underwoods and Royal Coronas. I noticed that Lillian was making eyes at Denis again.

"Are we decorating tonight?" she whispered. Several of us nodded. Sternly, Sister Katherine warned us to keep typing or there wouldn't be a dance.

"I almost have the snowman finished," I told Lillian as we were pouring from the school. "Make sure that Denis can get his dad's car to carry it to school."

Our theme for the Junior-Senior dance was Winter Wonderland. It was my idea. I still couldn't believe that I had become so popular. My theory had worked.

Once we got settled into our new home, I was enrolled in Mount Saint Agnes. Kindley Air Force Base had no school facilities for high school age dependents, so we had to attend local Bermudian schools. I was pleased that Mount Saint Agnes was within walking distance of our home. My old reluctance to make new friends threatened to assert itself on the first day during lunch break. A group of girls was laughing and carrying on. I thought, "They don't want me. No, by golly, I promised. No negative thoughts."

"Hi, my name is Marianne."

"Hi, I'm Rosalie and this is Jacqueline, Barbara, Nora and Jennifer. Where are you from?"

They had noticed my accent already; I started to withdraw. NO! I'm not going to fall for it. "I'm from Germany."

"Wow, that's groovy. How did you get to Bermuda?" They were actually interested. Nice girls.

In time, we shared our stories and studies. Our junior class consisted of only seventeen students. Sister Vincent was our English and history teacher. Sister Elizabeth taught Science and Math. Sister Katherine taught Religion, Shorthand and Typing. How I hated that typing! All the eleventh graders were attempting to qualify for the Cambridge Oversea School Certificate. This was a big deal. Only eight of us qualified. I got so stressed out over the science experiment and all the other stuff I had to study that I ended up in the hospital with pneumonia for two weeks.

Now the exams were behind us, and we were decorating for the dance.

"Are you bringing Bill to the dance?" Rosalie wondered.

"Yes, we're still going together," I hesitated a little. Bill was not educated beyond the eighth grade. He was the boy next door, good-looking and three years older than I. He was, however, somehow beneath Mount Saint Agnes students. Some of the girls openly snubbed him.

"It's okay. Don't feel bad. If you like him, that's all that matters."

"I know." In the hubbub of decorating the hall any doubts left me. My home-made paper-maché snowman had a prominent place on the stage and ivory soap snow was piled up in each small window pane. It has never snowed in Bermuda, so everyone was quite excited about our theme.

Bill and I had a great time at the dance. We usually just went to movies for fun. Even though there were many great beaches in Bermuda, we seldom took advantage of them. Movies, movies, movies. Bill was okay as a boyfriend; he would never become my husband. He had no job; as a result, he had no money to spend on our entertainment. I believed that he wouldn't have had any imagination even if he had enough money. I was going with him because he was good-looking and lived next door.

I was growing up. A senior in high school. Amid the fun thoughts about my future sobered me. There was no money for me to go to college. I wasn't sure I was ready to leave home, anyhow. I had found another comfort zone, and I didn't want it to end yet.

"You mean we won't wear caps and gowns?" I was a little disappointed.

"No, it's a tradition for Mount Saint Agnes girls to wear white formals for graduation. It's beautiful." Sister Elizabeth explained.

"Mutti, you have to make me a white formal!"

"What? Why? Are you getting married?" my mother was stunned.

"No. They wear white formals for graduation here. Jacqueline Soose wants to know whether you can make her one too," I blurted out.

My mother made two beautiful gowns. Graduation was a hit.

1955 Mount Saint Agnes Graduation

DISOWNED

"Oh Hi, Tom! It's great to have you back!" Flo's voice caught my attention as I was sorting the subscriptions to the newspapers brought in daily from New York. I looked up, and a wave of warmth swept over me. There stood God--tall, dark and fantastic—talking to the manager. Though our eyes didn't meet, my heart began to beat noticeably. I quickly bent down and concentrated on my work.

My job at the Kindley Air Force Base Terminal Exchange had become comfortable for me. Graduation from high school was just behind me, and now I was taking care of the stationery department in a small shop in the terminal. My duties included counting out the subscription newspapers, putting the leftovers out for sale, and trashing the out-of-date ones. I also had to keep my station neat and display merchandise in a glass case which I was expected to keep sparkling. I loved my eighty-one cents an hour job. I was now officially grown up!

"Hi!" Coal-black oriental eyes, beautiful teeth and a disarming smile approached my counter.

"Oh, my God, here he comes!" I thought as "Tom" brought an armful of newspapers. He had counted them for me. "So he's even helpful!" I felt the same funny little feeling I had felt the day before. Warmth. Maybe it was just the July heat in Bermuda washing over me.

"Thanks for doing those newspapers for me. I was just getting ready to go in the backroom to count them." I tried to be as nonchalant as my eighteen-year-old heart could manage. "You didn't have to do that."

"It's alright. I'm working here part-time again. I used to work here, but I went back to the States for a month."

"Are you a dependent, too?" I wondered out loud.

1955 Leighton Tong

"No, I'm in the Air Force, but I work here for extra money to send home to my folks. I'll be around. Bye."

Another thought flew by, "So he's generous, too. And he cares about his parents."

He was gone. I busied myself with my newspapers and soon forgot the gorgeous smile that had walked into my life. My dad came by later that afternoon to make sure that I had a ride home. I assured him that Edith was getting off at six o'clock, the same time I did. Our commute arrangement had worked out just fine for the past three days.

"Go ahead, Dad. You don't need to wait around for an hour." My dad had married my mom in Germany after the war, and he took his fatherhood seriously.

A few years ago, World War II had not only destroyed our home but also our family. My biological father and my mother never got back together again after his release from the German army. She met an American, and suddenly my life was changed forever. My dad, as I called the new man in my mother's life, remained in the Air Force and was now serving a tour of duty in Bermuda.

Life was good. Bermuda's great climate, my high school graduation, my mother's happiness, my own room, a boy friend named Bill, and a job was all I needed to make me believe I had landed in Paradise. Things were about to change.

"Gosh, I didn't expect you to do my newspapers again!"

"It's my pleasure." A quick smile, and he was gone.

Actually, it was **my** pleasure. I hadn't been dreaming; he was real. Somehow Bill's image was being replaced by Tom's.

Just before I got off work, he suddenly stood in front of my counter again. "I thought I'd buy one of those newspapers."

Tom was in uniform. His name tag read "Tong."

"I thought your first name was Tom. Isn't that what Flo Black, the manager, called you the other day?"

"My name is Tong. Leighton Hall Lai Tong."

"What nationality is that?"

"Chinese."

"I've never met a Chinese before. I always thought that Chinese people are very small. You're so tall. I thought you were Hawaiian. How tall are you?" My blabbering mouth proved I was obviously eighteen. I couldn't stop the gibberish. Blather, blather, bla...

"I'm six feet tall. I think my ancestors were mountain people."

"Like Genghis Khan? That's great. I think I have Attila the Hun in my background!" We both laughed.

"You look cute with that little black nose." His finger gently wiped away a smudge of newsprint. "See you tomorrow."

It was a little more difficult to forget the smile this time despite a number of other customers crowding around my cash register.

What should I call him? His name wasn't Tom. Oh, never mind. My boyfriend Bill was waiting to take me to a movie, and I didn't really have any business dreaming about a Chinese guy. Even if he was the most handsome, generous, considerate, and graceful creature I had ever met.

One of the most exciting holidays in Bermuda is the annual Festival of the August Moon. Two days of festivities including boat floats on the Hamilton Harbor were about to help me take control of my fate.

Bill and I had plans to go see the boat parade and dance in the streets. We had been going together for about two years. He was a Bermudian of Portuguese descent who lived two doors down from our home. We had no plans for a future together. His lack of planning a career made it clear to me that he had no intention of ever supporting a family. He was simply my boyfriend; I was simply his girlfriend. Until I met Tong my life was simple. Local events happened. Bill and I attended.

When Tong appeared at my newspaper counter with his friend Dave, I asked whether they had ever gone to the Festival of the August Moon in Hamilton. They hadn't.

"Oh, you should go. There is going to be all kinds of fun," I oozed.

"Well, if we both can get the night off from work, it might be nice to see what it's all about." Dave agreed.

"How will you get there?" I asked, smiling at Dave.

"Dave and I both have motorcycles. Transportation is no problem."

The seed had been planted. They would probably come to Hamilton. Now all I had to do was to go to town without Bill. This would not be easy. My parents would not let me go alone.

Saturday evening I suddenly developed a "headache." I told Bill I was staying home. I moped around for a while. My mother asked me what was wrong. I told her that Bill had called off our date to go to the Festival. She mentioned that our friends, a young American couple who lived downstairs, were going.

"Why don't you go with them?"

"That's a great idea, Mutti, but I don't have any money."

"Here's a couple of dollars. Have a good time, but don't get lost in the crowd. With so many strange people, you never know what could happen." If she only knew what I had cooked up!

The Glidewell's and I walked the two miles to downtown Hamilton. The town was aglitter with excitement. The boat parade was about to begin, and crowds were gathering everywhere. I lost no time in separating myself from my companions. As the Glidewell's were busy watching the boats, I was busy scanning the crowds for a beautiful head of black hair.

Nothing. It was turning into a depressing evening. What was everyone so excited about? Who cared about a bunch of boats with lights floating on some crummy water? I walked around aimlessly for about a half hour and decided to go home. It wouldn't be difficult to explain my separation from the Glidewell's.

Heading up Serpentine Road alone and miserable, I glanced up just in time to see two smiles.

"Oh, Hi! I see you were able to get off." My heart was louder than my words.

"Yeah. We decided to see what all the fuss was about." Dave was friendly but not my type. For now, however, I had to accept them as a matched set on one motorcycle.

Tong's eyes looked into my soul, "Would you like to go get a bite to eat?" Would I! He had no idea!

"That would be nice." Cool, calm and collected me.

"You're more familiar with Hamilton than we are. Why don't you suggest a place?" Tong reasoned. Was there no end to his good qualities? Generous, reasonable, considerate.

"Let's go to Little Venice. They have pizza and delicious sandwiches. It's just around the corner."

Moments later we settled into a booth at the small restaurant in the shadows of the Bermudiana and the Princess hotels. I was in heaven.

It was getting late, and I had to get home. After some discussion which included the explanation that Dave was not old enough to get a local motorcycle driver's license and that's why they were riding together, Tong decided to take me home while Dave would wait at the Little Venice. Perfect. Ever the gentleman, Tong drove very carefully and walked me to the door. I wondered whether he would try to kiss me goodnight. He didn't.

"Would you like to go to the beach with us next weekend?" He asked.

"Us?" I was a little disappointed.

"Yes. Dave and I have plans to go to Elbow Beach. I'm sure he would like to have you come along." I was beginning to become suspicious. Was he trying to set me up with Dave?

"I'd like that. Thanks for the pizza. I had a real good time. Say good night to Dave."

Walking into the house, I was confused. The signals I was getting were unclear. I thought Tong liked me. Maybe he is already married. Maybe he's shy. Maybe. Maybe. I collapsed onto my bed. Wow, my life had sure become complicated in just one week. My plan to get him to come to town had worked, but there was no encouragement on his part.

In the summer the convertible Bermuda cabs have bright umbrellas instead of tops. The twenty mile an hour speed limit throughout the islands made our ride to the beach an easy, laugh-filled adventure. The radio was playing "My Prayer" by the Platters. Crowded into the backseat, the three of us hummed along.

A news bulletin warned of an approaching hurricane. Ione. It would pass by Bermuda, but the turbulent seas had already claimed one life. A woman had been swept off a cliff in clear view of her terrified husband. We looked at each other. Sure, it was a bit windy, but the sun was shining.

"Let's go anyway. Who knows when we'll get another day off."

I agreed. We would be safe on Elbow Beach which was located in a sheltered cove. We would avoid standing on cliffs.

The cab driver mumbled something about crazy Americans, but he didn't refuse to earn the fare for a ride to the beach.

Sand whipped around us, and any hope of swimming was dashed. Yet no one wanted to give up and go home. Dave was determined to brave the wild waves at least once. Our towels and blankets had to be anchored down with shoes. I was cold. We were having the time of our lives! Three idiots.

I lay down on the blanket to keep it from getting air-borne. I was scared of the hurricane and the roiling ocean. I was cold and hungry. I was worried about Dave running in and out of the waves. Tong lay down beside me and put one hand on my shoulder. Suddenly I was filled with a calm warmth that spread all the way to my toes. I dared not look into Tong's eyes. I lay there pretending to be resting.

Dave yelled, "Hey there you two. Why don't you come in the water?"

"No thanks. We're thinking of heading back home." Mr. Reasonable.

"Okay, let's go. I don't want to become a statistic anyway." Dave grumbled as he came out of the water.

We ate our sandwiches and huddled together, chatting until the wind got loud enough to drown out our voices.

"This is fun. We ought to come to the beach some time when there's no hurricane."

We laughed and sang all the way home despite the storm clouds which threatened to break. All the cabbies had rolled up their umbrellas and pulled up the roofs. The guys were happy and seemed perfectly content to share our dates, but I wasn't at all thrilled about this threesome arrangement. Who needed Dave?

The cab dropped us off at my home. I had introduced the guys to my folks when they came to pick me up, so I invited them in for a drink before we called it a day.

After their motorcycle roared off, my mother surprised me with, "Boy, it sure is obvious which one you favor. I don't think it is a good idea for you to see him anymore."

There it was. The race thing. The issue.

Before long it even became obvious to Dave that he was not the one I wanted to date. Bill also realized that another man had come into my life. I was a goner.

The only one who didn't seem to realize the burning within me was Tong. Days went by without the slightest move toward intimacy.

On the job he was all business. Pleasant but business. We ate lunch in the terminal cafeteria and worked crossword puzzles together. We talked about our respective families. We decorated my stationery counter together. We avoided touching each other. I almost exploded with the tension. Something was going to happen even if I had to make it happen!

"Hey, Edith. My dad is working late today, so I'm not riding with you. He'll be by pretty soon to drive me home."

"Okay, Marianne. See you tomorrow." As Edith drove off, I got a sinking feeling. What if Tong didn't stop by this afternoon? Moments later, he showed up.

"Gosh! I'm sure glad to see you. Edith drove off and left me and my dad has already gone home. I don't have a ride home. What am I going to do? A cab is so expensive." I must have looked helpless.

"All I have is a small motorcycle, but I'd be glad to take you home." Tong offered. "You're lucky this is my day off." Lucky? No. This was a planned emergency. I knew it was his day off.

"A motorcycle is fine. You know how to drive very well, and I know you'll get me home safe and sound."

Only two short weeks ago when he had taken me home from the Little Venice, I sat way back on the seat and held onto the handle for dear life. As the motorcycle roared to life this time, I put both arms around his waist and gushed, "My life is in your hands." A half hour of bliss.

"Would you like to go to a movie one of these days?"

"Yes." Yes, yes, yes!

"How about next Saturday night?"

"Yes." Yes, yes, yes!

At home no one suspected a thing. The subterfuge had begun. Still no kiss, however.

"Are you still seeing that Chinaman?" my dad roared.

"We go to the movies once in a while. What's wrong with that?"

"I'll tell you what's wrong with it, young lady. The base commander called on me today and told me to stop letting you hang around with that Chinaman. You've been seen all over the base with him."

"I still don't see what's wrong with that. I'm over eighteen, and he's a member of the United States Air Force."

My dad got red in the face. I tried to remain calm and logical, but I started to cry. "I don't care about your stupid old base commander. He should take care of his own stupid kids. They're all over the base causing trouble." My voice got shriller with each word.

"What he does about his kids is beside the point. This could hurt my Air Force career. You are not to see this guy again. He is not of our race. Don't you realize what you're getting into?"

"He's human and he's better than any of the other guys around here." I countered. "I can't imagine what this has to do with your career."

"Come on, Marianne. You're blond and pretty. Don't do this to me." My mother pleaded.

"You did what you wanted to do even though your mother didn't want you to." I knew it hurt her to be reminded of her heart-wrenching decision to leave Germany and her family. Tears were flowing freely.

"Bitte. Lass das doch sein." In moments of stress my mother felt more comfortable in German. There were no words in any language strong enough to convince me to leave Tong.

"I'll try." In my heart I knew that trying was useless. Tong and I had kissed. We had decided to call each other "Love." We did crossword puzzles together at lunch every other day. I dated other guys when they asked me out, but my heart was no longer free.

On Christmas Eve 1955, I attended the 10:00 p.m. mass with Al Falzon. He was a lieutenant and the right race. My parents approved of him. He was nice, but there was no spark. Al dropped me off around eleven. Merry Christmas. See you tomorrow. Blah.

"If I asked you to marry me, would you say yes?" Tong asked me under the oleander tree.

"If you asked me I might answer."

"Would you marry me?" Soft. Loving.

"Oh, Love. I would if I could, but we're not the same race. It's impossible." I couldn't see over the man-made obstacles.

"It's mind over matter." He calmly stated my entire philosophy in that simple sentence. I felt that calm warmth again.

"Yes." Yes. Yes. Yes. Yes. "Now I'd better go in. My folks think I went to church with Al Falzon. They have no idea that I had a date with you after church."

"It's too bad that your folks are giving you a hard time. I like your dad. We're in the same squadron.

"Love, I'm sure they'll be okay once I tell them that I intend to marry you." I was sure my mother would understand, but I kept my fingers crossed about my dad. "We'll cross that bridge when we come to it. Let's talk about it tomorrow. Goodnight and Merry Christmas, my sweet Leighton Tong."

"That's a man's prerogative!!!" My dad was livid.

In our argument about interracial marriages and the social problems of the resulting children, I had just pointed to the fact that American servicemen had brought lots of Japanese and Korean wives to America and that their children could become the spouses of any children Lee and I would have.

"If you insist on going through with this marriage, we'll disown you!" roared my dad.

My mother ran to the bedroom to cry just as I was screaming, "Tong is worth a lot more than I could ever inherit from a poor Air Force sergeant!" Ouch! Forty years later, he retaliated.

THE CHALLENGE

So here was my challenge: If I married my beloved Leighton, I would be disinherited. This did not scare me. After the war I had seen plenty of people start over from nothing. Some people had lost all their wealth. There was nothing to inherit, anyway. My perspective on what I might inherit from my parents was affected by my history as well as my future. I was certain that my wonderful Leighton would provide a secure life for me.

"But, Mutti, I need your approval and permission to get married here in Bermuda. Besides, I love you, and don't want to fight with you."

"Sorry, Marianne. If you insist on going through with this marriage, you'll have to do it without me. I can't do this to Daddy."

How often I would have to hear this disclaimer throughout my life. "Doing it to Daddy," was my mother's guiding light. She had left her own parents, her country, and, in fact, her daughter behind to please this man. Her explanation for her decisions included giving me a better life in America where freedom and opportunity would make my life into heaven on Earth. "Daddy" continually expounded on the virtues of the human rights we had under American laws. Everyone was equal. Unlike other countries, America valued human life. He had me convinced. When I found the man I wanted to marry, he back-pedaled. And my mother was blind to his hypocritical bigotry.

By Valentine's Day Leighton and I were engaged but unable to make wedding plans. By my nineteenth birthday in May, I had made up my mind. I had to leave Bermuda. The atmosphere had become more and more intolerable. My heart could no longer endure being alternately subjected to vitriolic arguments and passionate encounters. I took up my aunt's offer to come live in California. Leni was my mother's sister. I appreciated her compassion in her letters even though I suspected she would try to talk me out of my relationship with Leighton once I arrived in her home.

A tearful good-bye just three days before the date we had originally set as our wedding day closed one chapter of my life. I would never again feel the unconditional child-like love for my mother. Alone and penniless, she had nurtured me through unimaginable difficulties. Now she turned her back on me, denied my love and supported my adversary. I had to do what I had to do!

SO THIS IS INDEPENDENCE

When Lee and I had to separate, we promised to write daily letters to each other.

This time, I had no mental conflicts about writing. My loving words flowed freely onto the paper, expressing my thoughts and feelings with ease. At last, I discovered the power of words that I had long suspected as a forbidden secret. My world opened up, and though I didn't write much besides the letters to my love, I no longer felt the resentment previously associated with writing.

"Long Distance phone call for you, Marianne. You can take it in the office." I had been working at the Magan Clinic in Covina, California for six months. My heart had been broken in Bermuda, so I decided to live with my aunt, who had gotten married in California until I could regain my senses.

Daily letters flew across the Atlantic to keep Leighton and me in touch. My mother's sister tried her best to help me forget him, but my heart just wasn't ready to give up my true love. Being a nineteen year old girl, however, I still wasn't convinced that the rest of the world was wrong about my relationship with Leighton, so I was willing to go along with the ideas of others. My aunt introduced me to a young man who would have pleased my entire family as an appropriate mate for me.

Rudy had graduated from Cal Tech with a degree in Electrical Engineering. He had all the blond qualifications, except that I didn't love him. I let him take me to fancy restaurants, the State Fair in Pomona, to San Juan Capistrano, to Big Bear and various other places. My engagement ring remained prominently displayed, and I continued to remind Rudy that I was not available. He kept telling me that he didn't mind.

"You have a call from Bermuda." For two minutes I cried after I recognized Leighton's voice.

He finally said, "Love, this call is costing $8 a minute. Please stop crying so we can talk. I called to find out whether you want me to come to California to get married, or whether we should break up. I can't go on like this."

"Yes! Come! We can get married in Los Angeles." I had been ready to get married in Bermuda, but the law required my   parents' permission there. In California there was no such restriction. With promises of undying love, we ended our expensive conversation.

"You're going to Germany with us!" my mother insisted. My parents had come to my aunt's house in California after their tour of duty in Bermuda was over. Their new Air Force orders would send them to Ramstein Air Base in Germany. It would be the perfect opportunity to find me a proper German husband. I let my mother buy me a warm winter coat and obtain a visa to travel to Germany on my passport. I still hadn't made up my mind. Finally, I realized that I could not continue to please all the people I loved. No matter what I decided, someone was going to get hurt. And it wasn't going to be me.

"Leighton is coming, and we're planning to get married here in California." I tried to be matter fact, but I was going against all I believed in. For years I had cooperated with parents who were no longer married to each other. I had been an obedient daughter, braving an ocean voyage to be with my mother. For five years I had accepted the rather bigoted ideas of a German-born American step-father. Several times in my young life, circumstances forced me to be courageous beyond my years. I had already survived serious illnesses in the midst of a war, fought for my rights in a foreign language and traveled unaccompanied across the Atlantic on the promise of being reunited with my mother. It was definitely easier to defer to adult authority than to live my own life, but here I was, standing up for my own heart again.

Leighton had just driven up in a borrowed car to come pick me up.

"Mutti, he's come to pick me up. We're going to get married." I was very sad as I realized that my mother would not be at my wedding. Again there was crying. My aunt and my mother tried to cajole me into another mood. My dad got physical. He knocked me onto a couch and kicked me in the behind. My aunt's husband Jack was storming around, "Leave the girl alone!"

I ran out of the house with my mother after me. She was still sobbing as she was begging Leighton to be sensible. "Please don't do this." She tried to reason with him, "Think of the children, think about what you're doing!"

We drove off. Somewhere in the distance a sound of breaking glass resonated our breaking hearts.

The lady who handed us our marriage license asked me, "Do your parents know what you're doing?" I said yes, so she had done her duty.

A couple of Leighton's boyhood friends were our witnesses at our wedding, and about thirty friends or so even made a reception for us at Tate's restaurant in Los Angeles. His parents and his uncle received me cordially, and I began to feel comfortable in my new life.

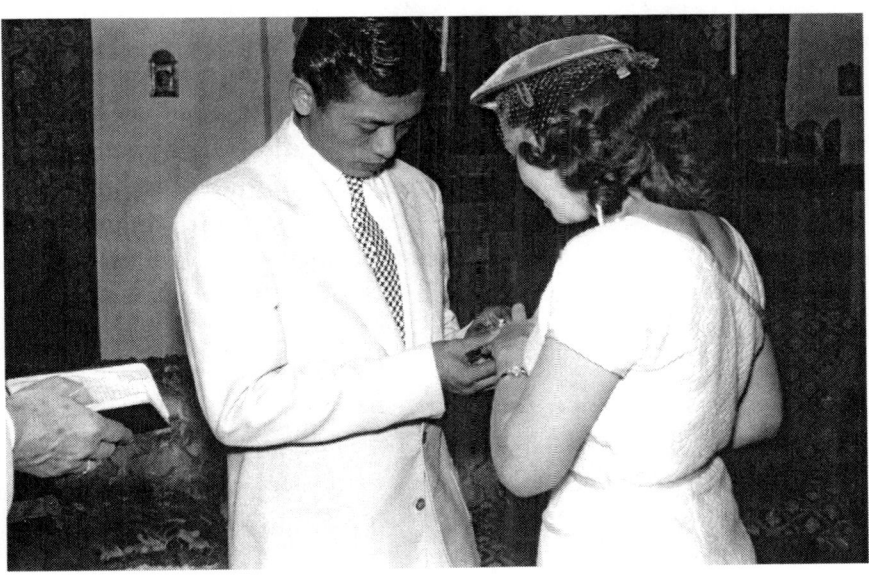

We would be leaving for Bermuda in a couple of days. I went back to work at the Magan Clinic until our departure. For lunch I usually walked downtown to a small diner. Just as I was turning a corner on the last day my mother "accidentally" appeared in front of me.

"Well, hello, Mrs. Tong." She smiled, "I knew you'd actually do it. Let's go have lunch."

My dad had already left for Germany, so my mother was staying with her sister until she could leave. We made up that day, and she wished me all the luck in the world. She had realized that her example of leaving Germany and her entire family for a man who was not the father of her child had influenced my decisions. She had made independent choices, and now it was my turn.

Fortunately, my mother and stepfather benefitted from my new attitude about writing. They would be in Germany for four years, so I kept in touch with them through frequent letters. For a few more years all my writing was of a personal nature.

Leighton and I flew back to Bermuda with practically no money in our pockets. There was no family support. I had never had a job which made more than $1.10 an hour, and he was a simple sergeant in the Air Force making the grand total of $250 a month. Most of his reserves had gone to our tickets, and we would arrive in Bermuda before the next paycheck. Like it or not, love would have to be enough.

Panipinto, one of Leighton's co-workers, knew we were coming, so he had found a very small apartment for us. We asked the landlord whether we could pay him for two weeks. We didn't have enough for a whole month's rent! He agreed, and we were set. Both of us knew how to be frugal, so we ate simple meals and played cards or Monopoly for entertainment. Soon we were celebrating life among our friends. By Christmas and New Year's Eve we had established ourselves as an old married couple.

In fact, I didn't realize just how married we were until the doctor confirmed my pregnancy. Our first baby would arrive in September, just ten months after our wedding. I was ecstatic but apprehensive. Would he still love me once I became a mother instead of his attractive playmate? He laughed, "Did you ever see a Chinaman without a large family trailing behind him?" That set my mind at ease.

We had talked about these things before. The vision of our life together definitely included children, grandchildren and a loving home with perhaps a picket fence. Had we not gone to the movies? Had we not seen images of just how idyllic American life could be? We resolved to live the dream.

My young husband and I discussed the possibility of reenlisting for another four years in the Air Force. The two thousand dollars reenlistment bonus and the sheltered life as a military dependent looked awfully good to me. We wouldn't have to worry about prejudice, and medical care would be provided. With a baby coming in a few months, we would need a car. Yes, staying in the Air Force was a good idea.

We bought a Roliflex camera and a Necchi sewing machine. We also made a down payment on our first car, a yellow Nash Cosmopolitan convertible. I thought I had gone to heaven.

Our "Lovebaby" arrived in September. We called her Vivienne, and, boy! Did she live up to her name! What a lively one! Only three weeks later, just as I was nursing her, Sputnik was announced on the radio. I realized that our children would live in a different world. The space race had begun. The so-called cold war, after all the hot ones, made the whole world jittery. People's imaginations were taken up with unimaginable scenarios of superpower versus superpower nuclear holocausts.

My little Vivi kept me from worrying about world events. Her baby demands left little time for me to think about much else. Besides, a few months later, I discovered that another baby was coming.

Our tour of duty in Bermuda was almost over. I really didn't like airplane travel, so we requested concurrent travel by surface carrier to our next station, and it was granted. Five months pregnant and carrying a ten-month old baby we boarded an ocean liner and sailed toward New York. Our new assignment was Homestead Air Force Base in Florida. Leighton and I both felt the need to make contact with our families. He had plenty of leave time saved up, so we jumped in our little car and headed toward Florida via California. This was not a trip I care to remember. It was nice to see his family and my aunt, but the discomforts of traveling with a baby in a tiny car in the heat of summer was almost too much for us.

After a month of travel, we arrived in Florida. What now? We checked in at the base, but they had no available homes for us. We had no money for hotels, and at the time, credits cards had not yet become the custom. We called around, and a small trailer was ready for occupancy just a couple of miles from the base. I was so travel-weary I would have bedded down in a pup tent! The 27-foot trailer seemed like a castle to me. Just let me sleep.

Our household goods were not due to arrive for a couple of months, so we had time to think about what we wanted to do about living arrangements. The trailer park was a friendly place. It had a swimming pool, playground and a large laundry facility. The people were nice, and there was a larger mobile home for sale. Homestead Air Force Base was building new base housing. For a few days we couldn't decide whether we wanted to remain in Kingman Road Mobile Home Park or move on base. Finally, the hard terrazzo flooring in the new housing became the deciding factor. I could just see a couple of babies cracking their heads on the floor, so we bought a ten-foot wide 47-foot two bedroom mobile home. Leighton built a screened-in patio room, and we were ready for our new baby.

Kathy arrived in November, three days after our second anniversary. She was the opposite of her older sister. She slept through the night, smiled a lot and cried very little. What a pleasure! Vivienne thought I had bought a new doll for her and immediately loved her little sister. In fact, I had to work extra hard to keep my fourteen month old Vivi from treating the infant like a rag doll. She wanted to play with the baby, so she tried to stuff things into her mouth, pull down the bassinette, and push a pencil in her belly button. One of Vivi's favorite tricks was to vault out of her own crib into Kathy's crib which was only eighteen inches away in the tiny bedroom. Okay, so my heaven proved to be more difficult to live in than I had envisioned, but I was absolutely contented with my sweet husband and my two little babies. 1959 was a very good year. Then came 1960. My parents were due to return from Germany in October. I wanted my mother to have the full experience of being a new grandmother, so I talked Leighton into letting me have another baby. What was I thinking?

There has never been any regret. Our Lisa turned out just as perfect as the other two. Her timing was a little off, though. My parents came back from Germany in October, but Lisa was not born until January 1961. We took her to Washington, D.C. to see my folks who were stationed at Andrews Air Force Base. The babies made a great hit with my mother and all the acrimony of the past was forgotten. Shortly after we got there, the Bay of Pigs debacle made the news. I was almost afraid to go back to Florida, but in our new larger car, a bare-bones Nash Rambler, we arrived in Homestead just in time to find out that we were moving again.

Leighton had the opportunity to be retrained in Illinois to work on missiles. Since the training would take four months, the Air Force would let me travel with him as long as we made our own living arrangements. "Let me go, Love. I'll stay there with you for a couple of months, and then I'll go to stay with my folks in Washington for a while."

"Okay, we'll find a small place to live in Rantoul, so we can be together," he agreed. The man is a saint, always trying to please me.

With two little girls and a six-month old baby, we set off toward the Midwest. Our "small place" was a trailer not much bigger than a shoe box. The five of us barely had room to breathe. It was summer, so we spent a lot of time outdoors. Leighton and I knew it was temporary, so we were happy just to be together with our little clan. Never mind the morning we woke up to screaming.

Vivienne had found my sewing shears and was practicing her hair dressing skills on herself and baby Lisa. Kathy was screaming because she didn't want her hair cut. My heart pounded as my mind envisioned the humungous scissors piercing my baby's head. In reality, I simply took the scissors away and yelled for a while. I think I traumatized all three of them that day because they all refused to let me cut their hair and let it grow long and straight as they were growing up. Of course, those were the hippie years when everybody wanted to look like Cher, anyway.

Finally, it was time for me to go to my folks. I decided that we would travel by train from Illinois to Washington D.C. It didn't look very far on the map, so off we went. The train ride was exciting for the girls for about fifteen minutes. Then everybody got antsy. Somehow I entertained my girls for a few hours. It seemed like a good idea to go to the dining car to give my daughters the full benefit of the railroad experience. The look on the porter's face as I dragged my brood into the dining car was worth every penny I spent on the trip. There had to be some way to wipe that smirk off his face!

We ordered food and had the baby's bottle heated up. My well-behaved family caused no trouble, but the porter remained cold and aloof. I left him the biggest tip I could afford and thanked him for his patience and kindness. Then I got up and left like a queen with three little princesses. He followed me and offered to open the door. I swear, I saw him smile and bow a little as we moved past him. I, who had never put much stock in being wealthy, gained a whole new perspective that day on what money could accomplish.

For six weeks the girls and I threw my parents home into turmoil. They had no experience with little children. They tried to be patient, but when Vivi and Kathy climbed on the back of a large swivel recliner and twirled around holding onto the drapes my mother lost it. I was in the shower at the time and thought the house was on fire because of all the screaming.

Now and then my dad gave my mother and me a break. He offered to baby-sit while we went to play Bingo at the NCO (Non-Commissioned Officers) Club. One such Bingo evening was especially exciting. My mother and I had purchased our cards and went to sit at a small round table. We sat down without realizing that the table had been saved until we noticed a set of bingo cards that weren't ours. We looked around for someone, but no one claimed the cards. I took them to a bingo worker for safe-keeping, and my mother and I chose another table.

Suddenly, a woman with a heavy German accent came over to us and started yelling, "You took my table! Now someone else has it. Why are you so stupid? Didn't you see my cards?"

I tried to explain that we had made an honest mistake, but she kept yelling. Finally, I said, "Leck mich am Arsch!" This remark is highly insulting in German.

Throughout the evening, she kept looking over to us and pointing us out to her friends. We ignored her.

After Bingo, the Club manager invited us to his office. He wanted to clarify the incident. Again we tried to explain. She was upset about the German insult and wanted an apology. My mother tried to appease everyone, but I refused to relent. When I stated that she didn't need to come yell at us for making a simple mistake, she took off her shoe and threw it toward my mother, yelling, "I would be ashamed if I had raised a daughter like that." The shoe sailed past my mother's head and banged against the wall. The manager told us all to go home and forget about it.

When we got home we told my dad what had happened. To my surprise, he blamed us and yelled, "Why are you always trying to cause trouble? Stay away from there. My dad.

Eventually, we heard that this lady had been banned from ever coming to Bingo at the NCO Club again. She apparently had proved to be a trouble-maker on several other occasions.

Not all our time together was this much fun. My mother gradually began to pry into our financial affairs. I got quite agitated one day when she hinted that my husband had told her that his parents rather than his wife and children had been named as the beneficiaries of his survivor's benefits. How would she know something like that? Why would she bring something like that up? I didn't know whether she was right or mistaken, but I didn't like the idea that my mother was trying to set me against my husband. This was something I would have to discuss with Leighton in person. It was a good thing that my three little girls made the six weeks go by quickly, or we would have had a big fight.

I could hardly wait for Leighton to come pick us up and return to Florida.

Overall, it was a good visit, and I was happy that my parents had a chance to get to know my daughters. However, I realized that I could depend on my mother to keep me on the defensive the rest of my life.

CALIFORNIA OR BUST

Life with three little girls in a Mobile Home Park in Florida was simple. Sunny days were spent in the swimming pool. The girls were too young for regular school, so I enrolled Vivi in a private Kindergarten; otherwise, I had nothing to worry about except my daily routine of meals, laundry and pleasing my sweet husband.

We wanted to go to California, so Leighton kept requesting a transfer. In early 1963, he finally got orders. We would move to Travis Air Force Base in June. Meanwhile my dad had retired and moved to Glendora, California. My parents were eager to see us all again, so we looked forward to our cross-country trip.

We took ten days, stopping early every day to get plenty of swimming time in the motels. Except for some extremely hot Southwest hours in our bare-bones Rambler (no air conditioning in those days), our trip was very pleasant. We had sold our mobile home and no longer had to count the pennies. By this time, we were rounding our expenses off to the nearest dollar.

"Wow, look at the nice house my folks have!" They were waiting for us in the front yard. Lots of hugs, and a fresh cup of coffee, made us feel welcome. My aunt also showed up to see the girls. In the excitement Lisa barfed all over the kitchen floor. My mother explained, "The poor little girl had to sit too long in the car."

For a few days we enjoyed Glendora together, and then Leighton left for Travis. He planned to scope out the area and rent an apartment, so we could join him soon. I could hardly wait to set up housekeeping again. I had gotten used to being my own boss, and the old tensions of being my mother's child had started to creep into our conversations. I did not want to destroy our relationship, so I avoided any discussions that might result in an argument.

In July Leighton came to get us. We had talked many times of choosing a place to settle down after he retired from the Air Force. When we saw Northern California, we both knew that this would eventually be our home if fate allowed. One month after we arrived, we purchased our home in Fairfield.

I was not too happy about Leighton being on the night shift. I still had many demons to deal with and needed assurance that someone would wake me out of a deep sleep in case of an emergency. The solution was "Happy," a dog from the SPCA. With a backyard for planting stuff, a friendly neighborhood and a school within walking distance for our first grader and Kindergartener, I had landed in heaven again.

"You know, Love, we should really try to have a son!" I approached Leighton right around Christmas.

"What if we have another girl?" he looked me straight in the eye to see if I was serious.

"That would be okay, but I'd love to have another baby, and each time it's a 50-50 chance." I rationalized. "Three is an odd number. Let's make it an even four children. That's a nice size family."

We were soon expecting our fourth child.

In April, I spent a lot of time in the yard digging and planting. The dust made me cough, but I didn't mind. This piece of the earth was ours, and I reveled in the thought of making things grow like my grandmother had in her vegetable garden.

"Love, I don't feel so good! I didn't sleep well all night." I yammered one morning.

He made an appointment for me. After listening to my complaints, the doctor gave me some sleeping pills and told me to get some rest.

I took one of the pills that night and promptly had a nightmare. A fence had fallen on me in my dream, and I couldn't breathe. As I was still gasping for air, Leighton woke me up.

"Love, what's wrong?" he wondered.

"Man, my chest hurts. I had a bad dream about a fence falling on me." I could barely get out the words. "I'm scared! I'm pregnant, and I'm in pain. Maybe it's just from the dream. Let's try to get some sleep." I lay back down on my pillow.

The pain didn't go away, though. Leighton called my neighbor Gisela. "I'm taking Marianne to the hospital, could you help watch the kids?" Gisela was always ready to help.

"This young lady has to be admitted. She has pneumonia in both lungs." The doctor in the emergency room declared.

"But I'm pregnant! What about my baby? I can't let you give me all those X-rays and medicine! It might hurt my baby!" I protested between painful coughing.

"First we have to keep the mother alive, and then we'll worry about the baby!" The doctor was firm with me. "Let's get you healed up first!"

For a couple of days, I was in and out of consciousness and gladly followed orders. When I started feeling a little better I was put on a salt-free liquid diet. Yuck! How did they expect me to get better with the kind of stuff they brought me? Jello and salt-free bullion! The pain in my stomach got worse than the pain in my lungs. When I complained to the doctor, he relented and put me on a salt-free soft diet. The stuff they called my breakfast, lunch and dinner was still awful! I couldn't eat, sleep or anything. I was even too weak to cough even though the doctor wanted me to, so my lungs would get stronger. Every time Leighton came to visit he made a sadder face. I must have looked terrible!

"Love, I wish I could help you! What can I do?" he wanted to know one afternoon.

"You could bring me a big juicy hamburger!" I suggested.

He was stunned. "I didn't expect that!"

"I'm serious. I'm starving. Either bring me a hamburger or bring the undertaker! I'm dying here."

At dinnertime, he reappeared with a sheepish grin on his face. "Look what I have here!" He unwrapped a big Dairy Queen hamburger and we dined together, being careful not to get caught.

For the first time in over a week, I slept well that night. The next morning I told the doctor what happened. He laughed, "Well, I guess we can put you back on a solid diet, but it still has to be salt-free. I also want you to cough as much as possible. You're still congested and running a fever. We can't let you go home yet."

I agreed to try coughing although it hurt a lot every time I made the effort.

Finally, one night, I woke up and felt my chest loosening up. I coughed a little. It didn't hurt! Happily, I coughed a little more. Yay! The doctor would be happy! Suddenly a nurse came in with a little medicine cup. "I heard you coughing. This is just a little cough syrup to give you some rest."

"But the doctor wants me to cough!"

"It's the middle of the night, and you're disturbing the other patients." She explained.

I refused the cough syrup and told her to get out of my room. The next morning, the doctor smiled, "I hear you're giving the staff a hard time. You must be getting better."

A few days later I went home to recuperate. I was still worried about my pregnancy, but with good food and the tender loving care from my husband, it went without any further problems.

We even restored an old piano so the girls could take lessons from one of Gisela's daughters.

In September our son, John, was born. What more could I want? I wanted this wonderful life in my own home to go for a long time, but this was not to be. Soon Leighton got orders to retrain into another career field near Denver. His expertise in missiles was no longer needed, but they needed people to work in precision measuring equipment. His training would take nine months, so the Air Force would move us. I didn't really want to go, but neither did I want to be without my Leighton. Jackie Kennedy had just lost her husband, and I didn't want to lose mine. I decided to keep our family together. Reluctantly, we turned our house over to a realtor, packed up and moved bag and baggage—four kids, a dog, a piano and miscellaneous stuff-- to Aurora, Colorado.

Within two weeks we had our family settled in. Vivienne and Kathy went to school, I had made friends with the strange kitchen stove and we experienced our first snow. Before we left the Denver area, the girls were playing the piano, Johnny had learned to walk, Leighton was ready to run a Precision Measuring Equipment Laboratory, and I had all my upper teeth pulled. I discovered I shouldn't have gone to Denver, but who knew?

We had free dental care in the Fitzsimmons Medical Center. This type of service was not available in most military hospitals, so I thought I'd get my teeth taken care of while we were there. Innocently, and still respecting authority, I went to my first appointment. A retired dentist working part-time looked at my teeth and said, "We should pull them and fit you with a nice prosthesis."

I was shocked and tried to argue back, "I just came in here to get my teeth checked and cavities fixed.'"

He was very convincing, "We can fix you up for free. You have lots of cavities, and it'll cost you thousands of dollars over the next few years. As you get older, your bones will shrink and you'll lose your teeth anyway. Do it now while you can get it done for free."

With a trembling heart I thought about all the money my teeth would cost in the future, so I said yes.

As he was pulling the first four teeth on my right side, a young assistant said, "Look at those roots, they could have been saved." The old dentist ignored him and continued to finish the job. I had to make two more trips to take care of the rest of my mouth. The second appointment took four teeth on the left side and the third, my four front teeth. I was devastated, but I thought I was doing the right thing. My sweet Leighton felt bad for me and wished I had talked it over with him first. Sometimes, independence is not so good.

For more than a year, I had nothing but trouble with the prosthesis, but life went on. With his training completed, Leighton got orders for Bangor, Maine. I had hoped we would be able to move back to California, but Maine it was. Luckily, I found a wonderful dentist in Bangor. Dr. Mouridian fitted me with new dentures that have served me faithfully for years.

There were many other wonderful things about Maine. We had a nice two story house on base and great neighbors with children about the ages of ours. We played cards on those snowy evenings and enjoyed many comfortable weekends with our friends. The weather reminded me of Germany. It got cold enough to make an ice skating rink out of the back yard by spraying water across the ground in the evening. By morning, it had turned to ice. I made warm coveralls out of military wool serge purchased at the clothing sales, and the children enjoyed their sleds and ice skates. We enrolled the girls in a Catholic school in Bangor where they also got piano lessons. We spent a very pleasant summer and enjoyed the beautiful Maine autumn with our friends. We looked forward to the holidays and celebrated a bountiful Thanksgiving. So close to the original Pilgrims, I felt very patriotic.

That feeling was put to the test in one phone call. "How would you like to spend Christmas with your folks?" For a moment I was stunned into silence. In 1966, this could only mean one thing. He was being sent to Viet Nam. I began to cry.

"No, no, Love! Don't tell me."

"No, I'm not going to Viet Nam. I'm being sent to Thailand. That's a little safer," he tried to assure me.

I didn't buy it, "But you'll be gone for a whole year. What'll I do?"

"You'll be fine. You're strong. Think of all you've already gone through. Besides, you can live with your folks." I cried even louder. I could already imagine how my mother would take over and boss me around. "We'll talk about it when I get home, okay?"

What choice did I have? It had to be okay. We were serving our country. We had only two weeks to get ready for the move, and we had accumulated a lot of stuff. One thing I made up my mind to do was move back into our own home in Fairfield. I was not staying with my folks. I wanted to remain on good terms with them, and I was sure that a year of being with them would destroy our relationship forever.

We arrived in Glendora on Christmas Eve. For a few days we enjoyed the holidays, and then we drove to Fairfield. Despite my brave front, I felt empty as I hugged my husband one more time before he boarded the plane that would take him far away from me. My home seemed strangely alien as I was cooking dinner for the kids. Suddenly, I thought about my grandmother and my mother, those two brave women who had raised their children through World Wars I and II. Somehow, that thought made me feel a little better, but...

I was back in California, but I might just as well have landed on the moon.

ALONE IN A CROWD

The year 1967 went by very slowly. My four little children, our dog, Happy, and my home kept me busy. Gisela, a neighbor who was also from Germany tried to cheer me up, and my mother made frequent phone calls. I even enrolled in two college classes on Travis Air Force Base (an extension of Vallejo Junior College) and took piano lessons from Gladys, a Bolivian lady. Nothing helped. I missed my husband terribly.

Vivienne and Kathy were attending Anna Kyle Elementary, just two blocks away from our cul-de-sac home on Coolidge Street. Lisa had started Kindergarten in Bangor, Maine, but there was no room for her at Anna Kyle. She was already six years old and plenty smart at reading and doing math, so I insisted they test her to see whether she could get into the first grade. The counselor explained that such an exception was very rare because the child would have to test at the upper two percent to qualify. A couple of days after the testing, the vice principal called me to let me know that they'd be happy to have Lisa attend first grade. Good. The three girls would be attending schools and little Johnny was only two and a half and easy to take care of.

Writing a letter to my sweet husband became part of my daily routine, and time somehow went by. The days were filled, but the nights were lonely.

My mom and dad's visit in the spring almost ended in disaster. I was preparing dinner and watching the kids through the kitchen window. They were waiting for "Oma and Opa" in their big car, so they went to sit on the sidewalk in front of Gisela's house with a couple of friends. Suddenly I heard brakes squealing and kids screaming. I ran outside and saw my girls come running toward me. "Johnny got hit by a car!"

I remember screaming, but there is no way to describe my emotions at that moment. I flew toward the street. Someone was coming toward me carrying my beautiful boy who looked just fine. Relief flooded over me, but I was skeptical. What had happened? Apparently, the driver, seeing the flock of kids on the sidewalk had slowed down. Johnny, thinking it was my folks' car, jumped up and hit the side of the car as it went by. The driver stopped right away, and another car braked quickly enough to make the tires squeal. I couldn't stop crying and insisted on going to the hospital to have Johnny checked. Gisela promised to watch the girls and make my folks welcome when they arrived. It took me a few days to calm down, and I kept the incident a secret from my husband who had enough to worry about with a war going on.

Summer vacation was coming, so I planned to take the kids to my folks for a couple of weeks. We could go to Disneyland while we were there. Our big Chevy station wagon had plenty of room for all of us, including the dog. I was sure everything would be fine. We left early one morning with enough money to stop halfway there if I couldn't drive the whole way at once.

We stopped for ice cream at a stand shaped like a big orange on highway 99, and everybody was still happy. The long drive was boring, but we sang and played word games. Suddenly, one of the girls yelled, "Happy pooped on my pillow!"

The smell reached my nose, and everyone was yelling. Finally, we reached a gas station. We threw away the pillow, aired out the car, filled the gas tank and refreshed ourselves. This was turning out to be an exciting trip.

Just as we approached the grapevine, the car sputtered once or twice but kept on going. I was wondering whether there might have been a drop of water in the gas we just got and kept my foot on the accelerator. Up the hill next to a big rig, "Sputter, sputter." We kept on going. What in the world was happening? I got in line with the traffic on the far right.

I thought, "If the car stalls, at least I won't be in the middle of the highway causing a traffic jam." Naturally, in the back of my mind I feared the worst, but there was no way I would let my kids watch me panic. I just smiled and told them there was nothing to worry about. Inwardly, I worried plenty. We would be hitting Interstate 10 during rush hour. How would my station wagon act at 65 mph in bumper to bumper traffic? Now and then the engine gave a little cough but no stalling. I prayed.

By the time we arrived at my folks' house my shoulders were tight and my right leg cramping. I told my dad how the car acted, and he analyzed it right away, "It must be the fuel pump."

The next day we took the car to my uncle who owned a garage in Covina. He replaced the fuel pump and explained that the old one had been working at only about 10%. I prayed some more. It was amazing that we had not stalled right in the middle of all that traffic.

For the rest of the time we enjoyed being spoiled by Oma and Opa. Their new house had space for all of us, and the atmosphere remained pleasant. My mother had stopped making snide remarks about my husband, and she thoroughly enjoyed our sweet children. It seemed that she had finally respected the fact that I was a grown woman with a family. I was very comfortable in our new relationship. We made plans to get together at Christmas before my little clan headed back to Fairfield.

School started again in September. One day I got a phone call from Leighton. He would be arriving at Travis Air Force Base this afternoon at 2:00. What??? His year was not over. Why was he coming back already? My imagination had him coming home on a gurney. Instead, he was simply bringing some equipment to be repaired at Newark, Ohio. Travis AFB was the entry point for military aircraft, so he scheduled a two-day layover on this trip. I went to the school to get the girls, and we piled into the car. They wondered what the emergency was, but I just kept smiling without saying a word. At the terminal I couldn't keep the secret any longer. "Daddy will be coming off that airplane. He will only stay for a couple of days, and then he has to leave again."

We were ecstatic. The two days went by far too quickly. Phone calls from Newark kept us in touch, and another quick stop at Travis on the way back to Thailand helped to pass September and part of October. Halloween and Thanksgiving also kept us busy, but the hole in my heart had widened. While I had gradually gotten accustomed to being the one in charge, I realized how much I missed my husband after he left for the second time. Christmas without him was a dismal prospect. The wintry weather didn't help either, and I was diagnosed with strep throat which was treated with penicillin.

My folks came to Fairfield as promised and tried to make sure we enjoyed the holidays. I couldn't get into the spirit despite their best efforts. Two more months before my husband's return seemed an eternity. The war in Viet Nam was raging, and I was afraid that he might never come back. My mother kept nagging that I had to stay strong for the children, but I was tense and depressed. My folks left the day after Christmas, and I noticed an itchy bump on my right shin as I was waving good-bye to them.

Within days the blue-green bump grew to the size of an orange and two more developed on my legs. The pain was intense. I could barely drag myself to the hospital while Gisela watched the kids. It turned out to be a severe allergic reaction, erythema nodosum, to the penicillin. The doctor explained that this kind of reaction often takes six weeks to develop and just as long to go away. He gave me medicine to relieve the symptoms, but I was very sick. Again, I didn't want to worry Leighton and didn't tell him anything about my condition.

Presumptuously, I had assumed that the future of the world depended on my stoicism. If I became weak and my husband had to be brought back, the war effort might not succeed. If the war effort did not succeed, the Communists (God forbid!) might take over the world, and then what? My little bump was insignificant compared to such an imagined cataclysm. Somehow I managed to live through the following month. The fate of the world depended on me!

When Leighton finished his tour of duty in February 1968, he returned just in time to fish his wife out of the maelstrom. My health gradually improved. Together we grappled with moving to Indiana, an unfamiliar place to both of us but a place where a family could grow in peace.

MOM, THE HOOSIER HERO

We had hoped to stay at Travis Air Force Base. We had our home and extended family in California, and moving again was an unwelcome prospect. Our orders, however, were for Bunker Hill Air Force Base in Peru, Indiana. I had become philosophical: "Well, at least it wasn't the country Peru!" We would still be in the same country on the same continent with our families. After having been separated by oceans from people I loved, this was important to me. Our time in Indiana turned out to be even better than I thought possible.

After the movers packed up our belongings in the Fairfield house, we piled into our big blue '64 Bel Air station wagon and went to visit our families in the Los Angeles area one more time before setting out on another cross-country trip toward an unfamiliar goal.

At Bunker Hill, we had to stay in transit quarters for a couple of weeks while we were waiting for Base Housing. The waiting list wasn't very long, and with Leighton being a Master sergeant, we were soon assigned a split-level home on Schilling Blvd. "Oh, Love, it's beautiful. Look, there is a basement, and all the bedrooms are upstairs!"

"We'll be happy here. There is plenty of room for the kids to play, and we can get some furniture from base supply until our own stuff arrives," Leighton assured me.

It didn't take us long to get settled. Our stuff from Fairfield arrived a month later, and I used my sewing machine right away to upholster the dining room chairs and make a matching table cloth. I had already made friends with the kitchen stove and arranged our home to my personal preferences. There were always some things that had to be taken care of right away in a new home: register the kids in school, connect the telephone, order a newspaper, and get a piano teacher for the girls.

While Leighton was getting settled into his new work environment, I had time to make all the arrangements. Calling around, I found out that Mrs. McIlheny was considered the best piano teacher in Peru,

Indiana. I went to see her. "Sorry, I only have one opening. The best I can do is a half hour lesson. I'll take your oldest daughter."

Reluctantly, I agreed, but I could see the disappointment on Kathy's face. I found another teacher, Mrs. Anderson, who lived on base. While Vivienne was making excellent progress on the old piano, Kathy and Lisa seemed to be going nowhere. From the daily practice, I knew that they were just as talented and motivated, but I had to find a new teacher and perhaps a new piano. The new Cable piano and a huge library of music books helped a little, but the girls weren't even happy with the new teacher. By June, it had become apparent that I had to do something. Suddenly, something was done for me.

On the first day of school vacation, Kathy came home with a broken arm. She had fallen off a swing. For six weeks, her right arm was in a cast. So much for piano lessons.

That summer Vivienne and Lisa competed and won trophies using Kathy's new bicycle in a bicycle rodeo organized by the NCOA (Non-Commissioned Officers Association). Kathy had received the bike because we bought Vivi a saxophone to play in the school band. Poor Kathy! This was not her year.

Kathy's cast came off, and she started practicing the piano again. One day as she sat down on the bench, her hand went up to scratch her scalp. Then she asked me to scratch her back. Then I noticed her arms turning red and itchy. I rushed her to the hospital. Hives. The doctor suggested Calamine lotion and asked me about her nerves. There was no problem that I knew of, and Kathy seemed happy. The hives had completely disappeared by the time we got home. The next day, the same thing happened. Her hands swelled, and her skin itched all over her body. I realized right away that the pressure of trying to please me was too much for my sweet little girl. We had a long talk. I promised her that I would not make her practice or play the piano anymore. Her health and happiness was much more important to me than her ability to play the piano. One thing I requested, however was, "Kathy, if you ever want to start piano lessons again, you have to tell me. I will not bring it up."

"Okay, Mom." Kathy never had the hives again.

Even though it was extremely difficult for me to ignore Kathy's lack of musical interest, I stuck to my promise. Lisa started lessons with a young teacher recommended by Mrs. McIlheny and finally seemed happy. The summer went by, and we had plenty of other diversions.

Through the NCO Club we had made friends with a number of other nice young couples. For years, Leighton had to beg me each time to get a baby-sitter and attend his social affairs. Although he was patient with my stubborn insistence on being the Earth mother in my own home, he liked going out to dinner and dancing once in a while. In Indiana, I finally loosened up. Notably, John and Joan Pascuitti were particularly compatible with us. We played cards and went to parties together. Their little boy, Christopher, was about the same age as our four-year-old Johnny. Joan and I would take the boys to the base nursery while we attended NCO Wives functions once a week. I finally felt that it was okay for me to develop a life outside of my home. I even accepted a nomination for Assistant Treasurer and was elected. Leighton gladly supported my new enthusiasm for the social events planned by our club.

With my usual vigor, I threw myself into my new social life. My sewing machine almost groaned under my demands. I made three formal dresses, two wool traveling suits, Hawaiian outfits and other costumes for our various functions. When Leighton and I showed up as Captain Hook and Peter Pan, we were the hit of the Halloween party. I also made nearly all the kids' clothes. From morning to night, my hands were always busy, and I expected the same from others. There was one incident that shocked me back to reality: the first time I ever was truly disappointed by my wonderful husband.

In Thailand, Leighton had gone to see a lot of movies. One of his favorites was <u>Dr. Zhivago.</u> When this movie came to the base theater, he suggested I go see this movie. He would stay and watch the kids. Leaving the dinner dishes in the sink, I rushed out of the house to pick up Joan and make it to the movie on time. For nearly three enchanted hours, I was enthralled by the images on the screen and the memories of my own war experiences. I had been alternately homeless, frozen and in love, much like Lara. The main difference was that my romance had been transformed into a loving marriage with four children and a comfortable house. Gratefully, I floated home with dreams of a welcoming smile and romantic embrace.

Instead, I opened the door to a messy kitchen and a husband already snoring.

At that moment, I couldn't think of anything romantic about my situation. Couldn't someone have washed the dishes? Couldn't someone have waited up for me? Couldn't someone realize that I would be emotionally charged by this movie? Couldn't someone understand how much a war survivor needed to sort out her own past in a "debriefing" after seeing such a movie? The silent house with the dirty dishes overwhelmed me. I sat down and cried and cried. For nearly three days, I couldn't speak civilly to Leighton. He didn't know what he had done wrong, and I couldn't tell him. There was no fight, but even the kids realized that we were mad at each other.

Our anger had to stop because our little boy got very sick. Johnny just wanted to sleep. He didn't or couldn't eat. The doctors couldn't determine exactly what was wrong and assured me that he just had the flu. Neglecting everything else, I sat by him hours at a time trying to get his mouth to accept a little Jell-O or chicken broth. With his pale baby-face and closed angelic eyes, he seemed so vulnerable and weak. I was numb with fear. This went on for two weeks. I was sure we would lose him. Then one afternoon, when I had him upstairs to clean him up, he made vomiting noises. I quickly leaned him over the toilet, and he up-chucked a mass that looked like a shapeless sponge. Both Johnny and I were fascinated by the mass as it floated in the toilet bowl. There were no loose pieces just the porous mass. Johnny smiled at me and said, "I'm hungry." He had no idea why I began to cry as I prepared him some food.

With our busy social life, this crisis was soon forgotten. The NCO Wives had another luncheon, and the golf pro had been invited to speak. He was inviting the ladies to try golfing on the base golf course. Leighton had already tried to get me to golfing with him after work. The summer afternoons were long enough to get in nine holes before dark, but I was not interested in golf. When a half dozen ladies, including Joan, Virginia Thompson and a French woman named Monique coaxed me to join them in the free golf lessons, I relented. Leighton was impressed. He was hopeful that I would get involved in a sport that he particularly enjoyed.

Of the four women accompanied by the golf pro, I was the one with the lowest score at the end of the day. The facts that the reasonably-priced golf course was on base, and cheap day-care was available at the base nursery, kept me enthused. I even won a couple of trophies in golf tournaments. After getting off work at four o'clock, Leighton took me golfing for a couple of hours before dinner. Was there no limit to the things I could do? I was truly expanding my horizons. Indiana was good, and I was thoroughly enjoying my life there.

In the evenings, we often played cards with friends. Our children were close by playing games while the adults enjoyed pinochle or bridge. Two particularly memorable games almost (emphasize almost) in disasters. Joan invited a group of us ladies to play bridge at her house. One of the ladies was Virginia Thompson, a neat-freak. After the bidding in bridge, one player out of four gets to sit out and be the "dummy." I had won the bidding, and my partner Virginia was the dummy. There was nothing unusual about her getting up and straightening things.

After she sat down for the next deal, we all started to smell smoke. Alarmed, we searched around Joan's house for the source. There was a pantry in the kitchen where Joan kept her garbage bucket. Billows of smoke oozed through the cracks. We were afraid to open the door and afraid not to open it. Finally, we stood ready with a couple of buckets of water while Joan cautiously inspected the damage. Flames shot out, but we quickly extinguished the fire Virginia had started by emptying an ashtray directly into the garbage can.

On another evening Leighton and I hosted a pinochle party. We had invited three couples and planned a tournament where partners alternate until each person has had a chance to be partners with each of the seven other players. With good food and lots of laughter, we were having a great time until the Stewarts became partners. This husband wife team was known for their rambunctious relationship, but we expected them to be able to play four hands of pinochle without incident. Wrong! The first hand didn't even get finished before the loud shouting began. With doors slamming behind them, the Stewarts left the rest of us to complete our tournament. I was extremely embarrassed, but everyone was gracious enough to make the remainder of our evening enjoyable.

Despite our expanding social life, our focus remained on our children. Vivi, Kathy and Lisa attended school regularly. They brought home excellent reports. Vivi enjoyed learning to play the saxophone and Kathy continued with her clarinet in the school band. John was a growing boy who kept me hopping. One evening, the kids were upstairs noisily getting ready for bed. Suddenly, one of the girls shouted, "Mom, Johnny fell asleep in the bathtub!" I almost fainted. Asleep? Probably drowned! I raced upstairs. There was John, lying on his back in about three inches of water with his whole face out in the air. He was breathing normally, but I wasn't. Luckily, I had already trained the girls never to put much water in the tub when Johnny was going to take a bath.

That boy gave me another scare when he and a couple of friends took the dining room chairs outside to build a fort on the front lawn. Somebody screamed, "Johnny's eye is bleeding!" I was afraid to look and slapped a towel on his face. A neighbor rushed us to the hospital for stitches. The small cut was above the eyebrow, and the eye was safe.

Leighton's club, the NCOA decided to put on a Fourth of July Carnival for the base. Various organizations, including our NCO Wives club were invited to have our own fund-raising booths. It took months of preparations to get the permissions and materials together. The Base Commander rationalized that it would be beneficial to keep the people as close to the base as possible for the long Fourth of July weekend, so he approved and supported the event. The NCO Wives decided to have a "Taco Stand" because one of our members was a Mexican lady who was known for her delicious tacos. I was selected as the "Taco" chairman for this three-day event. Someone had a small travel trailer that served as our "kitchen." Under a decorated awning, we sold the tacos at three for a dollar. Business was brisk. All the other booths were also making money and there were lots of games to be played before the culminating fireworks on the Fourth of July. Unfortunately, in the aftermath of this successful event, the Base Comptroller, accused the Base Commander of misappropriating funds for the event. Proper channels had been by-passed. Bureaucracy prevailed and people were reprimanded.

Meanwhile life went on in our home. My mother came to visit for a month. It was a very nice visit, but she told me that she had recently been diagnosed with rheumatoid arthritis. I realized that this was a very serious disease and tried to stay brave. When I told my friend Joan what kind of medication my mother was taking, she advised me to try to talk my mother out of it. As a medical technician, Joan had access to information regarding this medication. It was still experimental and considered very dangerous. My mother didn't listen to me because, "You're not a doctor." She had apparently not lost her edge. With just a few words, she had always been able to remind me of my lowly status. All in all, the visit was very pleasant.

My mother missed the fun of the tornado season in Indiana. We spent several afternoons in the cellar anxiously peering out the window at the lead-colored sky. Heavy cloud formations and radioed tornado warnings were enough to keep us alert. Fortunately, we never actually experienced the full fury.

The excitement wasn't enough for the girls. The three of them were always thinking of mischief to keep me going. One sunny afternoon one of them yelled into the front door, "Lisa is trying to start a fire!" I ran outside and found Lisa under a tall Juniper watching a little fire. I quickly pulled her out of the way and stomped on the quickly burning dry branches on the ground. She remembers the event but not the reason other than curiosity about using matches. I made a terrific commotion and restricted Lisa's activities for several weeks.

One day Kathy said, "Mom, I want to talk to you." I was apprehensive. What now?

"Yes, Baby, what's wrong?"

"Mom, if I could get Mrs. McIlheny, I'd like to start piano lessons again."

I almost knocked a chair over in my haste to get to the phone. I explained to Mrs. McIlheny what had happened with Kathy's piano, the broken arm and the hives. My patience had paid off. Mrs. McIlheny made time for Kathy, and soon the girls were playing duets again.

Before the end of the summer, our friends planned a picnic at Indiana Beach. We packed lots of goodies and bathing suits. Between the Thompson's, Pascuitti's, Tong's and two other families, we had about ten children. We had great fun all day, and I got my reputation as "The Hero." The whole crowd was sitting high up on the beach while I was watching Johnny and Chris (the two four-year-olds) splash around in the sand near the water. A few yards away from us was a group of young men (perhaps around twenty years or so) playing catch with a football. Everyone was having fun. Suddenly the ball got away from the guys and flew toward my two little guys. One huge guy lunged after the ball and got a little too close to my little group. I reached out and hit the guy on the shoulder with the loud comment, "Careful, you could have hurt my two little boys!" The guy fell down, more from his momentum than from my weak tap. He went back to his laughing friends who pointed at me and cheered.

That tap made quite a hit. My little Johnny said, "Wow, Mom, you Karate-chopped that guy." Chris gave me a big hug, and our friends who had watched the whole thing from the beach clapped and cheered for me. I was quite embarrassed by all the hullaballoo, but I loved the attention.

The twenty months in Indiana passed too quickly. We were looking forward to another nice winter and the Christmas holidays when Leighton came home with some news. "We're going to Germany!"

For years, I had not-so-secretly wished we would get orders for Germany. I still had family there, knew the language and needed to exchange my old memories for new ones. Now that the time had come, I was hesitant. Was I really ready to face my father again? How would my Chinese husband be received? Would our children like Germany? The answers would have to be experienced. I couldn't guess them ahead of time. There was nothing to be decided. The Air Force was sending us. Only our attitude toward the experience was in our own hands.

I organized our household goods and made us some traveling clothes. In October 1969, we drove to McGuire AFB in New Jersey to catch our flight to Frankfurt. Another adventure was about to begin.

BACK TO MY ROOTS

Once we arrived in Germany, I looked up my father whom I hadn't seen in nineteen years. Many difficult memories had to be overcome, but my sweet husband and children helped to bridge the chasm that had become deeper than the Atlantic Ocean. My father and I developed a mature relationship and I grew to love him despite our past.

My father immediately fell in love with his "Jungche", (little boy) John. We frequently went to his home-office combination, and John played with the typewriter. I taught the children to call my father "Großvater" because they had known my dad as "Opa," the usual German for grandpa. He and his wife "Tante Lotti" came to our home a lot, and we often made sightseeing tours to Luxembourg, Bernkastel, Vianden, or other places around the area. They also enjoyed playing Bingo with us in our little NCO Club.

The four years in Germany were filled with activity. There were ski trips, sight-seeing tours, baseball tournaments, pig roasts, skating parties, and teen club events. John always fitted in despite his age. Whatever was in the plan, his good sportsmanship, appropriate behavior and cheerful disposition could be depended upon. The girls were becoming wonderful young ladies. Leighton enjoyed his job of managing the Precision Measuring Equipment Laboratory in Bitburg, and I loved helping my father in the office two times a week.

With so much to do, we needed a second car. My father found a friend who wanted to sell his small Opel. It was perfect for us. When I thought I needed a phone to keep in touch, my father pulled some strings to get us to the top of the waiting list. It was definitely an advantage to have my German father living in the same city where we were stationed.

I wanted to make sure that they wouldn't lose their piano-playing skills, so I scouted around for a good piano teacher. Through Kathy's school teacher, I became acquainted with Frau Unger. She was supposedly a wonderful teacher, but she couldn't speak English. Even though I could speak German, I had not taught my children the language. I asked Frau Unger to try teaching them despite the language problem. At first I went with them to interpret instructions, but soon I was no longer needed. Music is universal, and the girls benefited enormously from the experience of learning to play the piano and speak German at the same time.

Frau Unger brought out the best musicianship in the girls. Vivi and Kathy became especially adept at four-handed classical pieces. Frau Unger even facilitated a very special experience: she managed to get tickets for us to a performance by Philipe Entremont on Beethoven's birthday in Bonn. I made blue velvet dresses with white lace collars for the occasion. The difficult trip through a snowy night was well worth it. The winter weather couldn't dampen our spirit as we sang, "Happy Birthday, dear Ludwig!" in the car.

John joined the WEBELOS, the youngest level of the Boy Scouts. He proudly wore his uniform to meetings, but carried his official wallet wherever he went, for a while. One day he came from the playground crying. He had noticed that his wallet was gone. I asked him where he might have lost it. He explained that he had it in his pants pocket just a little while ago. I said something about being a little more careful with things in his back pocket. All his frustration was expressed in the outburst, "Next time buy me some BIG pockets!" I couldn't help laughing out loud as I hugged him and promised to sew some huge pockets on the inside of his coat.

That summer my mother came to visit us. For a few days we enjoyed each other's company, and then the old stresses came back. She had brought some divorce and child support documentation from twenty years earlier. I wasn't sure what she wanted me to do with this paperwork, but I suspected that she wanted me to approach my father with it. I was not willing to get involved in legal battles that should have been fought a long time ago without me.

Even though we tried our best to make this visit as pleasant as possible, the tension between us was growing. My mother also spent time with her older sister in Trier and her younger brother in Koblenz. My grandmother was still alive and happy to have my mother back in Germany. I was doing a balancing act trying to please all my relatives without neglecting my own family.

In late fall I began to feel the strain on my system. I tried to manage a persistent pain in my right side with a heating pad, but nothing helped. Just before Christmas I had to have emergency surgery to remove my gallbladder. By New Year's Eve I had sufficiently recuperated to celebrate in a restaurant with my family.

That spring John became interested in baseball. Our housing area had a solitary baseball diamond that was used for men's and women's softball, teen club games, major and minor Little League games and all the practices. We signed John up in the PeeWee League. His first team was called the Pirates. We were incredibly proud of our little slugger.

Vivi, Kathy and Lisa also participated in softball, and I was a happy spectator. One day one of the other young mothers asked me to join the women's softball team. "Oh no," I begged off, "I don't even know how to throw a ball. I'm terrible at sports."

"Come on. We'll teach you. We only have eight players, and we need another person, or we can't play."

Since she put it like that, I agreed to come to the next practice. The welcomed me as a needed right-fielder. They worked hard with me as I attended all the practices and games. During the last game everybody cheered when I made a catch in right field. The crowd, composed mostly of friends and neighbors, went wild when I made a base hit. I got a standing ovation when I caught the winning out. I was tickled pink to receive the most improved trophy at our banquet.

For the next couple of years, our softball team traveled regularly to Ramstein and several other U. S. Air Bases to compete against their dependent wives' teams.

MY WATERMELON LETTER

"Love, I'm so angry I could scream!" I yelled and slammed the door as I returned from our small commissary. We lived in a base housing area just outside of Trier, Germany. The main commissary at Bitburg Air Base, was located twenty-five kilometers away in the Eifel mountains. Housing was limited on the main base, so the ninety units in five large apartment buildings served the American families stationed in Bitburg. Lee was the ranking NCO on this remote site and therefore in charge of overseeing the support activities, such as the movie theater, the cleanliness of the buildings, the Teen club, and other things. His actual Air Force duties had to do with the Precision Measuring Equipment Lab in Bitburg.

"Wow, calm down, Love! What got you so upset?" Lee tried to give me a hug.

"You can't fix this with your charm!" I yelled so loud that our daughters came out of their rooms to check on us. They weren't used to us fighting.

"Okay, okay, just tell me what happened," Lee was really curious by now.

"Eve is pregnant, and she's from Texas, and she likes watermelons, and we're supposed to save gas by not driving to Bitburg unnecessarily, and, and…" I was getting out of breath with outrage.

"You're not making any sense," Lee held my hand. "Now explain it to me again, but talk a little slower. Start from the beginning. Why are you so angry?"

I took a deep breath, "For the past couple of weeks, watermelons from the States have been shipped to the main commissary, and Franz, the German manager of our little branch commissary was allowed to bring a few for sale here. Last week he put up a sign that said 'Watermelons need to be ordered ahead of time for Saturday delivery'. As you know, Eve loves watermelons, so she ordered one for today. The only thing is that she forgot she had a family trip to Luxembourg planned, so she

115

asked me to pick up the watermelon for her. When I talked to Franz, he told me that the commander of the main commissary wouldn't let him bring any more watermelons to Trier. Eve will be very disappointed"

"Ah, so that's why you're upset," Lee said calmly, and the girls went back into their rooms. The excitement was over.

"Love, that's only part of my outrage. What really gets my goat is that the base commander had an article in the base newspaper just last month about saving gas during this energy crisis of 1972 and not driving back and forth unnecessarily. And now we here at Trier Housing have to waste gas because of some stupid arbitrary rule about watermelons. It's disgusting! Eve is going to be very disappointed. She's pregnant! By now, you should be quite experienced about how women get when they're pregnant." I was finally getting calm, but I couldn't let go of my thoughts about the situation. "I just want to slap somebody!"

"Love, now it all makes sense. Why don't you write the Base Commander and explain your feelings just the way you explained them to me?" Lee asked.

"Are you sure? Won't you get in trouble? Won't that reflect badly on you? We wives shouldn't be making waves, especially not overseas," I had never complained about military matters before, and I considered the commissary and all other support services part of the military.

"If you don't use any profanity and explain your point of view as logically as you've explained it to me, nothing bad will happen. You might not get what you want, but there is no harm in trying," Lee assured me.

I wrote a polite note to the Base Commander, explaining my concern about the waste of gasoline and the unfairness of not getting our fair share of the produce that comes from the States. My hands were shaking as I deposited the stamped envelope in the mail box.

A few days later, I received a copy of my letter with the Base Commander's handwritten comment to the Commissary Commander, " What about this, Bill?" I wasn't sure what to make of this brief note, but I noticed that our Trier Housing Commissary had watermelons for the rest of the season. I assumed my little note had achieved the desired result and made up my mind to hone my writing skills as much as possible. I might have to move someone else into action in the future.

EXPLORING EUROPE

One winter our family took a trip to Bavaria. We went sight-seeing in Vienna and Salzburg and even went to St. Wolfgang so I could show my husband where I had spent the last year of the war. We also went skiing in Berchtesgaden. Johnny was only six years old. On the slopes he acted as if he knew what it was all about. He kept up with his sisters even though he was quite a bit younger than they.

Leighton and I took our parental responsibilities very seriously. When the teen club director in our housing area quit, he encouraged me to apply. I got the job. For the next eighteen months we spent time planning and carrying out activities and trips with the teenagers on Trier Hill. Leighton even got a bus driver's license, so he could requisition base buses for day trips. We took the twenty or so teens to various places in the surrounding area. We went skating in Luxembourg, exploring the large Ehrenbreitstein fort in Koblenz, dining in a German restaurant, and clowning around in a circus.

We also raised money to make longer trips. After obtaining the necessary documents, we went on a train through East Germany to Berlin. The director of the AYA (American Youth Association) Teen Club in Berlin guided us all around the city. The Berlin Wall was still up at that time, and the teen club members were quite impressed. There were many other interesting things to experience. On our way back to Trier, someone mentioned, "We ought to go skiing in the Alps next time."

I couldn't let a challenge like that go by. Soon we were raising money for a ski trip to Garmisch. With the train travel discount for club members, room and board in youth hostels, and low-cost rental ski equipment through the U.S. Air Force recreation services, a ski trip was definitely within the realm of possibilities.

The high school principal peered at me over his glasses, "I can't just let my students take a few days off, even if it is an educational experience to ski in the Alps."

"Isn't there some way that I can arrange to get the students out of school for three days? It'll be an experience of a lifetime," I probed. "We can't get reservation during school vacation."

"Well, if you can get the parents to write requests for a short period of independent study, I could give my approval."

I went to each teenager's parents, and the trip was on!

The train took us to Garmisch. We went on local buses to the low-cost youth hostel, where we had to split up into two large dormitories, one for males and one for females. For the very small price of staying there, we would have to help serve our own food and help in the kitchen with clean-up. We also had to keep the dormitories clean and neat. I had instructed the teens on what to expect, so everybody was cooperative.

Early the next morning we rode the bus to the ski slopes. We had reserved the rental ski equipment ahead of time, so it didn't take long for us to get into the spirit. After I fell a couple of times, I decided that as leader of this group, I couldn't afford get a broken leg. I spent most of my time near the ski lodge helping the kids with their equipment or making sure they weren't hungry or thirsty.

When we got home four days later, the only injury was one broken leg. Oddly, the one girl who wasn't allowed to go on the trip with us because her parents were afraid she'd get hurt, was on crutches. She had broken her leg playing basketball while the rest of the teen club was skiing unscathed.

The teen club also made a trip to Paris. French train service was not nearly as efficient or pleasant as German rails. Our group of eighteen teenagers and five chaperones had to spend several cold hours on a platform in Metz waiting for a connection to Paris. The way back also had its ups and downs. Even though the sightseeing and transportation in Paris was wonderful, our kids couldn't get used to the French cuisine. It was expensive and

not to our taste. When we found a McDonald's on the Champs d'Elysee, I thought our kids would go crazy. We finally got something decent to eat.

The four years in Germany went by far too quickly. My relationship with my father was cemented, but it caused the rift between my mother and me to widen. This, however, is material for another book.

In November 1973 we flew back to the United States.

NORTH CAROLINA

Our first assignment back in the continental U.S. was Seymour-Johnson Air Force Base in Goldsboro, North Carolina. We only stayed in North Carolina until August 1974, but in that time we did quite a few interesting things. We viewed the U.S.S. North Carolina Battleship Memorial in Wilmington. We also took a short vacation to Washington, D.C. to show our children the Nation's Capital. Since we had bought a camping trailer we spent some time in at a camp site near Manassas, Virginia to view the battle field where the First and Second Battles of Bull Run were fought during the Civil War.

There was school, softball, Sunday afternoon Kiddie bingo at the NCO Club, and golfing to keep everyone entertained. John joined a Little League baseball team and soon found that he had been taught well in Germany. The girls played softball and took piano lessons. We had a nice house in base housing, and we should have been very happy. Unfortunately, Leighton and I were not happy to be in North Carolina. We were far away from any other part of our families and were suddenly notified that Grandpa Tong had died. We hadn't even heard he was sick, and his death was quite a shock to us. Our hearts yearned to get back to California.

Lee was still in the Air Force, so we didn't really have the freedom to leave. After talking it over for a long time, Lee made the decision to retire with twenty-two years in the service. He would get out in November 1974, but school would start in September. We took leave and moved the family during the summer vacation.

We had bought a travel trailer, so we made a very pleasant cross-country trip. We set up housekeeping in our house on Coolidge Street that had deteriorated because it had been rented out for more than eleven years. Lee had to go back to North Carolina to finish out his tour of duty, and I did the best I could with the house. The yard was also a mess, and the kids and I lived out of boxes for a while. But we were home

PRUNES

That same summer I got acquainted with some Guamanian people across the street. The German wife of the oldest son was living with them. She was childless and intended to get divorced as soon as she could afford to live separately. She tried to get a job, and got me caught up in the effort to "work". When she finally got a job in the fields in Winters, she needed a ride. Since I had a car, idiot me fell into the trap of volunteering to drive if I could also work there. What an experience!

I was reasonably sure the kids were old enough by this time to take care of themselves during the day. Viv was almost seventeen; Kathy, sixteen; Lisa, thirteen; and John, ten, so I really wasn't needed for baby-sitting, anymore. I told them I'd really appreciate it, if they would take care of things at home, so I could earn a little extra money for their school clothes and other things they'd need during the coming year. I had never worked outside of my home before, and I loved being with my kids, but this was something I thought I needed to do at the time.

Vera, the German woman, told me that I could start on Monday. I was to bring a lunch and wear old clothes because there were no fancy facilities where we were going. She also surprised me with the fact that I would have to pick up a couple of other people in Vacaville. The two women we picked up were either Philippine or Guamanian, and their brown bags contained pungent lunches that smelled up the car. Even though my relatively new car had air-conditioning, the ride was very unpleasant for me. Despite my usual bravado, I didn't have the nerve to tell Vera not to smoke one cigarette after another or to tell the others to put their lunch into the trunk. Anyhow, we finally arrived at our destination.

Most of the others on our work crew had already arrived. I noticed the stares when they saw me. They must have figured that a soft white house-wife like me would never make it through the day. I could sense their amusement. Well, I was determined not to break. I thought, "This

Marianne has endured more difficult days, and she is going to make it through this one, too."

The first day we were to sort prunes. The work area was a large concrete pad with a tin roof for shade. There was a strong odor of prunes everywhere. Large wooden containers were stacked on one side, and a huge conveyer belt system lined the other side. The foreman told us to take up our stations at the belt. Actually, there were two belts directly in front of the workers. Each belt was about eighteen inches wide. The nearest one to us moved from left to right and moved all the prunes past us. We were to leave the good ones and toss the bad prunes to the second belt which moved from right to left.

After about ten minutes of looking at the moving belts, I started to feel dizzy. I forced myself to retain my equilibrium, swallowed a few times, and stubbornly kept sorting the prunes. Pretty soon I felt as if I were on a ship. The belts kept moving in opposite directions, and I kept sorting. There was very little talk or camaraderie because the motor that moved the belts made a terrific clatter. The heat started to roll in about ten o'clock. I kept thinking of the money that would roll in and how proud Lee would be of me for "working". As the noon-day heat got more and more oppressive, I also started thinking about the kids at home without their mother or their father. They were probably rolling around in front of the TV. The belts kept rolling like great waves on the ocean, and the prunes smelled like the stuff they supposedly facilitate. But I stubbornly kept at my task.

A half hour for lunch and ten minute breaks every two hours helped to pass the time. At the end of the workday, I drove the ladies back home in my dusty, smelly car. The next day there would be more prunes for us to sort, but after that we were to transfer to the tomato crop. I was employed!

The girls and John had taken care of themselves quite well, and I slept like a baby that night to prepare me for what was to come.

When I picked Vera up the third day, I was already anticipating the worst. Sure enough, she lit up a cigarette as soon as she was buckled in. She talked and smoked all the way to Vacaville. At seven in the morning it was already 85 in the shade, and my air-conditioned car was the only thing that seemed half-way civilized. The two Vacaville riders had packed a particularly powerful lunch that included boiled eggs and some kind of salted fish. They were all chattering happily while I was keeping a wary eye on the Freeway traffic, a tight rein on my stomach and an imaginary clothespin on my nose. I don't know to this day whether I was more annoyed with the three ladies for being so inconsiderate or myself for being so stupid as to let them stink up my car.

I was not in the best frame of mind when we arrived in the tomato fields. Again I noticed the sly smiles as the others warned me to wear a mask because it was going to be dusty on the harvester. Someone also smilingly mentioned that occasionally rats or snakes get caught up and warned me to look out for the little critters. I remained undaunted.

As we walked toward the harvester, I didn't think it was particularly impressive, but as we got closer it grew to enormous proportions. In fact, by the end of that day it had filled the entire universe.

A tomato harvester is a monster machine with a balcony on each side and an awning. A tractor pulls the contraption along the furrows, and a truck with receiving crates for the tomatoes follows closely behind it. The two drivers coordinate their efforts to keep the wheels between the plantings. The harvester itself straddles the furrow on huge wheels. A great paddlewheel in front scoops up entire plants as the entire entourage moves slowly forward. The tomatoes are jostled loose inside a large rectangular box in the center of the harvester and allowed to roll onto parallel conveyor belts that are approximately and conveniently waist-high to the crew. Thirteen workers are stationed on the narrow balconies that sway and creak in rhythmic defiance to the clatter that emanates from the monster's bowels and the noise from the two trucks. Six crewmembers stand on each side and sort the tomatoes as they roll out of the box, and one stands at the back to supervise a perpendicular inclined belt with swiveling containers that transfer the tomatoes onto the truck.

I was quite excited when I climbed up to the balcony. Imagine me on a harvesting crew! As the engines cranked up, the machine jerked and with a great lurch we were off. Protected with bandanas, gloves, and sunglasses, we began our work. The tomatoes, great and small, whole and smashed, came out of an opening at the bottom of the metal box. Only the "good" tomatoes were to be left on the belt. Everything else, the "bad" tomatoes, the leaves and stems, and the clumps of dirt had to be returned to the ground through an opening between the belt and the worker. Sometimes an entire tomato plant was pulled through.

Such a treasure had to be flung over the shoulder to be discarded. I found the work interesting and the environment vibrant. As a unit we moved like a belching, clattering monster from one end of the field to the other. Momentarily, I had the sensation of having left planet earth. I had become part of a great machine. Conversation was impossible, but not thoughts.

My mind turned to the often-expressed criticism about the people who come to work in America. I was surrounded by the very people who had been criticized for not learning English. Among the thirteen members of our crew were Germans, Philippines, Guamanians, and Koreans. A second harvester crew on the same field was composed completely of Mexicans. We all did the same work despite the severe rattling of our brains. At the end of one of those workdays under the hot sun, who could possibly be motivated to grab the books and study strange words with child-like enthusiasm? Does this type of work make one lazy or just tired? Why isn't one language just as good as another? I waxed quite philosophical as my eyes watched for perfect tomatoes and my hands disposed of the flawed produce.

At the end of two furrows, we took our first break. Ten minutes were just enough to freshen up at a faucet over a rusty tub. The water was cool, and the soil on our faces yielded. The impressions remained, however.

Each furrow took approximately an hour, and twelve o'clock couldn't come soon enough for me. Gratefully, I jumped off the machine and got into my car to eat my lunch. I turned on the engine, so I could run the air-conditioning for a little while. Surprise, surprise, my carpool buddies got into the car with me. Without the slightest hesitation, they unpacked their pungent delicacies. Vera lit up a Chesterfield. The ambience in my car was indescribable.

I turned off the engine and left them sitting in their peculiar atmosphere. The anger began to rise in me, but I was still too polite to say anything. A half hour of heat and food later, we boarded the machine for another shift of two furrows.

When it was time for our afternoon break, two or three members of the crew insisted on going on "No Break!" It wasn't clear to me why they didn't want their break, but it was clear that I wanted one. I jumped off the machine and told the foreman to go on without me. I was quitting and did not expect to get paid for the day. He simply nodded.

For two hours I sat in my car which had aired out by then. When the ladies came back, I told them they would have to make other transportation arrangements. I was through.

COOLING THINGS DOWN

With Lee still in North Carolina, I had to be very resourceful. My experience in the prunes proved to me that I would not be able to earn money any time soon. As a result, I made do with what we had. When our household goods arrived, I was disappointed to discover that the refrigerator no longer worked. No problem: I used it as an icebox by keeping it stocked with purchased bags of ice until I could afford to buy another refrigerator.

"Mom, why can't we get this house a little cooler too?" one of the kids asked.

"Well, we do have this big old window air conditioner in the garage, but with your dad not here, I can't install it."

We all looked at each other. There must be a way to make use of that machine. Together the girls and I schlepped it on boards to the door between the kitchen and the garage. It fit nicely into the opening at the bottom, but now we could not close the kitchen door!

"Let's hang some blankets up to keep the hot air out and the cold air in," little Johnny suggested.

"Good idea!" the girls chimed in. We grabbed some blankets and tacked them onto the door frame. Sometimes, creature comfort is hard to come by.

As the summer was coming to a close and school was about to start, the kids were making friends in the neighborhood. During one of their rough-and-tumble games in the park, Lisa broke a toe. I was surprised to discover that no cast was required, but the toes were taped together. She was given some crutches and asked to keep her weight off that foot. Sounds simple enough.

"I'm never going to wear a dress again!" Lisa yelled after her first day back at school.

"What happened?"

"Mom, you have no idea how much trouble it is to walk on crutches while you're wearing a dress!"

I secretly thought, "Well, the style of dress had something to with it." Hemlines in the mid-seventies were just under the panty-line. Outwardly, I empathized with Lisa and made a few suggestions about some nice pants and tops while her toe was healing.

"Guess what, Mom! Viv is going to be our choir accompanist!"

"How did the high school choir director find out that you can do that?" I asked Vivi.

"Kathy opened her big mouth!" Viv explained. "Mr. B. asked whether anyone in the choir could play the piano, and Kathy volunteered me."

"This is a very good opportunity for you, but if you don't want to accept such a responsibility, you don't have to." Viv knew that with that word "responsibility" I implied that she would have to see it through if she accepted. Somehow, she managed to juggle her senior year schedule to include a variety of endeavors: softball, library aide, marching band, choir accompanist, DECA club, and an active social life.

HOUSEWIFE OR COLLEGE STUDENT?

When Lee returned in November, we spent several months remodeling the house and getting settling into a routine. Our children had become independent teenagers and didn't need the constant supervision of a stay-at-home mother. I had my eye on a beautiful local Community College and wished I could take some classes there.

"Love, when Vivi graduates from high school she wants to go to Solano Community College, and I'm thinking of taking a class or two with her. What do you think?" I approached Lee very gingerly.

"I don't know why not," he answered. "I've been looking through the catalog Viv got from the counselor, and they have some wonderful classes. As far as I know, there are lots of adults taking classes there."

I knew I could count on Lee to be supportive, but I was so accustomed to asking his advice that I hardly made any decisions without first consulting him. This time, too, he whole-heartedly encouraged me to take advantage of the available facilities.

"What kind of classes do you want to take?" he was curious.

"I want to take English, so I can learn how to write!" I remembered my struggles with the perfect circles and the typewriter keys. "Maybe I'll improve if I have the motivation of getting good grades. "Also it would be fun to take Spanish with Vivi. We could practice together," I was suddenly filled with enthusiasm. I could sense a new world opening up to me.

Not everything I found in that new world was to my liking. Even though I earned A's in every subject, I saw that there were tremendous deficits in the education system I had so long admired. I signed up to be a tutor and found several adults who were practically illiterate. Also many of my younger classmates had minimal skills despite their high school diplomas. Instead of an orderly progression of growing knowledge, chaotic opinions about politics, big industry, the military, big oil, stay-at-home housewives and various other concepts were freely aired in classes.

My essay in response to an assignment in "Mass Communications" earned a "B" with the hand-written comment "this is an elaborate cop-out."

> *"Every time I am asked to write a review I feel like Sancho Panza being asked to become Don Quixote. I am realistic enough to recognize the powers that be, my status as one of the masses, and my desire to enjoy whatever I'm allowed to have. Occasionally I am outraged at a piece of trash or delighted by a true work of art; however, to strike at individual creations within the system goes against the principles I hold most dear.*

> *I doubt that any other form of government has ever granted its citizens so much freedom of expression. The individual in the United States is limited only by his own abilities or motivations. Granted, the opportunities have not always been equitable, but this is largely the result of man's inhumanity to man rather than of legal obstacles. Most important is the right to express one's hopes, fears or dissatisfactions; the quality of each expression is secondary and subjective.*

> *The media are, of course, tools of a government by which to control or "mediate" the masses. This control may range from absolute propaganda reinforced by violence to the dissenters to absolute freedom of expression circumscribed only by the tastes of the audience. All the nations of the world subscribe to some form of control consistent with their political convictions. In the People's Republic of China the news media as well as entertainment media are highly nationalistic and designed to instill certain attitudes in the masses. I shall reserve my judgment (or lack thereof) on the merits of such a system, though I know that it can be only as "good" as its leader.*

> *Under Hitler I personally experienced what it is like to live with highly controlled media. Even though I was very young I sensed that something was amiss when Hitler was screaming through our black table model radio, and I saw my parents wide-eyed with fear*

one minute and disagree in hushed voices the next. Opinions were never openly expressed, and many of my questions were met with evasions. All music was of the nationalistic type and large rallies were held to arouse the masses. Children were popular entertainers reciting very inspiring new poems. I made my debut at age four at a firemen's dinner-dance with a poem about Hitler's "Eagle's Nest" in the Alps. I remember my family treasuring books from the pre-Hitler days. They had been hidden during the collection of books which had been declared "verboten". Those books published in that era were total propaganda, and, as I recall, very dull to a young enquiring mind. It is difficult for me to imagine to what extent these media might have influenced my mind if Hitler had not been stopped in his insanity. Somehow I believe that my mind would have remained my own as it has under the influence of the opposite extreme of nearly unrestrained media.

In our political system it suits the government to let the masses be opiated by the relatively harmless daily fare of television. Those that have a little (or a lot) of talent can become the entertainers or the financiers and the rest of us are the audience. This does seem to be the ideal way to keep the masses happy and in line. Should the masses overreact to the freedom and get out of line, the government would soon control the media by regulation or strangulation.

The real value of this system is that it also gives the dissenters freedom of expression. Those that see wrongs being committed by the government or other factions can use any medium to persuade others to their points of view. Those that wish to make financial profits may also use the media to entertain. This gives rise to wide choice of media, from live entertainment of the rawest kind to mild comic books; from classical music to "payola" recording companies, from underground newspapers to sophisticated textbooks.

As a member of the masses I appreciate the opportunity to choose according to my own tastes; I also appreciate the efforts of others, be they financially or altruistically motivated. While I can tell the difference between what I like and don't like, I feel totally unqualified to judge on the value that one person's offering may have to another person. It is particularly difficult for me to take an isolated book, television program, magazine or movie, criticize its statement, and evaluate its influence on the masses because I see each as an example of a priceless freedom.

I only hope that I may always be free to choose for myself how I should be informed and entertained and that wiser people than I are allowed the opportunity to voice their opinions in any medium whatever."

The professor's comments started a chain reaction within my brain that very nearly cost me my life. I looked up "Cop-out" in the dictionary and found that it was someone who doesn't do what he should do. This was my turning point: I promised myself I would never be a cop-out again!

When I say that being called a "cop-out" nearly killed me, I'm being completely truthful. I tried to please everyone around me by meeting **their** needs. I had taken my duties as homemaker, student and tutor far too seriously. Also, since my figure had become somewhat matronly, I began to diet myself into a skeletal shadow of my former self and refused any kind of food or medical help. Within a few weeks at this pace, all I could do was sleep for hours and stay up for a few minutes at a time. When I was at the point of death, my husband sat sadly by my bedside and listened to my incoherent whisperings. Suddenly I felt a rush of warmth throughout my person. For a moment I was stunned. Then I said, "I'm going to take a shower." Then I got up, took a shower, ate a decent lunch and took up life where I had left off.

I decided to write a rebuttal and deliver it to the professor in person.

"Mr. Siegel,

I fail to see that my paper was an elaborate cop-out. To the contrary, if I had reviewed someone else's creation just to get a grade, I would have to consider myself a cop-out! I probably could have pretended to be sufficiently critical to suit you, but that would have compromised my principles. I tried to demonstrate in my paper how I feel about mass media, and if I failed to do that, I deserve an "F". Talk about copping out! Instead, I got a "B" and few snide remarks, such as, "Are you serious?" You bet I am! Deadly serious! The very reason for my attending school, and the mass media class in particular is to attain the skills needed to make a judgment or a contribution. Right now, I don't even know exactly what I have in mind, but I do know that any improvement of the world must start with me improving myself. With that I do not mean to say that I don't care what anyone else does; quite the opposite, I care, I care, I care. As a matter of fact, I see clearly the injustices, the misinformation, and the infinite examples of man's incredible ineptitude.

I also see my own limitations and my potential. I am not an expert in sociology, psychology, anthropology or any other kind of...ology. I am, however, gradually expanding my knowledge. By attending your class I had hoped to gain an insight into the workings of mass media; instead I found myself listening to various and sundry opinions of other students. Valuable class time was spent discussing the relative merits of "Jaws", bantering small talk about "Engelbert Humperdinck", or whether or not Susan Carpenter "thinks so, too." I learned one thing from this class, though, and that is, if one can appear to have all the answers even before the questions are asked, one is considered qualified. I'm not sure what you consider an "A" paper, since it is obviously not based on anything presented in class. Oh, oh, I can feel myself getting carried away...I digress!

You asked me if I was serious. The answer is yes, I feel very strongly about the power of communication. Every culture (or form of governing) must somehow communicate with constituents. A totalitarian system uses the media to tell its members what they must do to survive. Its leaders suppress any attempts at two-way communication because they recognize the power of language. Once released, this power changes the masses into people: talking, writing, and thinking people. This same power of language is accepted and practiced in our culture. I have not denied it. In fact, I am aware that our culture is a dynamic entity. We are members of a society which, as a whole, is greater than its individual parts. This society or culture is not a finished product; it is a living, and as such mortal, being. Each member has a responsibility to use self-respect, self-restraint, and self-discipline to prevent the destruction of the culture. All this sounds very idealistic, and it is. That is precisely my point.

Unfortunately or fortunately, we are all human and as such subject to human weaknesses, the seven sins: greed, avarice, etc. If we somehow corrupt our culture through our two-way communications, there can be only one foreseeable outcome. Someone will have to protect us from ourselves. This protection may take on some very unpleasant forms.

Alright, so where does that leave me? Am I to be totally despairing or blithely optimistic? Should I start at the top and work down or start with myself and work my way outward?

Sincerely, Marianne

I got an A for the course!

Yes, the power of the word was impressive! I had found a new weapon with which to fight the world! For the next few weeks I wielded my weapon so much that I nearly drove my husband and children to distraction. Fortunately, my habit of practicing logic and calm in a storm throughout my life prevailed and pulled me back from the brink. Instead of simply throwing words around, I began to write letters to people I considered experts on various subjects. I asked them questions rather making statements. I received lots of answers. Sometimes a lengthy correspondence developed; at other times, one sharp response sufficed.

One particulary interesting set of letters ensued after I asked a cardiologist, "What is the human heart?"

WHAT IS THE HEART
OF THE MATTER?

"A busy life is a happy one," I declared to myself one day. I had just enough interests of my own with a French class at Solano, volunteering in a convalescent hospital, advising the Junior Music Makers and enjoying a social life with my husband who had recently joined the Elks' Lodge.

As I was driving along listening to the car radio, another puzzle headed my way. Hadn't I had enough of things I heard on the radio? Well, this was just a Country and Western song that made me perk up, "Open up your heart and let my love shine in." Now what kind of nonsense is this, I thought to myself.

It was time for another letter. "I'm going to write to a cardiologist to find out whether opening up your heart is actually possible," I told Lee. He just smiled. By now my family had become accustomed to my letter-writing.

I found an ad in the newspaper where three cardiologists were opening a branch office right here in town. Perfect. I'll find out whether they have a different notion about the heart from the Valentine's Day one.

September 26, 1978
Dear Doctors,

Before you think that my question is facetious, you should know that English is not my native language. Ever since I first learned the word "heart", I've heard people use it in many different ways: you've broken my heart, bless your heart, the heart of the matter, have a heart, and so on.

Since you are specialists in heart disease, perhaps you can clarify this term for me: just what IS the heart of a person?

Respectfully,
Marianne Tong

Harold Kane. M.D.
October 2, 1978
Dear Ms. Tong:

Thank you so very much for your very thoughtful and concerned letter. I appreciate the differences of opinion and interpretation of the word "heart." However, in terms of the physical or organic the heart is an organ in the chest that pumps blood to all the organs or structures in the body. Enclosed is a picture of the heart so that you can graphically appreciate it, in the words of Confucius...
Thank you so very much for your interest.

Sincerely,
Harold Kane. M.D.

October 5, 1978
Dear Dr. Kane,

Thank you so much for taking the time to answer my question.

Now I wonder just what part of the body the composer (probably male) of the Country and Western song, "Open up your heart and let my love shine in" was referring to. There are many parts one can open, but the heart as you describe is not one of them.

After twenty-seven years of actively studying the English language, I find I do not understand it.

Thank you again.

Respectfully, Marianne Tong

I laughed out loud when I received the following response:

Dear Ms Tong:

The heart is an abstract organ as well as being a vital one.
Respectfully, Harold Kane. M.D.

October 1978
Dear Dr. Kane,

It has been a pleasure corresponding with you.

I shall cherish your letters as evidence that we both have one of those abstract, vital organs (even if some of the other parts are not so perfect, painful, or missing altogether).

Sincerely,
Marianne Tong

For a few months there were no more letters. When I read a newspaper article about President Jimmy Carter's "bottom of my heart" comments, I couldn't resist writing Dr. Kane again.

Dear Dr. Kane,

You may recall our correspondence concerning the term "heart".

As a serious student of the English language, and a tax-paying citizen of this country, I feel I have the duty to understand the words our President utters.

I did not understand his speech of July 15, and now I do not understand his statement about that speech. He mentions the "bottom of his heart". Is that located anywhere near his well-publicized hemorrhoids?

Sincerely,
Marianne Tong

On August 7, 1979 Dr. Kane wrote:

Dear Ms. Tong:

President Carter apparently has a heart and hemorrhoids, but doubtful whether he has any brains. Recent history has amplified these points. Keep searching for the ultimate meaning.

Sincerely,
Harold Kane. M.D.

My response was concise:

August 13, 1979
Dear Dr. Kane,

Never a doubt! Mr. Carter has at least two brains: yours and mine.

Sincerely,
Marianne Tong

Dr. Kane and I didn't correspond for nearly a year, then one day I found a poem I just had to share with him.

April 18, 1980
Dear Dr. Kane,

Recently I found the enclosed poem by an anonymous poet in a UNA (United Neighbors in Action) Newsletter. At first, I thought it quite touching, but then I realized that the author had given a description of her own heart. Perhaps you would be interested in reading it.

I guess it stands to reason that a person's vital signs change drastically as one relives one's memories. But I can just imagine what happens to those vital signs when a well-intentioned nurse or aide interrupts a waltz or polka by wrapping the cuff of a sphygmomanometer around the arm that is resting on the shoulder of one's beloved.

Having been a volunteer in a convalescent hospital, I can also guess what happens next when a patient's heart rate, temperature, blood pressure, etc. don't measure up to the accepted standards.

Good nurses quite naturally respond with the prescribed medications to bring such data back to conventional figures for the charts.

Naturally, uncredentialed people like me get ever so politely removed from the premises for questioning such practices. Fortunately, until now no one has forced a tranquilizer on my person whenever my memories cause me to cry. (And, believe me, I have some terribly sad ones)

Sincerely,
Marianne Tong

(from "Guide for Volunteers"--Jewish Family and Children's Services, San Francisco) There was no copyright.

> What do you people, what do you see?
> Are you thinking when you are looking at me
> A crabbit old woman, not very wise
> Uncertain of habit, with far away eyes.
> Who dribbles her food and makes no reply
> When you say in a loud voice--"I do wish you'd try"
> Who seems not to notice the things that you do,
> And is forever losing a stocking or shoe.
> Who unresisting or not, lets you do as you will.
> With bathing and feeding, the long day to fill.
> Is that what you are thinking, is that what you see?
> Then open your eyes, folks, you're not looking at me.
> I'll tell you who I am as I sit here so still
> As I use at your bidding, as I eat at your will.
> I'm a small child of ten with a father and mother.
> Brothers and sister, who love one another,
> A young girl of sixteen with wings on her feet.
> Dreaming that soon now a lover she'll meet.
> A bride soon at twenty -- my heart give a leap,
> Remembering the vows that I promised to keep.
> At twenty-five now I have young of my own.
> Who need me to build a secure, happy home.
> A woman of thirty, my young now grow fast
> Bound to each other with ties that should last.
> At forty, my young sons have grown and are gone.
> But my man's beside me to see that I don't mourn.
> At fifty once more babies play round my knee,
> Again we know children, my loved one and me.

Dark days are upon me, my husband is dead.
For my young are all rearing young of their own,
And I think of the years and the love that I've known.
I'm an old woman and nature is cruel,
"Tis her jest to make old age look like a fool".
The body it crumbles, grace and vigor depart.
There is now a stone where I once had a heart.
And now and again my battered heart swells
I remember the days, I remember the pain.
And I'm loving and living life over again.
I think of the years all to few--gone too fast.
And accept the stark fact that nothing can last.
So open your eyes. people. open and see
Not a crabbit old woman, look closer--see ME!

Dr. Kane answered:

June 20, 1980
Dear Ms. Tong:

You have a sensitive eye and a human heart. Keep on living as you seen and feel.

Sincerely,
Harold Kane. M.D.

On June 25, 1980 I wrote back.

Dear Dr. Kane,

Thank you for your kind note. I'll certainly try to keep on living as I see and feel, but if my sensitive eye is forced to continue perceiving the preparations for World War Three on this planet as well as some of the other happenings, my human heart will soon be broken.

I do hope you will take good care of yourself; not only because I may require your professional services one day, but because you also have a human heart.

Sincerely
Marianne Tong

For more than a year, no more letters were exchanged between us. Then I found a newspaper article regarding Hoagy Carmichael's death. Hoagy was one of my favorite song writers, so I wrote to Dr. Kane again.

December 28, 1981
Dear Dr. Kane,

You may remember our correspondence concerning "the Heart". Well, here I am again.

The first and last paragraphs of the enclosed article, "Hoagy Carmichael dies" demonstrate a shocking dichotomy. Apparently, hospital officials consider the melodies in Hoagy's heart an ailment and a cardiac problem, while he thought they kept him young.

Is there no end to the tragic misunderstanding between doctors and patients; scientists and artists?

Sincerely,
Marianne Tong

Excerpts from Newspaper account:

Songwriter Hoagy Carmichael, famous for such relaxed songs as "Stardust," "Lazy River," and "Georgia on My Mind," died Sunday of a heart ailment, hospital officials said. He was 82. Tanned and dapper in his latter years, he said songwriting kept him young. When he turned 70, he said "I'm too busy following the melodies in my heart to feel it."

In June I suddenly received a letter from Dr. Kane

June 3, 1982

Dear Ms. Tong:

I want to apologize for this long delay in not responding to your sensitive thoughts regarding the article "Hoagy Carmichael Dies."

In his own words "but song writing can sometime be murder" should not be interpreted that it's an occupational disease that afflicts the heart. Trials of such nature can also be very inspiring, and for him as well as other creative individuals made their minds more demanding and their "hearts" more vibrant.

The tragic misunderstanding between doctors and patients is, very simply stated, due to the lack of sensitivity and superficial communication. Unfortunately no philosopher can bring together this unfortunate gap, and we will have to await the warm and pure winds.

Please keep me informed. In enjoy your remarks.

Sincerely,
Harold Kane. M.D.

I was very happy to receive such an encouraging letter and answered:

June 9, 1982
Dear Dr. Kane,

Your timing is absolutely great: your kind words arrived just when I needed them most: my remarks are not exactly the most popular literature in the UC Berkeley English Department, and my grades have been quite depressing.

Speaking of warm, pure winds: they blew cheerfully in Fairfield this afternoon to enhance my son's graduation from Armijo High School and gave me a palpable reason for hope.

Thank you again.

Dr. Kane responded with a welcome note:

September 10, 1982

Dear Ms. Tong:

One's profound principles are not necessarily intertwined with popularity, and one's grades are not necessarily the mark of a scholar. Keep up your fine individuality and purpose.

I am happy for your son's graduation from Armijo High School and I hope that he has some pure winds, much hope and a kind environment in order to survive and learn.

My best wishes to you.

Sincerely,
Harold Kane. M.D.

September 29, 1982
Dear Dr. Kane,

Thank you for your kind wishes. I'm back at school hitting the books harder than ever. Your encouraging letters have really helped me through some rough times.

Fondest regards.
As ever,
Marianne Tong

Shortly after that I received a handwritten note from Dr. Kane. He advised me to stay healthy and spiritually strong and recommended I read the book, If you Meet Buddha on the Road, Kill Him!
On September 22, 1983 I responded:

Since I'm neither therapist nor patient, I read If You Meet the Buddha on the Road, Kill Him with the moderated interest of the lay person. I appreciated your believing me capable of understanding the language and absorbing the information and loved the librarian's guarded smile when I asked for the catchy title.

Have you ever read Keyes' short story, "Flowers for Algernon"?

As ever,
Marianne Tong

On October 27, 1983 I received another letter from Dr. Kane:

Dear Mrs. Tong:

I was pleased that you read the book <u>If You Meet The Buddha on the Road, Kill Him!</u> *A flashy title but still the content had some good points to reflect upon. Another fine book, which I you would get a great deal out of, is Robert Persig's work* <u>Zen And The Art of Motorcycle Maintenance.</u>

I haven't been able to find Keyes' Short Story, Flowers For Algernon. I need a heartbreaker in my life at this moment.

As ever,
Harold Kane. M.D.

I wrote on February 4, 1983

Dear Dr. Kane,

I didn't know what to make of your last letter--the one about needing a heartbreaker. I tell you, if recent newspaper headlines don't break your heart, it isn't breakable.

As ever,
Marianne Tong

On August 1, 1984 Dr. Kane explained in a handwritten note:

Dear Mrs. Tong, There are different kinds of hearts and heartbreakers. A deep sense of loving life and our natural survival

instincts help, but even the most bold of us need somebody.
Keep up the fine writing
I responded on August 19. 1984

Dear Dr. Kane,

You are right about even the most bold of us needing some
body, and that is why it was so neatly arranged for each of us
to have one.

I must admit that it takes a certain degree of boldness to
own up to the naked truth as the heart relentlessly beats on.

Thank you for your encouragement.

As ever,
Marianne Tong

Dr. Kane responded with another handwritten note in December
where he tells me that the heart can be a very lonely organ and that it
needs the sensitive soul to be aware of it and a kindly environment to
bathe it.

Thus ended my correspondence with Dr. Kane.

I'LL CALL IT A HELICAR

The mood of the country has changed subtly since September 11, 2001. An enemy turned America against itself and used American aircraft to destroy American life and property. We have become alert and suspicious. Our innocence is gone. Those with ugly intentions toward children have become more brazen; those with honorable intentions, more intense.

Although none of my family was directly affected by the catastrophe of 9-11, my mind's eye goes back to a time when I saw something like this coming. The panic I experienced **then** almost cost me my life:

More than thirty years ago I was a forty-year-old mother of four. Despite efforts to interest me in world politics on the part of my German father who had served in WWII, and the fact that my husband was a U.S. military man, I had no enthusiasm in political matters. All I knew was that I had absolutely no power to affect the decisions of those leaders who had their hands on the nuclear buttons, anyway. My attitude toward politics was, "Leave me alone and do what you want!" The idea of such powerlessness caused me some uneasiness about the future, but I had to find my personal raison d'être. I loved my family and didn't want it destroyed, so I cared for each child as if the future of the world depended on his or her survival. I loved America (warts and all) because I was free to do that here, so I gladly subjugated my own desires to the needs of my country. I had packed up and moved my home seven times in seven years. I gladly went where the Air Force sent us and eagerly restarted our routine. Suddenly, my simple patriotism and heart-felt love were shaken to the core: a professor I respected called me a "Cop-out."

My mind wandered back to my grandmother's place in German society before Hitler proceeded with his evil deeds. Could she possibly have affected the outcome of the holocaust if she had publicly expressed her private displeasure of the events of the time? She probably would have been dragged off to a concentration camp or even killed. She had no power then, just like I had no power now. Despair overwhelmed me, and I began to die.

The faces of my family lost their smiles. Their only concern was that they might lose their wife and mother. They didn't worry about war, pollution, crime, or the energy crisis. They couldn't understand why those things meant anything to me. Their love healed my soul, and soon I was ready to take on the world.

My choice of weapon was a typewriter. I had not learned to type very well in high school. When I was trying to type my first letter to a U.S. Senator, I started to cry after I had pulled the third messed up piece of paper out of the typewriter carriage. My ten-year-old son asked me innocently, "Why don't you just write it?" I knew that my penmanship wasn't much better than my typing, but I was immensely comforted by his naiveté.

Once I gained some confidence in my typing, spelling and composition abilities, I wrote letters to lots of important people. My main purpose in writing to manufacturers was to learn **why or whether** some things hadn't been tried in the solution of the energy crisis. The ensuing correspondence is the subject of this chapter.

I've lost my copy of the original handwritten note that I sent to United Technologies on February 29, 1976, but it had something to do with building a vehicle on the principle of a motorized "Frisbee" for human transportation. At the time, I was sure that someone, somewhere was already developing such a vehicle, and I was merely curious. (Friends had confused me by telling me that **we** don't know and won't be told about the things that are being manufactured, but I couldn't quite believe that a woman like myself—wife, mother of an American family, citizen and taxpayer—was to be kept in the dark).

The answer I received convinced me that should pursue my quest for information a little further, but I had no idea that I would subsequently encounter so much opposition to a novel application of natural phenomena: centrifugal and centripetal forces. Nor was I prepared to encounter so many confusing interpretations of my question:

"Is someone, somewhere working a 'Flying Saucer' made on Earth? And, if not, why not?"

In March I received a reply from United Technologies:

Mr. Maxiome Tong (apparently, my handwriting hadn't improved much since my perfect circle practice failed so miserably. They couldn't tell the difference between Marianne and Maxiome)

We have your letter of February 29, 1976 addressed to our Sikorsky Aircraft division.

We are always glad to consider suggestions which may lead to improvement in our products.

However, in view of the fact that we did not solicit or agree to accept a disclosure of the information which you sent with your letter, we did not have an opportunity of telling you in advance of the condition under which we would feel at liberty to receive and consider what you have sent us. Our policy, like that of many other companies in such matters, is to receive and consider such information, whether it turns out to be old or new, only under the condition stated in the fifth paragraph of this letter. We make this request on the advice of our patent counsel, in the light of decisions of the courts in cases involving submissions of what people may have believed in good faith to have been novel suggestions, but which proved upon examination not to have been new or inventive, but lacking novelty in fact and already in the public domain.

We feel that the condition state below is a reasonable and proper one, but suggest that you consult your own attorney before accepting it.

> *The only condition under which we are willing to consider the information you have already sent us, and any further information that you may wish to submit to us in the future, is that you agree with us that your rights and remedies (and those of anyone who may be associated with or claiming through you in the matter)arising out of the use or disclosure of any information that you have submitted or may submit to us, shall be only such as you and your associates may be entitled to under the patent statutes of the United States or foreign countries.*

Your letter has thus far been examined only enough to indicate that it may include a disclosure of a suggestion, and we shall not examine or consider it further unless we receive your acceptance of the condition stated in the fifth paragraph of this letter.

If available, we would much prefer to have you furnish us a copy of an issued patent, or a copy of some other publication, disclosing whatever you ask us to consider. Nevertheless, if neither such publication exists, we would be willing, but only under the condition stated in the fifth paragraph of this letter to receive a copy of a patent application as filed in the Patent Office, or even sketches or descriptions, provided they are signed and dated, and of which you should keep exact copies for your files. You would not need to furnish us working drawings or models, nor would you need to come to see us, at least for the present.

Among many reasons for our adopting the policy stated in this letter is the fact that a suggestion, honestly supposed by the person submitting it to be new, often turns out in fact to be old or not to have any inventive quality. The suggestion may have been previously submitted, published or patented, sometimes even in an expired patent, or be one which, for some reason, anyone is free to use. It often happens also that, especially in our own particular fields of manufacture or research, the same or a similar idea has previously originated with one of our employees.

We must tell you also that if it should turn out that we have previously worked or are now working along lines similar to your suggestion or if we have learned of such subject matter from other sources, we would not feel obliged so to inform you, since we usually do not make our own work public until it is well advanced or in production, and even then the requirements of military secrecy might prevent us from tilling what we are doing.

If the condition stated in the fifth paragraph of this letter is acceptable to you, will you please confirm your acceptance of that condition by signing and dating the enclosed duplicate of this letter in the space provided at the end. We ask that this be done in the presence of two witnesses, who should then sign their full names and their addresses. If you will then return the signed duplicate of this letter to us, we undertake to consider the material which you already have sent us, and to tell you whether or not we wish to pursue the matter further with you.

If the condition is not acceptable to you, please let us know promptly, so that we may return to you the material which you have sent us.

Very truly yours,
UNITED TECHNOLOGIES CORPORATION
By Russell M. Lopez, Jr., Assistant Secretary

I warrant that I have the authority to accept the condition set forth in the fifth paragraph of the above letter which condition is hereby accepted and agreed to

Marianne Tong, March 27, 1976

Witnesses: Bob and Kay

Even though I realized right away that my letter would eventually end up in a wastebasket, and my ideas were futile, I decided to pursue the matter a bit further. I signed and had two friends sign the letter and sent it back to United Technologies with the following reply.

Marianne Tong
March 28, 1976

Russell M. Lopez, Jr. Assistant Secretary
United Technologies Corporation
United Technologies Building
Hartford, Connecticut 06101

Dear Mr. Lopez,

I was overjoyed to receive your answer to my letter and that you did not dismiss me as a nut. I am happy to comply with your request of signing the enclosed form.
Your helicopter division was the obvious choice to address my ideas. I want no personal recognition; publicity, too, would probably shatter my tranquil home.
I am a homemaker with four happy children, ages 18, 17, 15, and 11. My husband makes an adequate income, and we have

only one wish: that the world be a happy, unpolluted place for all mankind, our children, and our children's children. I have no intention of becoming a scientist, inventor or engineer.

The entire idea of a helicar without a gasoline engine stemmed from my enrolling in a Junior College Descriptive Physics course recently. When I learned that there is no shield against gravity, I began to wonder if there isn't something that my have been overlooked in scientific research. I thought perhaps gravity is the result of the earth's spin and its revolution around the sun, within the galaxy and the universe. In other words, the rotational forces of all the heavenly bodies create a magnetic field which holds everything in place.

If that is the case, then any other object that spins fast enough has its own created center of gravity and thus counteracts the earth's gravity. If the spin can be sustained or increased by mechanical means, such as an engine or battery-generator, the object can fly. If the spin can be made relatively frictionless while the object is still on the ground, lift-off should be accomplished with little effort. My idea may not work, but it is certainly worth a try.

Respectfully yours,
Marianne Tong

In April 1976, I received a reply from Mr. Lopez:

Dear Mrs. Tong:

Thank you for returning to us, with your acceptance of the condition of disclosure state therein, a copy of our March 23, 1976 letter.

The helicar proposal described in your letters of February 29 and March 28 have been carefully considered by one of our senior engineers. He advises that repeatable experiments show that there is an attractive force between two bodies (e.g., earth and helicopter) with is proportional to the masses of the two bodies whether they are rotating or not. Thus your interesting thought that "gravity is the <u>result</u> of the earth's spin" does not have experimental support of which we are aware. He advises further that the spinning of *a helicopter rotor causes the rotor blades to exert a downward force on the air and a corresponding upward reaction on the rotor, in accordance with Newton's III law, which counteracts the downward pull of the earth's gravitational attraction. No evidence is to be found that the spin of the rotor produces a counteracting gravitational force.*

We believe that no reason exists to expect your proposed helicar to be practical, but we do thank you for having written to us about this matter.

Very truly yours,
Russell M. Lopez, Jr.
Assistant Secretary

Marianne Tong
April 30, 1976

Russell M. Lopez, Jr., Assistant Secretary
United Technologies Corporation
Hartford, Connecticut 06101

Dear Mr. Lopez,

I appreciate your prompt reply to my correspondence. It was very difficult for me to accept my own new concept of gravity, also. And I'm not surprised that your senior engineers are clinging to the secure theory espoused by Sir Isaac Newton. Can you, however, truly prove to yourselves that Sir Isaac's apple was not pushed toward the Earth by the net centripetal forces exerted on it? After all, we exist in a world where everything, from the mammoth or the minute, spins.

The sap within the stem of the apple had spinning atoms which exerted enough forces to withstand the forces around it but eventually the stem couldn't withstand the pressure, it shriveled up, let go of the apple, and the freed apple was pushed toward the Earth. And Mr. Newton thought the Earth pulled it down.

The Earth itself spins also (or so it seems) and thus the centripetal forces it exerts upon any free molecules may be added to the forces of all the other spinning bodies.

Can you prove to yourselves why the air molecules near the Earth's equator are hotter (that is, spinning faster) than those in the upper atmosphere or those near the poles, if the reason is not the net centripetal forces of all the rotating bodies in the Universe?

I can well understand Mr. Newton's assumption that the apple was pulled to the Earth; after all, it certainly seemed to be so. He simply assumed that something magical, mystical or supernatural was in the middle of the Earth pulling down flesh, air, water, metal, and what-have-you. I wonder what he would theorize in this day and age if he could see an airplane fly but a dead bird fall; a helicopter rise, but a non-spinning Frisbee lie dead on the ground; electronics pushing beautiful music against our ears but our own human energies going to waste. We kill, rape, terrorize, seek refuge in ski resorts, play in executive sandboxes and find outlets in other seemingly nonsensical activities. What can all these activities be if not a release of energies built up from the energies pushed against us? As human beings, we have a choice, we can accept all the pressures, social or natural, and make the most of them, flying high and straight, or we can stand with two feet on the ground, learn from past mistakes, plan for the future realistically, and enjoy the present, or we can die.

If the human beings in control of technology are not willing to try all new avenues, they should not send out scare messages to the public about oil depletion, radiation of nuclear wastes and various other frightening phenomena. Let's not depend on some mystical superman from the planet "Krypton" to come show the world how to save itself. If a creature does come, it may well be one that is looking to us for help. What will we do? Panic or rise to the occasion?

Sincerely,
Marianne Tong

Mr. Lopez was kind enough to reply to my letter on May 12, 1976.

Dear Mrs. Tong:

Your letter of April 29 contains interesting observations and concepts. Perhaps your physics class will provide an opportunity for you to test your concepts and theories and to weigh their validity against the generally accepted concepts of those such as Mr. Newton.

Very Truly Yours,
Russell M. Lopez, Jr.
Assistant Secretary

Marianne Tong
May 17, 1976

Russell M. Lopez, Jr. Assistant Secretary
United Technologies Corporation
United Technologies Building
Hartford, Connecticut 06101

Dear Mr. Lopez,

There seems to be a slight misunderstanding of my motives. As I mentioned in one of my earlier letters, I have no intention of testing my concepts and theories in Physics classes. It is absolutely immaterial to me whether you accept or reject my ideas. Sooner or later someone will invent a flying saucer!

I do not have designs on a career in science or technology; my only reason for taking that Descriptive Physics class was to provide my brain with a little stimulation so that I would not become a boring, stagnant wife and mother but remain a stimulating companion for my husband. There is already a surplus of scientists and technicians who seem to be treading water. Why should I add my person to the ranks of those who are clinging to "generally accepted" concepts?

I prefer the challenge of maintaining a balanced life, or as we say in German, "Licht, Luft, und Leben". Since I am a logical, natural being, I can concentrate my efforts on any point I wish, and I wish to remain,

Just plain Marianne Tong,

With that I closed the book on United Technologies for five years. Then I decided to write again.

Russell M. Lopez, Jr. Assistant Secretary
United Technologies Corporation
Hartford, Connecticut 06101

October 13, 1981

Dear Mr. Lopez,

You may remember our correspondence of 1976; if not, perhaps the enclosed letters will refresh your memory.

This afternoon I found a picture in a local newspaper of the rotorhead and transmission of our newest commercial helicopter, the "S-76 Spirit" in our local newspaper. I am certainly happy to see that you people have incorporated my ideas into your product after all. I hope that some of my friends took my advice to invest in your corporation after I told them that it was bound to become a winner, but it doesn't really matter, does it? America as a whole will be the beneficiary of your efforts.

Best wishes for continued success.

Sincerely,
Marianne Tong

Mr. Lopez, still working at United Technologies, answered on November 9, 1981

Russell M. Lopez, Jr. Assistant Secretary
United Technologies Corporation
United Technologies Building
Hartford, Connecticut 06101

Dear Ms. Tong:

Thank you for your October 13, 1981 letter enclosing the picture of the rotor head and transmission for the S-76 helicopter.

The technology and features used in the rotor head and transmission of the S-76, as well as other helicopters manufactured by our Sikorsky Aircraft division, embody principles and ideas based on those developed by Igor Sikorsky some 40 years ago. Of course, details in the structures are constantly revised and improved to reflect advancements in technology. The elastomeric bearings referred to in the text under the picture are an example of this type of progress.

We do appreciate your expression of wishes for continued success.

Very Truly Yours,
UNITED TECHNOLOGIES CORPORATION
Russell M. Lopez, Jr.
Assistant Secretary

I responded on November 9, 1981

Dear Mr. Lopez,

Thank you for writing.

I'm glad to hear that your helicopters embody principles and ideas based on those developed by Igor Sikorsky some 40 years ago because I embody principles and ideas developed by Jesus Christ, among others, thousands of years ago.

I understand what you're trying to tell me: sorry, but somebody else thought of "...." first.

It's alright, I already knew THAT before I ever learned to read.

Sincerely,
Marianne Tong

Three years later, I wrote again (I think I wrote just to validate the passage of time)

March 8, 1984

Russell M. Lopez, Jr. Assistant Secretary
United Technologies Corporation
United Technologies Building
Hartford, Connecticut 06101

Dear Mr. Lopez,

It's been eight years.

A lot of water has flown into the ocean, a lot of blood has been mixed with the earth, and a lot of American lives have been ruined since we first corresponded concerning certain laws of physics and the materialization of a vehicle that would utilize rotational forces more efficiently than the vehicles that presently traverse this planet.

Do you and your senior engineer still believe that no reason exists to expect my proposed helicar to be practical?

Sincerely,
Marianne Tong

I received a short letter (in contrast to his three-page dissertation of 1976) from Mr. Lopez:

UNTIED TECHNOLOGIES
March 27, 1984

Dear Mrs. Tong,

In response to your letter of March 8, 1984, I can tell you that we know of no reason to change the conclusion set forth in my April 27, 1976 letter to you.

Very truly yours,
UNITED TECHNOLOGIES CORPORATION
Russell M. Lopez, Jr.
Assistant Secretary

I answered:

March 29, 1984

Russell M. Lopez, Jr. Assistant Secretary
United Technologies Corporation
United Technologies Building
Hartford, Connecticut 06101

Dear Mr. Lopez,

While I appreciate your taking the time to write, I just want
to tell you:
If you know of no reason to change the conclusion set forth
in your April 17, 1976 letter to me, you should ask Sir Isaac
Newton for one.

Sincerely,
Marianne Tong

A year and a half later, I wrote to the CEO of United Technologies:

September 13, 1985

Harry J. Brown, Chairman and Chief Executive Officer
United Technologies, Box 360
Hartford, CT 06141

Dear Mr. Brown,

In behalf of my three daughters and three granddaughters,
I thank you for the Wall Street Journal Ad of Sept. 12, 85!
Almost ten years ago, I wrote to United Technologies with
an idea for a type of vehicle that was not yet in production.
As long as Assistant Secretary Lopez thought I was a man, the
correspondence reflected interest. When it became obvious that

he was dealing with a woman, the condescension became almost unbearable. But never mind; I endured!

If you're really concerned how we, as a nation, perform, I beg you to consider the Frisbee principle as a viable alternative for an aircraft.

Sincerely,
Marianne Tong

I finally received a response from the United Technologies Corporation I could relate to and believe:

UNITED TECHNOLOGIES

October 3, 1985

Dear Mrs. Tong:

Thank you for your letter of September 13, 1985 to Mr. Harry J. Gray. We appreciate your kind words concerning the Wall Street Journal advertisement of September 12, 1985.

I also reviewed the file concerning the concept of your helicar. The underlying problem with development of the helicar is that significant resources would have to be devoted to investigating your concept and then developing a vehicle that employed it. Because of the uncertainty of the return, a business decision was made not to pursue this matter with your.

Thank you again for having written to us.

Very truly yours,
UNITED TECHNOLOGIES CORPORATION
Gene D. Eisenhower

I did not continue after Mr. Eisenhower's letter and let the entire matter drop until I saw a picture in the newspaper of an unconventional vehicle being developed and tested in my neighboring city of Davis, California. I sent the newspaper clipping in May 1989.

May 11, 1989

Gene D. Eisenhower
UNITED TECHNOLOGIES CORPORATION
United Technologies Building
Hartford, Connecticut 06101

Dear Mr. Eisenhower,

We corresponded in 1985 (your letter to me is dated October 3, 1985) concerning an imaginary vehicle that had not yet been built.

Please look at the enclosed newspaper clipping very carefully and think about the fact that a simple housewife had contacted you about building a similar prototype in 1976.

If your letter proves nothing else, at least it shows that American men and women are far more adventurous than big business and big government give us credit for. We could be a shining example of the American Ingenuity to the rest of the world instead of having to keep humanity in line with an occasional atom bomb or two.

Sincerely,
Marianne Tong
cc: Paul Miller, UCDavis

I received a terse reply from a Mr. Howard at United Technologies:

May 22, 1989

Dear Mrs. Tong:

Your letter May 11, 1989 addressed to Gene Eisenhower was forwarded to me for response.

We thank you for bringing the information about the "Merlin Aircraft" to our attention. It was interesting to read about how the aircraft was propelled.

I have reviewed your file which started in 1976. Noting in the newspaper clippings suggest that the Merlin aircraft with its six to eight rotary gasoline engines operate upon anything other than Newton's laws. Therefore, our technical evaluation of your theory has not changed based upon Paul Miller's concept.

We can only wish Paul Miller success in his adventure and sincerely hope he will be a big business one day.

Very truly yours,
Robert N. Howard

I answered:

May 30, 1989

Robert N. Howard
United Technologies Building
Hartford, Connecticut 06101

Dear Mr. Howard,

Thank you so much for your thoughtful response of May 22, 1989. It's encouraging to know that you've kept a file on me. Sometimes I forget that medical records aren't the only files kept on an old woman.

Newton's laws, being what they are, will always explain every configuration of matter in motion. I certainly don't have any problem accepting that a priori. Whether the mass is in the shape of a bicycle, a helicopter, an aircraft carrier, or a laser beam seems irrelevant at this point in time. It's all the same to me.

You mentioned a technical evaluation of "your theory." Adam and Eve, as well as good old Isaac have used the apple, especially an Alar-free, organically grown one, as a symbol for temptation and gravity. Patients and students enhance their relationships with doctors and teachers through apples. Considering the many accomplishments of science, including the nuclear missiles, the very future of this planet as a viable biome for mankind hinges upon laws and theories based on applesauce. How could I suddenly have come up with a theory of my own?

When I began to write concerning a "helicar," I was merely trying to gain some insight into the mind of America which had become too confusing for me.

Believe me, Mr. Howard, I am truly grateful for people like yourself who wish Paul Miller success in business. His corporation is located within driving distance of my family which has in the meanwhile increased from four teenaged children to four married couples and six grandchildren who--God willing--will seek employment in Northern California some day.

Your good wishes on the East Coast may be all that it takes to swing the pendulum toward a brighter future.

Sincerely,
Marianne Tong
cc: Paul Miller

I had not limited my correspondence to United Technologies alone. When I first thought about contacting folks about my helicar, I thought I'd better write to an aircraft manufacturer as well, so I chose Northrop:

October 5, 1977

Northrop
1800 Century Park East
Los Angeles, California 90067
Re: your Advertisement in the Wall Street Journal, Oct. 4, 1977

Dear Northrop,

Yes, it certainly seems logical that in Aircraft technology, as in everything else, simplicity is the ultimate sophistication. And what could be simpler than a spinning aircraft which could also spin through water or skim the surface of the Earth? This craft, however must yet be built by people who are willing to utilize the centrifugal force of the spinning Earth rather than fight against it. (I assume that the motion of the Earth relative to the rest of the universe has been proven beyond the shadow of a doubt.)

How? Why not build a vehicle in the shape of a disk and make it spin horizontally to the Earth? Minimize contact between the landing pad and the vehicle with ball-shaped landing bearings. The vehicle will need only a minimal "push" to start its spin (less than is stored in the vehicle's batteries to operate the electric motor.) While the spin accelerates from standstill to the velocity required to achieve the vehicle's independence (usually an instability problem in forward-moving vehicles) from the Earth's gravity, electricity will be generated and regenerated wherever two surfaces are rubbing together, perhaps at the axis or at the out edges. Once the vehicle becomes airborne, it will be maneuverable according to established aero-dynamic principles, like a helicopter, or according to established electronic guidance systems, like spacecraft. The stabilized cockpit can be very simple, like the helicopter's, or extremely complex, like a spacecraft's; the choice is up to the designer of such a crazy "helicar."

Imagine gently spinning out of the atmosphere at minimum forward speed, circling the Earth slowly to avoid "heating up" the surrounding air. Imagine quietly spinning through water, moving forward ever so slowly to minimize the resistance and to avoid making waves. Imagine traveling along on an Interstate and rising above the crowd when the traffic gets heavy. What a ride! Lock onto a star, and awaaay you go.

Simply,
Marianne Tong

I received my own letter back with a nice note from the patent director at Northrop:

NORTHROP
3901 West Broadway,
Hawthorne, California 90250
October 20, 1977

Dear Ms. Tong:

Your letter of October 5, 1977 referring to the Northrop Corporation advertisement that appeared in the Wall Street Journal, and generally describing an idea for a spinning aircraft, has been referred to this office.

Actually the concept of a flying disc aircraft, moving through the atmosphere like a Frisbee is not new and a large number of patents proposing various design for these kinds of aircraft have been granted over the past fifteen or twenty years. Our company has never entertained the notion or design and develop such a craft.

It is a strict policy of our company to neither solicit nor accept for review for possible interest, ideas, suggestions or disclosures of inventions that are not protected either by a pending or issued U.S. patent.

Therefore we return herewith your letter with our sincere thanks for your interest in Northrop.

Sincerely yours,
William Grange
Corporate Patent Director

I replied:

October 25, 1977

William Grange
Corporate Patent Director
NORTHROP
3901 West Broadway
Hawthorne, CA 90250

Dear Mr. Grange,

Thank you for telling me the truth. I appreciate that.

My idea was not entirely unsolicited, however. I formulated this concept in response to the many scare messages in the media about the so-called energy crisis. As I see it, we have too much energy and too little money or skills to express ourselves in "socially accepted" ways, causing crises in almost every traditional human endeavor.

If you aren't willing to accept mail from a concerned American citizen (not to mention fellow Earthling) what are you advertising for, anyway? Are we readers of your ads supposed to be grateful to you for whatever you may have done for our safety and comfort? OK, I'm grateful! Now what?

I am curious about one thing, though: whatever made you think that I was interested in NORTHROP? Did I give any indication of that?

Respectfully,
Marianne Tong

P.S. I like your cute little stamped message on the envelope, "Use Less Gas & Light Ease The Energy Plight", but I can't comply with your request. There is gas and light all around me, and I have no choice but to use them unless I kill myself. And that would be a waste of a valuable resource and thus not in the best national interest.

I dropped the idea of correspondence with Northrop but wrote them another letter seven years later.

March 8, 1984

William Grange
Corporate Patent Director
NORTHROP
3901 West Broadway
Hawthorne, CA 90250

Dear Mr. Graham,

It's been nearly seven years.

A lot of water has flown into the ocean, a lot of blood has been mixed with the earth, and a lot of American lives have been ruined since we corresponded concerning certain laws of physics and the materialization of a vehicle that could utilize rotational forces more efficiently than the vessels that presently traverse this planet.

Isn't your company about ready to entertain the notion to design and develop a craft that moves through the atmosphere like a Frisbee? Perhaps I should tell you that I spent three of the past seven years as a student at UCBerkeley and discussed this concept with numerous other persons, many of which have returned to their homes.

Sincerely
Marianne Tong

This letter was returned as undeliverable because Mr. Grange was no longer locatable at Northrop.

March 20, 1984

Chairman of the Board, NORTHROP
3901 West Broadway
Hawthorne, CA 90250
or 1800 Century Park
East Los Angeles, CA 90067

Dear NORTHROP,

A few years ago I wrote a letter to NORTHROP and received the enclosed reply from your Corporate Patent Director.

As you can see, this man is no longer locatable at NORTHROP. Perhaps other changes have been made as well.

Would you please tell me about NORTHROP'S current plans to manufacture a life-size Frisbee for the Free World?

Sincerely,
Marianne Tong

I did receive a short reply that convinced me to forget about Northrop.

NORTHROP
One Northrop Avenue,
Hawthorne, CA 90250
27 March 1984

Dear Ms. Tong:

Your letter, addressed to Mr. Thomas V. Johnson, Chairman of the Board of Northrop Corporation, has been referred to this office.

As explained in Mr. Grange's letter to you, the company neither solicits nor accepts for review ideas, suggestions or disclosures of inventions that are not protected by either a pending or issued United States patent.

Thank you for your interest in Northrop corporation.

Very truly yours,
NORTHROP CORPORATION
John E. Poole, Jr.
Patent counsel

I was sarcastic in my response to the all-knowing Mr. Poole.

March 29, 1984
John E. Poole, Jr., Patent Counsel
NORTHROP
One Northrop Avenue
Hawthorne, CA 90250

Dear Mr. Poole,

Good for you!
Since the company neither solicits nor accepts for review ideas, suggestions or disclosures that are not protected by either a pending or issued U. S. Patent, it effectively resists fire, leukemia, leprosy, cancer, death, time, and the heartbreak of psoriasis, none of which are patentable ideas, either.

Sincerely,
Marianne Tong

I had begun to enjoy my sarcastic and snide responses to the letters I received from the bureaucrats sitting in their offices answering my unsolicited ideas. It was especially satisfying to imagine their faces as they read another remark from my point of view. Northrop and United Technologies were soon joined by other manufacturers: Porsche of America, for example.

May 27, 1978
Porsche of America, Corporation
Englewood Cliffs, New Jersey 07632

Dear Porsche,

I must congratulate you on your advertisement in Tennis Magazine.

You do have a great advertising writer who described your vehicle in such glowing terms that I was truly impressed. As far as I have been able to determine, however, your Porsche 928 is still a car with four parallel wheels which spin vertically to the ground, and an internal combustion engine which utilizes petroleum products. (A rehash of Henry Ford's idea, albeit a sophisticated one)

Don't you think that the writer of the ad may have been overly optimistic when he stated that "nothing will come close for the next ten years?" How can he be so sure that someone isn't building a vehicle at this very moment that will revolutionize the entire transportation industry and give the freedom of helicopter-type flight to its occupant.

I suppose, it has been relatively simple up to now for those who control the automotive technology and petroleum resources to thwart the development of a horizontally spinning disc-type craft by convincing the public of its inherent instability and other "hazardous" qualities. But under the control of a brilliant, skillful pilot, an electrically powered, stabilized, pressurized and otherwise aero-dynamically engineered "Frisbee" should prove to be quite an "automotive phenomenon"

Of course, your Porsche 928 is real, not imaginary, and if I owned one, I'd certainly hope that nothing would come close to it, especially a big truck.

Respectfully,
Marianne Tong

I've misplaced the first response from Porsche, but I wrote another letter to the lady who had sent it.

July 2, 1978

I certainly appreciate your thoughtful reply to my letter, and wish to thank you for the booklets.

You state that new ideas for basic transportation which look good on paper still present major problems when it comes to mass production and actual use. Well, someone has to present major problems to the scientists and engineers; otherwise, they wouldn't have anything to derive satisfaction from! I feel that my ideas may as well serve that purpose.

Furthermore, I figure if they can actually build and utilize such contraptions as Mariners, Apollos, Vikings, Enterprises, and other craft, they can construct (and gently glide around in) a vehicle that spins to produce electricity and maintain its balance; and if they put the whole thing on roller casters, its electric engine should have enough power to start the ball (somewhat flattened) rolling.

By the way, I believe the horseless carriage, as you called it, is here to stay; the Frisbee (helicar, flying saucer, or whatever one may call it) will **augment** rather than replace existing transportation systems.

It was a pleasure hearing from you, and I hope your wish for me to try a Porsche will come true.

Respectfully,
Marianne Tong

PORSCHE + AUDI
Englewood Cliffs, New Jersey 07632
July 17, 1978

Dear Ms. Tong:

We enjoyed reading your unique letter; although many science fiction fantasies are rapidly becoming realities, the horseless carriage – driven by a piston engine – still has a lot going for it. New ideas for basic transportation which look good on paper still present major problems when it comes to mass production and actual use.

Most automobiles, including our Porsche 928, do not require "a brilliant, skillful pilot," but a good driver can derive a lot of satisfaction from piloting such a vehicle. We hope you have the opportunity to try the new Porsche soon.

Sincerely,
Barbara Bennett

It was a friendly letter, but I stopped corresponding with Porsche. I had other fish to fry: There were a number of other manufacturers I had to contact. The Robert Bosch Corporation, for example.

September 23, 1977
Robert Bosch Corporation
2800 South 25th Avenue
Broadview, Illinois 60153

Dear Mr. Earl,

I have been gathering information about a vehicle which is at this point in time only a figment of my imagination. As far as I have been able to ascertain, it is not officially known to be in production anywhere, but there is no reason why it could not eventually materialize as have countless other ideas.

Your advertisement in the Wall Street Journal, Sept. 22, 1977, gave me the opportunity to write to you in the hope that we may benefit each other.

I would like some information, if possible, about the generator systems which are perhaps already available or could be developed to accommodate the vehicle I'm about to describe to you.

Basically, the entire vehicle will be a wheel, horizontal to the surface of the Earth. The stabilized interior cabin will contain the necessary equipment and space for crew, passengers, and cargo. I know! You're already way ahead of me, UFO's! Impossible! But what about lift-off?

The principal source of energy for this vehicle will be its own motion: kinetic energy to be transferred (via generators, transformers, etc.) into batteries as potential energy to be utilized to sustain the spinning motions. How? by minimizing contact with the Earth and utilizing the kinetic energy of the Earth. (I assume, its spinning and other motion relative to the universe has been proven beyond a reasonable doubt).

The wheel will spin on a central pivot, contact between the vehicle and the smooth landing pad will be minimized by bearing-type landing globes. The amount of "push" to start the vehicle's spin will be very slight--less than is stored in its batteries--and as the spin accelerates, electricity is being regenerated into the batteries wherever two surfaces are rubbing together. At a specific velocity of spin, the entire vehicle will acquire its independence (usually a problem of instability in forward-moving vehicles) of the Earth's gravity and will become airborne and maneuverable according to established aero-dynamic principles. Existing land, air, and water routes can be traversed under established traffic regulations.

A sophisticated version, of course, will be able to travel in "outer space" by gently gliding out of the atmosphere at minimum forward speed to reduce the "heating up" of the atmosphere around it. I have called this vehicle "helicar," since I was partly inspired by observing helicopters.

Thank you for affording me this opportunity to contact. I feel we may as well utilize the ever-available kinetic energy of the Earth, before we (human beings, in general) destroy our one common ground completely by digging and delving for potential energy, redistributing enormous amounts of weight and rearranging the Earth's face beyond recognition.

In Appreciation,
Marianne Tong

I received an encouraging response.

ROBERT BOSCH CORPORATION
Broadview, Illinois
October 10, 1977

Dear Ms. Tong:

WE are in receipt of your letter dated September 23, 1977. The ideas for vehicular propulsion you have proposed are indeed interesting.

As you have requested, we are enclosing information of Robert Bosch generating systems, which are currently in production.

As you may or may not realize, Robert Bosch Corporation is a supplier of components for use on vehicle systems. We therefore suggest, that you pursue contacts with manufacturers interest in vehicle development.

Although your ideas are just at their inception, we certainly wish you success with their development. We thank you for your interest in Robert Bosch Corporation.

ROBERT BOSCH CORPORATION
Original Equipment Division
Diane M. Wickham
Account Manager – Sales
Cc: Mr. Earl, President Robert Bosch Corporation

I responded:

October 13, 1977

Mr. Earl, President
Robert Bosch Corporation
2800 South 25th Avenue
Broadview, Illinois 60153

Dear Mr. Earl,

I received Ms Wickham's correspondence and the booklets with great interest and appreciation.

I have already contacted a variety of governmental agencies as well as private manufacturers and research corporations as you suggested. Many, if not most, of their responses reflect the same good wishes and suggestions to continue pursuing my concept. Of course, that is exactly what I'm doing. As wife of a working man and mother of four teenagers, I feel that writing letters is my wisest and least disruptive method of "being involved in world affairs".

The reasons I have distributed my ideas so widely and freely are that they may combine with those of knowledgeable and highly trained experts, that this distribution will give me a measure of personal safety, and that the variety of designs will promote healthy competition among the corporations. In this way, should something unforeseen happen to my person, the world would feel no loss.

If the various people I have contacted feel that a different form of transportation for offensive, defensive or recreational use would benefit their own situation, they will find a way to incorporate such a vehicle into the existing economy.

In the meanwhile I shall be content to be a beneficiary of modern technology and the freest form of government imaginable on our Earth. I'm sure I need not mention what the loss of our government or the destruction of the Earth would mean to all of us.

Sincerely,
Marianne Tong

Alright, The Robert Bosch Corporation didn't want to get involved either. No problem, there were plenty of other manufacturers to stir up. The Timken Corporation made bearings. Perhaps they would understand how spherical object could help get a helicar off the ground:

The Timken Company
Canton, Ohio 44706
September 12, 1977

Dear Sir,

For some time now I have been gathering information about various components for a vehicle which is not now in production but will, I'm sure, eventually materialize. Remembering that the gasoline-powered vehicles of today were only someone's imagination of a few years ago, you cannot deny the possibility of other means of transportation if we want or need them.

The vehicle I have in mind will be spinning on an axis which is part of the stable interior. The kinetic energy of the spinning will be transferred into generators, batteries, etc. to store enough potential energy (electricity) to sustain the spinning once the vehicle is airborne. The stabilized cabin will provide space for passengers and/or cargo. Now--to get this contraption off the ground without expending more energy than is available in its storage batteries: contact between the Earth and the vehicle must be reduced to a minimum. Think of the Earth as a spinning ball (proved, I suppose, sufficiently). The centrifugal and centripetal forces (kinetic energy?) of the Earth will work in favor of "lift-off" of the vehicle. Due to the BEARINGS between the smooth landing pad and the vehicle, and a central pivot point, the vehicle will require very little force to start its spinning motion. The velocity of the spin will gradually accelerate until the vehicle achieves its independence of the Earth's gravity. Once airborne, the vehicle will be maneuverable along established aero-dynamic principles over existing land, air, and water routes, constantly regenerating electricity wherever two surfaces (in the armature) are rubbing together.

Your company engineers would, of course, know about the materials and lubrication of the proposed LANDING BEARINGS and this is my reason for writing to you. I'll certainly appreciate any information you might share with me.

For want of a better name, I've called this contraption a "helicar" since I was partly inspired by observing helicopters.

With respect.
Marianne Tong

TIMKEN
The Timken Company
Canton, Ohio, USA 44706
September 23, 1977

Dear Ms. Tong:

We have received your letter dated September 12, 1977, requesting information on landing bearings for your invention, which you call a "helicar."

As you undoubtedly know, there are very many different types of bearings. What you may not realize is that The Timken Company manufactures only one type of bearing, that being the tapered roller bearing. From the information contained in your letter, we cannot make any recommendations on bearings. We would need quite detailed information in order to help you, and I fully understand that you cannot give this type of information on your invention until you have protected your ideas with a patent application. In fact, we have a long-standing policy in our Company of not reviewing inventions until we are assured that the inventor is protected by a patent or a patent application. This policy is for the protection of the inventor as well as for our protection.

I am enclosing a copy of a special issue of "Machine Design" on bearings with the hopes that it may be of some help to you. This is a 1974 issue, but the text is virtually unchanged in the last printing.

Sincerely,
A. W. Fading, Patent Engineer

As I expected, The Timken Company wasn't interested either, but I was enjoying my letter-writing campaign for its own sake.

September 27, 1977

A. W. Fading, Patent Engineer
The Timken Company
General Offices
Canton, Ohio 44706

Dear Mr. Fading

Thank you very much for your prompt response. Of course, I appreciate your concern about possible ramifications in using other people's ideas. My "helicar" is not based on a new concept, though; it is merely another vehicle operating on the same principle as a helicopter. I have no specific design on paper yet, since I am still in the component-finding stage. The only appreciable difference between my "helicar" and a helicopter as it is known now, is the fact that is will be powered by electricity generated by its own motion instead of gasoline. This principle is made possible by the minimized contact with the Earth's surface and the net centrifugal and centripetal forces of both bodies. For want of a better name, perhaps we could call it the principle of relative gravity or levity.

As you can probably understand by now, this principle is not patentable, and each person, company or industry will have to evaluate its application to their own products.

I have considered the effects such a vehicle may have on the economy as well as on the ecology, and have come to the conclusion that they will be less severe than the effects of nuclear installations, supersonic chunks of metal in the air, the redistribution of immense amounts of weight on this planet, or the total standstill of technological developments.

I thoroughly enjoy my life and simply want to make a contribution wherever I can to maintain or improve my family's lifestyle.

With respect,
Marianne Tong

A Wall Street Journal Ad gave me another opportunity to contact a manufacturer. My imaginary helicar would need an engine. Why not a General Electric Engine? I wrote:

October 8, 1977

General Electric
Fairfield, Connecticut 06431

Seeing your advertisement in the Wall Street Journal, Oct. 7, 1977, reminded me of my favorite "Why-don't-they?" Why don't they build an honest-to-goodness electric engine to sustain the spinning motion of a disc-shaped vehicle which could travel in and make use of the force field between the Earth and the rest of the universe? (Human beings and other living things have long been utilizing this force, energy, power, or whatever it's called) encountering more or less resistance in their environment.

The lift-off of this horizontal flying wheel could be accomplished with minimum effort, if the contact between the smooth landing pad and the vehicle is minimized by the use of ball-shaped bearings and a central pivot point. The "push" required to start the spin will be less than is stored in the batteries, and electricity can be constantly regenerated while the spin accelerates from standstill to the specific velocity required to achieve the vehicle's independence of the Earth's gravity. This independence is usually an instability "problem" in fast-forward-moving vehicles such as race cars.

No matter what the design of the vehicle or the use of it, recreational, defensive, or possibly offensive, the engine of the future may very well be completely electric.

I have been writing to different companies about the component parts of such a vehicle for some time. Often the replies make vague reference to Mr. Newton's laws which are as ineffective as most of the other laws people don't abide by.

I have no specific design, no model, nothing patentable, and no doubt that this idea will one day materialize. Neither am I in position to build such a machine myself, but the American technology is available if the various experts are willing to get their act together. (Hopefully, before Russia or China do.)

GENERAL ELECTRIC
FAIRFIELD, CONNECTICUT 06431
October 18, 1977

Dear Ms. Tong:

Thank you for your interest in General Electric as shown by your letter of October 9, 1977.

We are pleased to have you think of our Company in connection with your idea concerning a new type of engine.

Before you disclose your idea to us, however, we feel that you should carefully read the enclosed booklet, "Consideration of Submitted Ideas," and particularly the terms concerning submissions which appear on pages 1 and 2 of the booklet.

If you then find either of the two suggested bases of submission acceptable, please select and fill out the appropriate form provided in the booklet and return it to us with a description of your idea made in one of the ways suggested on page 6 of the booklet. Upon its receipt we shall be very happy to consider your proposal.

Sincerely,
A. Violet Lambert, Manager
Enc. (LS-1D)

GENERAL ELECTRIC
FAIRFIELD, CONNECTICUT 06431
November 2, 1977

Dear Ms. Tong:

Thank you for your generous action in authorizing us to use without compensation to you your suggestion concerning a new type of engine.

We are forwarding the suggestion to our appropriate people for their consideration and will let your know as soon as we hear from them.

Sincerely,
A. Violet Lambert, Manager

GENERAL ELECTRIC
FAIRFIELD, CONNECTICUT 06431
November 28, 1977

Dear Ms. Tong:

You will be interested to know that our people have now considered your suggestion concerning a new type of engine.

I am sorry to say that they did not find the suggestion usable at this time, but we want you to know that we sincerely appreciate your good will in writing to us about it.

Cordially Yours,
A. Violet Lambert, Manager

December 1, 1977
A. Violet Lambert
Submitted Ideas
General Electric
Fairfield, Connecticut 06431

Dear Ms Lambert,

Thank you for keeping me posted. There was no need to apologize; the result was just exactly what I expected. I never thought the suggestion would be usable by a corporation that already has all the answers, but it was fun corresponding with a real live human being at GE, anyway.

I'm glad to know that there is no energy crisis, after all. Maybe if the men who have brought the world to the state it is in, keep up the digging for gas, oil, and other sources of energy, they will one day discover that they have destroyed the very thing they should have treasured most: the ground they walked on.

With respect,
Marianne Tong

The response from General Electric was no surprise. By now, I had become quite accustomed to the brush-off. Whether or not a helicar ever materialized was immaterial to me. I was thoroughly enjoying my new-found skill of writing. The perfect circles of my youth, and the horrid typing classes had done their job. I had become a writer!

It was time to search for another manufacturer. What about batteries? My helicar would need some. ESB might have some.

September 14, 1977

Communications Department, ESB Incorporated
5 Penn Center Plaza
Philadelphia, PA 19103

Dear Sir,

For some time now I have been gathering information about the components for a vehicle which is not yet in production (anywhere on Earth as far as I can ascertain) but will surely materialize one day. Remembering that the entire automotive industry was materialized out of ideas, you surely won't deny the possibility of my ideas being materialized sooner or later (some of them already are.)

The principal source of energy for this vehicle will be its own motion: kinetic energy to be transferred into BATTERIES as potential energy to be utilized to sustain the motion. HOW? By minimizing contact with the Earth and utilizing the kinetic energy of the Earth. (I assume, its spinning and other motion relative to the rest of the universe has been proven beyond the shadow of a doubt).

The shape of this vehicle will be a horizontal (to a smooth landing pad) wheel. The stabilized interior cabin will contain the necessary equipment and space for passengers and/or cargo. I know! You're already ahead of me, UFO's? But wait! What about lift-off?

The wheel will spin on a central pivot, contact between the vehicle and the pad will be minimized by bearing-type landing globes. The amount of "push" to start the vehicle's spin will be very slight--less than its BATTERIES have stored--as the spin accelerates, electricity is being regenerated into the batteries. At a specific velocity of spin the entire vehicle will acquire its independence (usually a problem of instability in forward-moving vehicles) of the Earth's gravity and will become maneuverable according to established aero-dynamic principles. Existing land, air, and water routes can be traversed under established traffic regulations.

A sophisticated version, of course, will be able to travel in space by gently spinning out of the atmosphere at minimum forward speed to reduce the "heating-up" of the atmosphere around it. I have called this vehicle "helicar" since I was partly inspired by observing helicopters.

In response to your ad in the Wall Street Journal, September 14, 1977, I am asking you for any information you may be willing to share about the batteries and generator systems for the vehicle I envision.

We may as well utilize the kinetic energy of the Earth before we destroy our one common ground completely by digging and delving for potential energy.

In appreciation,
Marianne Tong

ESB INCORPORATED
TECHNOLOGY CENTER
19 W. COLLEGE AVENUE/P.O. BOX 336
YARDLEY, PENNSYLVANIA 19067
September 21, 1977

Dear Ms. Tong:

I am very sorry to stick pins in your balloon, but I am afraid your "UFO" will never get off the ground – at least not in the form you have described. There are two reasons for this. The first is that all of the known energy storage devices, including batteries (and also your spinning disk) are inefficient to some degree.

When a battery is being charged, some of the electrical energy is converted to heat because of the electrical resistance of the charging device and the wires connecting it to the battery. The battery plates and electrolyte also add to the electrical resistance and generate heat during bother charging and discharging. This heat is wasted because it is carried away by the surrounding atmosphere. Insulating the battery to prevent heat loss would not help reduce the power loss, and the fact that the heat could not escape readily would eventually cause boiling out of the electrolyte and destruction of the battery. The same principle holds true for your disk; you can put energy in and you can take it aback out, but there is always some loss in the process.

The second reason is that in our universe there is always a penalty or price to paid for everything we get. The forces of nature are very precisely balanced in very complex ways and if we disturb one of them without considering how it effects (sic) the others, we may start a chain of events of disastrous proportions.

Let us suppose that you were able to build a batter that was 100% efficient (ESB would be very interested in such a batters) and that you were able to build your vehicle and somehow begin to draw its kinetic energy of the earth for power. The price you would pay would be to gradually reduce that store of available energy. As you did so the rotation of the earth would gradually decrease and the speed of revolution around the sun would also slow down. As the rotation decreased, the days would get longer and the midday temperatures would get higher, the nighttime temperatures lower, until eventually one hemisphere of earth would become hot and arid and would bake in perpetual sunlight; the other hemisphere would be cold, snow covered and in perpetual night. There would be violent tropical storms generated by the overheated oceans on the warm side and tremendous glaciers formed by condensation on the cold side. Meanwhile as the speed of revolution around the sun decreased, the centrifugal force which holds the earth in orbit would no longer be strong enough to balance the pull of gravitational attraction between the sun and earth. The earth would be pulled out of its orbit into a spiral path that would lead to eventual collision with the sun. By that time, of course, all our troubles would be over, and we would be incapable of concerning ourselves about the effects of the collision on the rest of the solar system.

I hope the scary scenario I have sketched for you does not frighten you away from further imaginative thinking, because it is certainly true that the innovators in this world spark its progress, but before embarking on an ambitious project it is always well to learn as much as possible about the subject and also to consider the penalty or price of success and whether it would be worthwhile to pay the price.

To learn more about batteries, I would recommend the following books:

Alkaline Storage Batteries: S. Uno Falk and Alvin J. Salking;

The Primary Battery: George W. Heise and N. Corey Cahoon; Vols. 1 & 2

Zinc-Silver Oxide Batteries: Arthur Fleischer and John J. Lander;

Lead-Acid Batteries: Hans Bode, Translated by R. J. Brodd and K. V. Kordesch.

These books may well tell you more than you care to know about batteries, but they are authoritative. They are written under the sponsorship of the Electrochemical Society and are published by John Wiley and Sons, New York. If your local library does not have them, they can probably be obtained on inter-library loan from either Berkley or Sacramento.

Very truly yours,
W. J. Danielson
Head: Technical Information Services

September 1977

W. J. Danielson, Head: Technical Information Services
ESB Incorporated
19 West College Avenue
Yardley, Pennsylvania 19067

Dear Mr. Danielson (assuming your masculinity from your figurative language),

I loved your answer to my inquiry. Since I have no balloon, your pins didn't disturb a thing. I doubt that you are truly "sorry" in any case.

The scenario you sketched for me was not in the least "scary", since I am one of the forces of nature myself, and I have been disturbed plenty by other forces and lived to tell about it. Nearly all that you say about the universal balance is based upon theories conceived in the imaginations of other human beings, or perhaps your own. Who knows, perhaps the Earth isn't moving at all, and the rest of the universe, (if there is such a thing) is moving around us. On the other hand, perhaps we are the only moving objects in the entire universe, and it is up to us to keep it going.

I, personally, am well satisfied with the success I have already achieved, but there DOES seem to be a tremendous clamor in the media for "sources of energy", implying that there are some people who are not yet satisfied; besides, there DOES seem to be room for improvement in life on Earth. I have considered the effect my idea may have on the universe, and the responsibility frightened me to death. Now that I'm dead, not much else frightens me anymore. We might as well continue to "fool around" with gadgets such as the Alaska pipeline which shifts tremendous amounts of weight from one part of the Earth to another. We might as well continue to "heat up" the atmosphere with supersonic chunks of metal. We might as well continue to transform inanimate objects such as nourishment, into animate objects, such as babies and wildlife. Sooner or later, the animate objects will destroy their inanimate landing pad in their search for space to move freely, that is, if another object from the universe hasn't collided with them or their home base first.

No, Mr. Danielson, your letter does not frighten me away from "imaginative thinking". On the contrary, your letter is probably one of the most encouraging signs of the times, considering that a person in your position is willing to correspond with a person in mine, a wife of a MAN and a mother of four wonderful teenagers.

With respect,
Marianne Tong

I sensed a certain amount of satisfaction from my figurative yelling at this person. He meant well, but I was not in the mood to be patronized.

It was becoming increasingly clear to me that America, was not ready for revolutionary thinking. I was worried that an enemy nation, such as China or the USSR, who were still our enemies in 1977, would build a vehicle based on centripetal forces before the US. At the time, I was aware that the middle east also represented a threat to the U.S. due to the American way of life's enormous need for oil from that region. American Independence was more than a Fourth of July buzz word to me. American Independence was real. I had breathed it and lived it since the day I immigrated. I was not pleased with the American dependence on foreign energy sources. I wanted America to be self-sustaining and independent.

It was time to write to someone in Washington D. C. I chose the Energy Secretary.

May 4, 1977
James R. Schlesinger
Executive Office of the President
Energy Policy and Planning
Washington, D. C. 20500

Dear Mr. Schlesinger,

As Energy Chief, you probably have the answer to my question concerning a source of energy not usually mentioned as an alternative: Is anyone, in this time of political, social, and worldly confusion, working on a vehicle powered by electricity generated by the same geo-dynamic mechanism which keeps the Earth rotating and revolving in its orbit? And, if not, why not?

I have researched as much as possible from my limited situation, but have been unable to ascertain if my idea has ever been tried before. I keep getting vague answers, such as "I'm sure they're (?) working on it?" If "they", indeed, are working on it, then "we" need not be in this state of alarm about "energy"; and if "they" are not working on it, then "they" should welcome any suggestions during this time of "crisis.".

My suggestion for a vehicle for private use has been pooh-poohed, but weren't there also many who yelled, "Get a horse!" when the automobile first appeared? I do not discourage easily, and if I can be reasonably sure that "they" are at least willing to try new ideas, I shall be content to believe in the reality of the American Dream! I am not looking for personal gain other than the knowledge that exciting new opportunities will be available for all of us.

There may be certain factions in the business world who would not welcome a vehicle which generates, stores, and utilizes its own energy, but their losses would soon be offset by the gains to the "economy" in general, in that we could begin exploiting resources from uninhabited planets or asteroids and perhaps even populate them. Besides, the manufacture, maintenance and utilization of such a vehicle would create just as profitable an industry as today's automotive industry--without the ecological risks we have subjected ourselves to in this century.

Please let me know whether anyone is seriously involved in developing a motorized, guided "Frisbee" with a stabilized cabin. This "helicar" (as I tentatively named it for its similarity to helicopters) with ball-shaped landing bearings could easily be integrated into existing surface, water, and air routes. This "helicar" would need only a minimal "push" to start its spin (no more than is stored in its battery-generator component)while still on the ground due to its bearing-like contact with the earth. Once the spin starts, electricity would be regenerated at an armature at the axis or wherever two surfaces are rubbing together.

Surely, I couldn't be the only one this idea has occurred to, but I suppose, it is possible. Today's scientists and engineers may have become too specialized and programmed with theories; they may not have had time to put it all together and realize, "This is it!"

Respectfully,
Marianne Tong

EXECUTIVE OFFICE OF THE PRESIDENT
ENERGY POLICY AND PLANNING
WASHINGTON, D. C. 20500
July 8, 1977

Dear Miss Tong:

Mr. James R. Schlesinger has asked me to thank you for your letter regarding your ideas for the development of non-conventional modes of transportation.

At Mr. Schlesinger's instructions I have take the liberty of forwarding your correspondence to Brock Adams, Secretary of Transportation, where it will be reviewed, evaluated and receive every consideration. I am sure you shall be hearing from his office shortly.

Your interest and the sharing of your thoughts are appreciated.

Sincerely,
Frank R. Pagnotta

OFFICE OF THE SECRETARY OF TRANSPORTATION
WASHINGTON, D.C. 20590
July 25, 1977

MEMORANDUM FOR: *Ms. Francis Hooks*
Chief, Administrator Correspondence
Energy Research and Development
Administration
Room 8219C
20 Massachusetts Avenue, N.W.
Washington, D. C. 20545

SUBJECT: *Transferral of Correspondence*

After reviewing the attached correspondence, it has been determined that it contains a matter which comes under the jurisdiction of your agency. The writer has been notified of the referral.

It would be appreciated if this correspondence were given prompt attention and that you be in touch the writer directly.

Warren A. Henderson
Deputy Executive Secretary
Attached Correspondence From
Ms. Marianne Tong

Note to Writer: Please direct any further correspondence concerning your interest to the agency named above

UNITED STATES
ENERGY RESEARCH AND DEVELOPMENT
ADMINISTRATION
WASHINGTON, D.C. 20545

Office of the Assistant Administrator for Conservation

August 25, 1977

Dear Ms. Tong:

Your letter to Mr. Schlesinger dated May 4, 1977, has been referred to this office for reply.

In the general description of your "helicar" concept you stated that the device will generate, store, and utilize its own energy. Such a claim is in direct violation of the laws of physics which govern our natural environment. In principle, these laws state that energy can be neither created nor destroyed. This simply means that no device or system can provide more output energy than is available to it from its input source. Thus, your "helicar" must have some external energy source to keep it in motion and the energy required to do this will be much greater than that produced by the device due to the inherent losses associated with the motors, generators, controls, etc.

The Energy Research and Development Administration does have an active program underway to advance the technology for electric and hybrid vehicles. This program includes the development of advanced energy storage systems as well as improvements in the propulsion system components. Many advanced concepts are being evaluated, however, there is no effort being devoted to the development of a motorized, guided "Frisbee," as you have described it.

Thank you for your interest in energy conservation.

Sincerely,
D. D. Weidhuner, Assistant Director
Electric & Hybrid Vehicles Systems
Division of Transportation
Energy Conservation

August 28, 1977

D. D. Weidhuner, Asst. Director
Electric & Hybrid Vehicles Systems
Division of Transportation
Energy Conservation
Energy Research and Development Administration
Washington, D. C. 20545

Dear Mr. Weidhuner,

Thank you for your typical reply. It seems that I am always in direct violation of the laws, physics or otherwise. Since no one has given me a satisfactory definition of the word "energy", I cannot agree or disagree whether it can be created or destroyed. We may not even be discussing the same thing.

I have one more question, however: whatever makes you think that I'm interested in energy conservation?

Let's hope that the Russians and the Chinese don't believe their free thinkers, either.

With respect,
Marianne Tong

I couldn't just let the idea go this time, so I wrote another letter to Mr. Schlesinger.

September 7, 1977

James Schlesinger
Executive Office of the President
Energy Policy and Planning
Washington, D. C. 20500

Dear Mr. Schlesinger,

What will happen when research scientists discover that the centrifugal and centripetal forces of the Earth's spinning is the source of energy (continuous and free) for life on Earth? What if they find this after having blown the Earth to bits with their digging and delving? Or after humanity has destroyed itself, leaving little need for "energy"?

Think of the Earth as a giant spinning dynamo within the magnetic field of the rest of the universe. The net result is??? Now think of a spinning smaller body (a Frisbee, if you will) within the magnetic field of the universe (disregarding the presence of the earth). The net result is???

I suppose, in the frantic search for a source of potential energy, the obvious source of kinetic energy could easily have been overlooked.

Mr. Weidhuner's statement that "there is no effort being devoted to the development of a motorized, guided Frisbee" is not necessarily true. I am devoting considerable effort to the materialization of my idea. (As mother of four children, I have learned to cooperate with nature). Besides, another nation may already be in more advanced stages of development of this contraption. Weapon or boon? That remains to be seen.

With respect,
Marianne Tong

EXECUTIVE OFFICE OF THE PRESIDENT
ENERGY POLICY AND PLANNING
WASHINGTON, D.C. 20500
September 21, 1977

Dear Mrs. Tong:

James R. Schlesinger, Secretary of Energy, has asked me to thank you for your letter advising him of your idea to utilize centrifugal force in order to alleviate the Nation's energy problem.

In view of your interest in alternative energy concepts, I have enclosed a pamphlet from the National Bureau of Standards, which has the Federal responsibility to evaluate promising energy-related inventions, and I believe you will find it most useful.

Should you desire to pursue your concept, it is suggested that you please submit more detailed material directly to Mr. George P. Lewett, Chief, Office of Energy-Related Inventions, National Bureau of Standards, where it will be further reviewed and evaluated.

Your interest in America's energy problem is appreciated and I trust the enclosed information will be of assistance to you.

Sincerely,
Frank R. Pagnotta

September 24, 1977

Frank R. Pagnotta
Executive Office of the President
Energy Policy and Planning
Washington, D. C. 20500

Dear Mr. Pagnotta,

I feel that we have, indeed, established meaningful communication with the arrival of your response to my previous letters. Perhaps you have already noticed that there is no doubt in my mind that the "helicar" will work, but my obstacle, so far, has been my ability to use the right words to describe what I mean.

As homemaker, I have neither the time nor the money to pursue "my" concept in any way except to write letters to the people I feel are in the optimum positions to evaluate and act upon my ideas in whatever way they see fit.

As you may have also noticed, I have an unshakable faith in our government. Perhaps the motives and activities of some of the people have been less than admirable, but the "system" works for anyone who is willing to put it to work. I'm not so sure that my motive has been understood.

While I am definitely not opposed to a financial gain, I am more concerned with proving the possibility of gentler ways of "getting around" than the breakneck velocities of forward-moving vehicles that stir up the atmosphere, gobble up tremendous amounts of matter, and leave relatively useless debris in their wake, just to transport us from point A to point B and back again.

We humans do enjoy "flying", but we must not lose sight of the fact that we aren't really going anywhere except to different spots on the Earth; consequently, it is to our common advantage to cooperate in keeping the Earth a nice place to stay, unless, of course, we're just visiting!

Thank you for letting me have my "say". I shall take your advice about submitting my idea to Mr. George P. Lewett; what have I got to lose?

With respect and appreciation,
Marianne Tong

September 24, 1977

George P. Lewett, Chief
Office of Energy-related Inventions
National Bureau of Standards
Washington, D. C. 20234

Dear Mr. Lewett,

I have been advised by Mr. Pagnotta, a member of Mr. Schlesinger's staff, to contact you in regard to a vehicle I have described in letters to that office. If you can clear your mind for a moment of all the theories and/or so-called natural laws you have surely learned in your science training, you will understand my basic concept. It is so simple that it is no wonder it has been overlooked in the present frantic search for "sources of energy": the Earth is spinning, right? Therefore, it has centrifugal and centripetal forces of its own. Shall we assume this to be kinetic energy? Whatever we call it, there is more of it at the equator than at either pole. With your permission, I shall call this the net centripetal forces. (Heat, light, by any other name it's still the same, and there can be more or less of it) NET because all the other bodies in the universe are also spinning at various rates and distances, constantly changing their relative positions to each other.

Let me try to connect this not-very-original concept to the practical utilization of this force to power a vehicle. I have based my concept upon observable phenomena plus my own experiences, as well as established practices; and after considerable "soul-searching" I have come to this conclusion: We have only one Earth, so why not do what I can to cooperate with those who are in the best possible position to maintain it in its present peaceful condition. I have often wondered why there is such a great hue and cry about "energy" and what do these people want it for. Most of what is called "energy" is actually fuel (hence matter) for the vehicles we humans use to travel from point to point and back again for a variety of reasons. The most efficient vehicle, of course, is the human body itself, and since I have one, I studied it very closely. I do not wish to bore you the details, but somehow I envisioned the following mode of transportation to be the most logical in the light of all that is officially known about the Earth's motion relative to the rest of the universe and the technological advances that have already materialized since Mr. Newton made his famous observations:

The vehicle will be wheel or disk-shaped, horizontal to the smoothened landing surface. Contact between the vehicle and the earth must be minimized by the utilization of ball-shaped landing bearings and a central pivot point. To get this contraption off the ground, the spin must gradually be accelerated from standstill to the specific velocity required for the entire vehicle to achieve its independence of the Earth's gravity (usually an instability problem in forward-moving vehicles). The vehicle will become airborne and maneuverable according to established aero-dynamic principles. To start the spin, a minimal "push' is required (perhaps from a catapult or from an electric motor). Once the spin is started, electricity can be regenerated wherever two surfaces are rubbing together (perhaps at the stabilized axis or at the outer edges). A stabilized interior cabin will contain the necessary equipment and space for crew, passengers and cargo. The stabilization can be accomplished mechanically with stabilizers (like helicopters) or electronically with gyroscopes and delicate balances (like spacecraft).

I have no drawings or particular configuration in mind. Not all airplanes are shaped alike and neither will all "helicars" (the vehicle's tentative name, since I was partly inspired by observing helicopters). The principle will be the outstanding difference: while most vehicles as we know them now are forward-moving relative to their starting point and must be "pushed" to maintain their momentum, the "helicar" will be able to spin "in place" or gently glide through air or water once the contact between it and the surface of the Earth is broken. Imagine the achievable velocity of spin or forward motion in "outer space" where there is little or no resistance of a surrounding atmosphere!

I have, of course, considered the effect that the wide-spread use of the principle of relative gravity and net centripetal forces (choice of semantics) in powering a vehicle may have on the atmosphere and the Earth itself. I have come to the conclusion that the effects will be considerably less severe than the wide-spread proliferation of nuclear devices, supersonic machinery in the air, the back-pressure of rockets, the redistribution of tremendous weights of petroleum products and the general rearrangement of the Earth's face that is already happening.

Please let me know if my description is not sufficiently clear. I have reached a point where I have described the "helicar" so often that I could have easily left something out that would clarify my concept.

Thank you for the opportunity to be a concerned Earthling as well as a typical American homemaker.

With respect and appreciation,
Marianne Tong

UNITED STATES DEPARTMENT OF COMMERCE
National Bureau of Standards
Washington, D. C. 20234
November 15, 1977

Dear Ms. Tong:

We wish to acknowledge receipt of your letter of September 24 indicating your interest in the evaluation program of the National Bureau of Standards' Office of Energy-Related Inventions (OERI).

The purpose of this evaluation program, established under the Federal Nonnuclear Energy Research and development Act of 1974, is to select promising energy-related inventions for recommendation to the Department of Energy (DoE) (formerly Energy Research and Development Administration) as candidates for Government support. DoE will determine the amount and kind of support to be provided for the selected inventions. The enclosed brochure describes the program in more detail.

To submit an invention for evaluation, the enclosed NBS Form 1019 must be completed and signed. Upon receipt of the form and complete details of the operation of the invention, OERI will begin its evaluation.

Your letter will be kept in our confidential files pending receipt of your form. You need not send duplicates of this information, but please supplement it where necessary so that a complete and thorough description of your invention is provided.

Your participation in this program is welcomed.

Sincerely,
George P. Lewett
Chief, Office of Energy-Related Inventions
Enclosures

Office of Energy-Related Inventions
United States Department of Commerce
National Bureau of Standards
Washington, D. C. 20234

Dear Mr. Lewett,

I certainly appreciate your taking the time to correspond with me. After reading Form NBS-1019 and the "Guidance for the Submission" instruction sheet, I realized that there would be no use in my submitting any further information to you.

Your guidance sheet clearly states that "an invention disclosure will not be accepted for evaluation if (among other stipulations) it contains obvious technical flaws. Since nothing is perfect, not even myself, I shall trouble you no further.

Please accept my apologies for attempting to interject my ideas into an already troubled world.

I seek nothing but the freedom to rear my children, though society, government, compulsory education, and other systems have alleviated me of the responsibility. It doesn't matter; they'll be well provided for by the welfare system.

The Earth is dead; long live "the world"!

Best Regards,
Marianne Tong

November 25, 1977

George P. Lewett, Chief
Office of Energy-Related Inventions
United States Department of Commerce
National Bureau of Standards
Washington, D. C. 20234

Dear Mr. Lewett,

My family and friends have convinced me not to give up. They feel that I have a good idea and that I should submit the entire package to you for evaluation. I agree with them.

Perhaps I overreacted when I read the words "obvious technical flaws". After all, even the most beautiful Steinway Grand piano has an obvious technical flaw: it won't make music unless someone plays it. Thus it is with our government: it won't work unless we give it a chance.

The vehicle I offer is also worthless unless someone needs or wants transportation. Perhaps someone will want a ride.

With respect,
Marianne Tong

DISCLOSURE (NBS-1019, 4D)

PURPOSE to transport persons or cargo for recreation, defense or offense.

THE OLD METHOD most transportation today is accomplished by the use of forward-moving vehicles that need powerful engines to overcome the resistance of the surrounding atmosphere (including the friction and surface tension at ground level) the exception is helicopters which have a spinning as well as forward motion, but they nevertheless need gasoline-powered engines to break the inertia between he two bodies, the Earth and the vehicle. IF

THE NEW METHOD the contact with the ground were minimized with roller casters (such as under heavy furniture) the engine would be able to move the vehicle with much less resistance. The vehicle would become relatively weightless (much as a heavy couch on rollers) and maneuverable with much less power (energy). An electric engine would probably suffice to attain a spinning velocity needed to render the vehicle airborne according to established aerodynamic principles. this specific velocity must maintained to balance the entire vehicle with the atmosphere. Electricity can come from various sources, notable from regeneration at armatures within the vehicle itself (much like a generator on a bicycle)

CONSTRUCTION of vehicles utilizing this principle would be at the discretion of individual designers. Few automobiles, airplanes, helicopters, submarines or even bicycles are construction alike, and neither will all helicars.

DIFFICULTIES encountered or to be expected exist only in the minds of those who feel threatened by any idea not their own. Some people will be killed while testing, utilizing and enjoying such a vehicle; but then, no one ever said that any other mode of transportation was 100% safe. To bring this "invention" closer to use, someone with money must be willing to finance the building of a model.

I cannot in my wildest dreams imagine **why** it hasn't been tried before, or even **that** it hasn't been tried before. Perhaps the principle of relative gravity is already universally accepted, except on Earth.

UNITED STATES DEPARTMENT OF COMMERCE
National Bureau of Standards
Washington, D. C. 20234
January 5, 1978
Mrs. Marianne Tong

Dear Mrs. Tong:

We have completed review of the descriptive material concerning your "Helicar," which you submitted for evaluation in accordance with Section 14 of the Federal Nonnuclear Energy Research and Development Act of 1974.

We regret to inform you that the material you submitted is not acceptable as an invention disclosure suitable for evaluation under this program. While your ideas and concepts may be of interest, they would have to be developed in greater depth, and described in substantially more technical detail to be considered for potential Government support.

Your interest in our program is appreciated.

Sincerely,
J. R. Lepkowsky, PhD
Senior Disclosure Analyst
Office of Energy-Related Inventions

When I read "Regret to inform" my blood began to boil, so I replied sarcastically.

January 9, 1978

J. R. Lepkowski, Ph.D., Senior Disclosure Analyst
Office of Energy-Related Inventions
U. S. Department of Commerce
National Bureau of Standards
Washington, D. C. 20234

Dear Mr. Lepkowski,

What makes you think I'm interested in YOUR program? My interest extends much further than that. I submitted my ideas because I was convinced by the media that there was an energy crisis, and I was advised to turn to your office against my better judgment. Please accept my apologies for wasting your time. I accept your decision about this idea of mine.

One more comment, if I may: it is a strange coincidence that you used the same words, „we regret to inform you" which are used to inform parents after their sons have been killed in the violent consequences of senseless disagreements among world „leaders". I have a son and three daughters: four other ideas of mine which have materialized. I should not take kindly to receiving a patronizing rejection note about them.

With respect,
Marianne Tong

cc: Jimmy Carter, President, James Schlesinger, Energy Chief, Mr. Lewett, Chief, Office of Energy-Related Inventions

In retrospect, I feel very sad that there have been, indeed, violent consequences of senseless disagreements among world leaders since my outburst. Not long after this letter was written, the Ayatollah Khomeini took control of Iran, and American hostages were taken. President Carter was not reelected and Ronald Reagan became President. The Iran-Contra Affair with Colonel North also foreshadowed more trouble with the Middle East and other OPEC nations. Suicidal terrorists have flown airplanes into skyscrapers. Blood has flowed in the very streets of America and veterans are coming back from conflicts with mangled bodies and confused minds, yet the ideas in **my** blood have meant nothing to anyone but my sweet family.

Where, oh where is the soul of man? Perhaps it is located right in my neighborhood.

In early 1977 I sent a description of my helicar to Governor Brown. The copy of that letter was lost, but its content was similar to the one I sent to the U.S. Government

In May I received the reply from Mr. Lichten.

STATE OF CALIFORNIA—THE RESOURCES AGENCY

===

ENERGY RESOURCES CONSERVATION
AND DEVELOPMENT COMMISSION
1111 HOWE AVENUE
SACRAMENTO, CALIFORNIA 95425
May 6, 1977

Dear Ms. Tong:

Your recent correspondence to Governor Brown has been referred to me for reply. While the Commission is anxious to encourage research in the field of energy, it also has an obligation to the people of California to take all reasonable steps to minimize the risk of law suits against the State. Accordingly, it is our policy not to accept for consideration, and not to review, evaluate, or comment on unsolicited ideas unless the submitting party signs the attached submittal agreement. Basically, this agreement provides as follows:

- *No confidential relationship is to be established by the submission of any proposal to us, nor is the same to implied through our consideration of the submitted material.*
- *The State does not assume any liability whatsoever for reviewing and considering your idea. We do expect to use reasonable care in handling it, but we have right to obligate the State to pay damages if you were to feel that the actions we took were not adequate.*

- *During any consideration of your idea, you will be complete-ly free to submit it to any other agency, public or private, and to make whatever contract you may wish with them.*

The protection which you may look forward to as being the inventor of this idea (if in fact such is the case) should be established primarily by the patent laws of the United States. We therefore strongly recommend that before proceeding further and before resubmitting your idea to us, you apply for United States letters patent. Even if you do not choose to take this step, we would also strongly recommend that you consult a competent attorney to advise you of the legal implications of the agreement which we have submitted to you. After Receipt of the agreement, your proposal will be forwarded to our Research of our staff. Additional review and related activities will be undertaken to the extent that they may appear to be appropriate.

It is possible that our analysis will indicate that your proposal is of value to our program and feasible for our support, but that it involves neither proprietary material nor any other basis to justify our negotiating a contract with you without competition. In that event, we would be obliged to send out a competitive Request for Proposals. Your experience and capabilities then would be objectively weighed against those of others, and an award made on the basis of the best value per dollar within budgetary constraints. The circumstances under which we may negotiate a contract without competition are limited by statewide policies set by agencies who control our fiscal affairs, such as the Departments of Finance and General Services. Generally it depends on the proprietary nature of your ideas or another capability which is unique. Our requiting the submittal agreement is, of course, no determination of these facts.

Sincerely,
IRWIN R. LICHTEN
Staff Counsel
Contract services

CONFIDENTIAL DISCLOSURE WAIVER
and
AGREEMENT FOR SUBMISSION OF IDEAS

1. *The undersigned represents that he now has certain suggestions, inventions, and/or ideas and may in the future have other suggestions, inventions, and/or ideas (hereinafter referred to as "suggestions") relating to the responsibilities of the California Energy Resources Conservation and Development Commission (hereinafter referred to as "Commission").*

2. *The undersigned further represents that he is the sole owner of said suggestions, inventions, and ideas which are about to be submitted under this agreement and that he has not agreed to transfer any such ownership to any other person, firm, or corporation.*

3. *The foregoing representation and its acceptance by the Commission shall not be deemed to be an admission that any right of ownership claimed by the undersigned is a valid one, but merely is to be construed as a denial that any rights which may be valid are being shared or about to be shared between the undersigned and anyone else.*

4. *The undersigned acknowledges that the Commission cannot receive suggestions in confidence and will consent to the disclosure thereof to its representatives and will consider the said suggestions only under the conditions hereinafter set forth and not otherwise.*

5. *The undersigned acknowledges that the Commission has advised him to seek independent legal counsel regarding his rights in this matter and that he has been advised to apply for United States letters patent or copyright if in the opinion of such counsel such protection is available to his suggestions.*

6. *All rights and remedies of the undersigned and of his principals if any arising out of the disclosure of suggestions to or the used thereof by the commission or any of its representatives shall be limited to any rights and remedies which may now or in the future be accorded to the undersigned under United States patens or copyrights or expressly established by a subsequent agreement which may be entered into between the undersigned and the Commission upon mutually satisfactory terms if after evaluation of the suggestions the Commission in its sole discretion and judgment considers itself able*

> and willing to proceed further with a contractual relationship with the undersigned.
>
> 7. The undersigned expressly acknowledges that in the evaluation of his suggestion the Commission may employ not only members of its own staff, but personnel on loan from other agencies of the State of California or of the United States and persons employed by it under contracts to assist it in its work. The utilization of persons described in this paragraph shall not affect the scope of or the terms of this agreement.
>
> 8. The undersigned understands all the foregoing and hereby requests the said Commission to consider and evaluate his suggestion and/or proposal (the said terms being synonymous herein) and in consideration of its doing so hereby releases the State of California and all of its employees, agents, and officials from any liability arising out of disclosure of said suggestions to any other person, firm, or corporation whosoever whether accidental or deliberate and/or arising out of any utilization of said idea or suggestion except such claims as may arise by reason of any valid United States' letters patent owned by the undersigned and the undersigned further waives any claim such as that described in this paragraph which may arise in the future.

Upon receipt of this form, I went to an attorney and had him read and sign the form. As the aforementioned "undersigned" I also signed the form and returned it to the State of California Resources Agency.

STATE OF CALIFORNIA—THE RESOURCES AGENCY
==
ENERGY RESOURCES CONSERVATION
AND DEVELOPMENT COMMISSION
1111 HOWE AVENUE
SACRAMENTO, CALIFORNIA 95425
October 27, 1977

Dear Ms. Tong:

I wish to apologize for our delay in answering your letter and proposal to Governor Brown dated April 24, 1977.

The Energy Commission has received your proposal from the Governor's Office. It is our policy at the Energy commission to have the proposal analyzed by a consultant with background and expertise in proposals of this nature. His technical assessment indicates that the device your describe, a helicar, is not technically sound, and violates physical laws. For example, although a "minimal push" would start the rotors at the bottom of the "helicar" they would stop almost immediately because of friction if energy is not continuously expended in keeping the rotors rotating. Just as much energy would be required to spin these rotors fast enough to lift the car as would be required if the rotors were on the top of the cars as in a helicopter. The position, above, at the center, or below the main body, would not significantly effect the energy required. However, if the rotor was below, the craft would be unstable, with a tendency to turn over.

In addition, if the rotational motion of the rotor shaft is desired to generate electrical energy for storage in batteries or for utilization as needed, one must put at least this additional energy into the rotor, besides the energy needed to keep it rotating fast enough to lift the helicar. The device describe would turn out to be less energy efficient than present automobiles. One is unable to obtain energy from nothing.

In terms of your analogies energy from your body is mentioned, but must feed your body, and food is a source of chemical energy. The more you move, the more energy you are converting from chemical energy to other forms of energy, including heat energy which is usually unrecoverable for future use.

As to your question concerning the words "energy" and "conservation" as used by President Carter, he is using energy in the strictly defined sense as given in an elementary physics textbooks (sic) and conservation is used as defined in dictionaries.

If you have any further questions concerning the disposition of your proposal, please contact me. Thank you for your interest and ideas on energy resources and alternatives. The California Energy Commission appreciates and encourages your input.

Sincerely,
RALPH CHANDLER
Energy Analyst
Energy Systems Integration Office

October 29, 1977

Ralph Chandler, Energy Analyst
Energy Systems Integration Office
Energy Resources Conservation and Development Commission
1111 Howe Avenue
Sacramento, CA 95825

Dear Mr. Chandler,

Thank you very much for your thoughtful reply. I appreciate your telling me the truth. Never mind helicars, motorized "Frisbees", and all that; the whole thing was a ridiculous idea to begin with.

You are absolutely right about the fact that I must feed my body. Luckily my husband has plenty of what I desire most.

With respect,
Marianne Tong

Time-warp to 1982:

Mr. Wright, a local theorist, keeps me informed of his dealings with various agencies. The following correspondence includes a typewritten paragraph he composed in response to the newspaper clipping the upper right-hand corner of the collage. There is a hand-written letter by Mr. Purcell of Bell Laboratories and Mr. Wright's cute little comment "they talk in circles."

Dear Mr. Wright: I'm afraid that you've been misled in your reading of Hobble's Law. The expansion does not go faster. What happens is merely that the further out into the space one looks, the faster away from us the pieces are moving. This is exactly what happens in a race. The runners start all at one time, and at any later time, the fastest runners are the further away. It's really that simple. If you're interested, why not read Stephen Weinberger's book, The First Three Minutes," published by Basic Books.

The comment "They talk in circles" caused me to write to all the people mentioned An interesting correspondence ensued after Mr. Purcell scribbled a note at the bottom of my letter and returned it.

"I'm very sorry to note that you don't seem to have taken enough time to try to understand what I wrote. On rereading it, I see no contradiction with the newspaper article. If you see something circular in the two statements, why not write to me and I'd be glad to try to clear it up.

Arno Purcell

I decided to take Mr. Purcell up on his invitation to write to him.

February 13, 1982

Dear Mr. Purcell,

I don't want you to get the idea that I'm just joking around. I HAVE taken the time to try to understand what you--among others--have written, and I am still taking the time to do so. I am currently majoring in English at UC Berkeley where I have learned to read very critically, but that does not mean that I have forgotten my own common sense.

I meant to convey the idea to Mr. Wright that you people sit around (probably in circular formation in expensively furnished rooms) and there do your talking. Naturally, you get paid by the rest of us for doing this.

Whether we get our money's worth, of course, depends largely on WHAT you discuss. So far, I have no complaints; after all, with your help I have been able to keep in touch with my mother and my children. Note: I have left my husband out because I can keep in touch with HIM without your help.

Anyway, Mr. Purcell, I see nothing circular in the statements--I live in a three-dimensional world.

Just in case you run out of topics to discuss in your circles, please read through the enclosed correspondence and see what happens.

Sincerely,
Marianne Tong

Enclosures included the "helicar correspondence I had gathered together

Arno A. Purcell, Bell Laboratories
Murray Hill, N. J. 07974

Dear Ms Tong,

I get an „us and them" feeling from your note—„you people" makes me feel that I somehow have to prove myself before you're willing to treat my words with honest objectivity.

Having told you how I feel, let me try two things on you. First, your friend seemed to think the universe's expansion had somehow changed over the few years between the two measurements reported in the papers, when all that happened was that both measurements have some uncertainty associated with them (we're just human after all.)

As to your second point, you sound angry, or at least frustrated, because people won't take your idea seriously. I agree that the bureaucratic responses you've gotten leave something to be desired, but, honestly, they aren't being foolish in ignoring your idea. Please read and think about the second law of thermodynamics. It contains a kind of paradoxical mystery. Among other things, it tells you why your car's engine has to "waste" heat and can never be perfectly efficient. It also shows why you can't get out the earth's rotation energy any more than you can get the heat out of a bottle of milk without running a refrigerator.

Most of us go through a perpetual motion stage early in our scientific careers, but then realize the flaw. You're just not there yet.

Be well, Arno Purcell

February 27, 1982
Arno A. Purcell, Bell Laboratories
Murray Hill, N. J. 07974
Dear Mr. Purcell,

Alright, I'm willing to let the universe take care of itself for a while if you are. It has, apparently been doing quite well for a long time. However, I'll address myself to the rest of your remarks. You seem to have gotten the wrong idea about me, and I promise to treat your words with the utmost objectivity one point at a time in order to clarify my attitude toward "you people".

First of all, if I sounded angry and frustrated to you, you were very perceptive. I am angry and frustrated. I am also alternately in love, in motion, happy, sad, and any other adjective you care to think of. Unfortunately, my emotional condition is not the issue here, so please let's leave that out of our discussion also.

Secondly, you asked me to read the second law of thermodynamics, and I did that. Here is what I read: This law says, in effect, that the availability of energy within any system will never spontaneously increase and can never be increased by any external method which does not result in an equal or greater decrease in availability of a like quantity of energy. (Encyclopedia Americana, vol. 26, p. 537) I have to admit that I do not understand this sentence very well. It does not tell me anything about my car as you stated. This law was, I'm certain, formulated long before my car (a 1976 Dodge Colt) or its prototype (Henry Ford's brainchild) was ever built. I mean Newton and Carnot lived in completely different centuries, didn't they?

Thirdly, your example about milk and refrigeration was not exactly convincing to me either. Aside from the fact that I grew up in a village in Germany without refrigeration but with plenty of milk, I am a woman who has breast-fed all four of her now grown-up children. The second law of thermo-dynamics doesn't mention a thing about any of that.

Lastly, I am not concerned with what stage most people go through early in their scientific careers; I'm having enough trouble going through the perpetual motion stage of my humanities career. Most professors seem to think that my energy and money is inexhaustible and will not accept any excuses about anyone's "being just human, after all." Being human is no longer relevant at the University level. Students, including myself, are merely cute little computers with hair to be programmed with theories, hypotheses and laws. We are neither expected nor encouraged to synthesize the information thus received into anything useful for the rest of society.

Mr. Purcell, I appreciate the fact that you took the time to send me a hand-written letter, but I did detect a patronizing tone. Many of my professors also believe that I'm just not there yet, and they simply refuse to give me credit for already having been there several times.

All other rhetoric aside, I want to thank you for your good wishes. If there is one thing this country needs more than anything else, it is for us all to be well.

Sincerely,
Marianne Tong

Dear Ms Tong,

I can't say that the one sentence description in your encyclopedia means much to me either. In order to understand the second law, you'll have to some serious reading or asking questions of knowledgeable friends.—It talks about the difference between energy and available energy, only the latter can do you any net good when you need energy for some purpose. The rotational energy of the earth isn't available to us because of a law of nature, not because of some limit in our imagination. Imagine putting a pulley around the earth to turn a wheel. That would only work if something (our workbench, say) was standing still. Since everything on earth is already turning, we would first have to stop the rotation of that part, and that would take more energy than we would get back, one the machine was working.

I'm sorry if the above sounds confusing, but it's about as well as I can do in a few lines.—It may be that the laws of nature are really different from what it says in the science text-books, but I wouldn't want to risk the future of our society on such a remote possibility. I know of no substitute for serious energy conservation.

Sincerely,
Arno Purcell

March 11, 1982
Arno Purcell, Bell Laboratories
Murray Hill, New Jersey 07974

Dear Mr. Purcell,

It was a pleasure to find another letter from you in the mail this morning.

There was no need to apologize, however, because your letter was not at all confusing. People have been asking me to imagine all sorts of things for a long time, and putting a pulley around the Earth to turn a wheel is no more difficult for me to imagine than television, telecommunications, supersonic flight, and the spontaneous dissolution of human flesh.

Actually, it really makes no difference whether you--or I, for that matter--would want to risk the future of our society on the remote possibility that the laws of nature are really different from what it says in the science text-books. The future of our society was risked a long time ago: the day someone decided that $E=mc2$. How can anyone possibly stop the chain reaction of THAT little mathematical exercise? The cat is out of the bag, and mankind has so many machines working for it now that it has become impossible to name them without a program.

Believe me, Mr. Purcell, when the Time comes, Nature is not going to ask the two of us for permission to let 'er rip!

Sincerely.
Marianne Tong

And so ends the saga of my helicar. A fellow student at UC Berkeley once remarked to me, "Marianne, some people go off on tangents when they talk, but you go off on secants."

"What do you mean," I wanted to know. "Do I talk too much?"

"No it isn't that. When someone goes off on a tangent, they never return to the point of the discussion; when someone goes off on a secant, they eventually return to the point," she explained. "I meant that sometimes you talk a lot, but if we listen long enough, you come back to the full circle."

I took that as a compliment and smiled. Perfect Circles? Yes!

THIRD PERSON SINGULAR

Vivienne participated in a very special event in May, just before graduation. Throughout the year, three of her friends had come to the house to practice with Viv. Carol played the clarinet, Karen, the flute, and Vivian sang soprano to Viv's piano accompaniment. These four girls were organizing a delightful concert of classical music in a local church! I wondered how I could help them, and they asked me to record them. I used the Sony tape recorder that Lee had sent from Thailand to preserve this precious hour. All four girls performed exquisitely for an appreciative audience.

Kathy was in her senior year at High school, and Lisa was a sophomore. They also spent their time in band and softball practice. John was doing fine in Middle school, and didn't need a lot of supervision. Although I kept busy with my letter-writing, I had too much time on my hands.

I had decided not to return to college after my "Cop-out" experience, so I decided to devote some time to helping in the community.

An opportunity presented itself when I heard the Governor of California on the radio asking listeners visit residents in nursing homes or other institutions. For a year and a half, I spent lots of time and effort in a local convalescent hospital.

Because of my observations and experiences there, I was among the registered students at Solano College again the following year. This time, I presented a paper regarding convalescent hospitals to a professor that earned me an A.

What follows is the fictionalized story of my experiences at La Mariposa. Of course, Rosemarie Tong represents me. I called the Story "The Sudden Activist" because I had not intended to be an Activist; I just wanted to be useful in the community. After one whole year of being welcome by both the staff and the patients. Then the administration changed. With that change, I became unwelcome by the new staff.

The patients still wanted me to visit, so I endured an increasingly tense relationship with the staff, especially because I fought back in writing.

One of the skills I had learned in my English classes was that a writer does not have to use the word "I" all the time. It is possible to be a narrator and put oneself into a story as just another character.

The experience of thinking myself a "cop-out" had made such an impression on me that it was logical to write out this story in the third person singular. The Marianne who endured the sting of criticism from an authority figure was not the same Marianne who loved her family. Writing in this style was one way to separate myself from the event.

In fact, writing had become very therapeutic for me. As my family continued life at work and school, I remained vigilant. Although I no longer felt panicky or in imminent danger, my responsibilities as a mother of an American family were clearly in focus now. I kept a close eye on news events, especially those of a political nature, and sent lots of questions to the people who made confusing or contradictory statements. It was clear to me that a mother of an American family should not be misinformed or misled.

Since I realized that I could not depend on the media to give me the straight truth about nutrition, medical care, national defense, and a variety of other subjects relevant to the well-being of my family, I decided to investigate locally as much as possible rather than gather knowledge out of books at school. An opportunity presented itself one day on the car radio: Governor Jerry Brown made an appeal for volunteers. He emphasized the need for members of communities to visit residents in convalescent hospitals. I viewed this as a chance to see just how much impact good nutrition, and especially a laugh or two, would make on the overall health of a person.

Was I ever surprised!

THE SUDDEN ACTIVIST

Had the Honorable Grey Black, Governor of the State of Cauliflower not personally pled with people in local communities, the average, ambulatory, free citizens, to visit those who are institutionalized and unable to participate in the American Dream, Rosemarie might never have taken it upon herself to walk into The Butterfly. But, coming home from college one day, she heard Governor Black ask the radio audience to visit their institutionalized fellow humans. Having a little extra time, and a special place in her heart for grandmothers and grandfathers, she made a commitment to herself: Rosemarie would attempt to walk into this valley of death without becoming contaminated with the diseases that had brought those people to their current circumstance. She felt that her family, her citizenship, her medical insurance, and her quick wit would protect her from any unpleasantness that might arise out of her contact with The Butterfly, a place where old and infirm people go to die. She was not prepared for the unpleasantness she did encounter.

One ordinary afternoon, Rosemarie walked right up to the reception desk in The Butterfly. She explained that she had heard the Governor's call. If there was anything she could do, she was there to do it. The Activities Director, Sue, was called. She asked Rosemarie a few questions and then gave her a list of five names. They chatted a few moments about these individuals, and then Sue took Rosemarie through the facility to introduce her to each of the five ladies. There was Clara, a blind mother of ten who loved to sing hymns along with the radio. Jeffie, the grandmother of a large family, was hard of hearing but she loved to watch TV. Blanche, who had recently lost her husband, was an avid Bridge player. Nelda was just Nelda, and Lulu remained in contact with her dearly-departed husband through letters.

Rosemarie enjoyed meeting these ladies and also said "Hi" to their roommates. There were three patients in each room. Many sat in wheelchairs and waved; others lay in their beds. Some moaned; others talked. Rosemarie promised to visit them again soon. She asked the ones who had been specially assigned to her to let her know whenever there was anything special she could do. Rosemarie told them that she had a car and that she would be glad to run errands or write letters for them. This was around August 1976.

For nearly a year, Rosemarie was one of the happiest women alive. Not only did she have a supportive family, a home, and all the modern conveniences, she also had a meaningful new way to spend her leisure time. She loved her new-found friends and became their lead to the outside. She respected the staff at The Butterfly and never made a move without obtaining permission. As a result, they supported her efforts whole-heartedly. Several of the patients had their doctor's permission to sign themselves out for daytime outings. Among the things Rosemarie did with and for the patients during that year were shopping trips, outings at restaurants, Bingo games at a local Elks Lodge, visits to old friends, regular trips to the beauty shop, and hundreds of other big and little favors.

The patients began to thrive.

Helen Edsel, a widow and a Parkinson's disease victim, became outgoing. Rosemarie took her to the library for "big-print" books and to Long's Drug store for toilet articles. She especially loved to go to Sambo's for a hamburger. One time Rosemarie and Helen took a trip to Oakland to visit the Mausoleum where her husband is inurned. That day was a revelation to Rosemarie. Here was a patient with a disease that supposedly affects the mind, yet she confidently guided Rosemarie through unfamiliar streets. They took a look at the home she and her husband used to own and stopped to talk to a shop owner who still remembered her. Afterwards, they went to eat at a restaurant on the Oakland Embarcadero where Helen and her husband used to dine. Helen showed no signs of fatigue or even memory loss throughout the entire day.

Betty, another patient, was highly resentful of her daughter-in-law's insistence that the convalescent hospital was the right place for her. She gradually befriended Rosemarie, and eventually decided to let her take her along to play Bingo. Betty also allowed Rosemarie to drive her to the beauty shop once every two weeks, and asked her to stop at K-Mart so she could buy a few necessities. Betty especially liked the hot dogs that K-Mart served in those days. The three ladies, Betty, Helen, and

Rosemarie often went out together. They tried most of the restaurants in town, like Denny's, Sambo's, Lyon's, and others. Since they had over two hundred years of living behind them, they had lots to talk about.

Four or five times a week, Rosemarie spent several hours visiting the various patients who could not get out of their beds or wheelchairs. There were hundreds of opportunities to make her useful. She helped feed patients at dinner, walked arm in arm with them through the halls, rubbed sore backs with Dermassage lotion, wrote letters, brushed hair, and sang songs. The staff as well as the patients was delighted.

One fine day in May, as Rosemarie looked up from feeding a piece of cake to an elderly birthday party guest, she froze. The newly hired Director of Nurses was staring at her with the most disapproving pair of eyes she had ever seen. That look made Rosemarie feel terribly self-conscious and almost guilty about being friendly and helpful. Her old defense system, honed to a fine point during World War II, was activated; right then and there she sensed that her happy days at The Butterfly were over.

The very next day, Rosemarie was called into the office. Not wanting to appear prescient, she tried to remain calm when Nurse Rumple started talking about changes that would be made now that she had been put in charge. Rosemarie made some remark under her breath about new brooms sweeping well just before leaving. She reminded Nurse Rumple that she was simply a community member heeding the Governor's call for volunteers in convalescent hospitals. Nevertheless, Nurse Rumple told Rosemarie that her services were no longer necessary now that she had been hired.

When she told her friends, the patients, that she was no longer welcome and that she would not be coming to visit as much, they assured her unanimously that they still wanted her to continue their routines. There was a general consensus that Rosemarie was not to pay attention to the new Director of Nurses; she was not doing anything wrong. Privately she wondered, "If that is true, why am I feeling so guilty?"

One day when she went to pick up Helen for lunch at Sambo's, she told Rosemarie that her doctor had increased her dosage of L-Dopa even though it made her face draw up and made her feel "funny". Rosemarie didn't know what to say, so she suggested Helen talk to the nurse about it. The next time they met, Helen said that she had to continue to take the higher dose because the nurse had told her that she had to "stay ahead" of her disease. Neither Helen nor Rosemarie knew what that was supposed to mean. Helen only knew that the medicine made her feel "funny".

Because Rosemarie was not comfortable talking to the nurse, she decided to write her a letter about the situation:

Dear Ms Rumple,

May I ask just what kind of nonsense have you been programming into Helen lately? She mentioned to me that you had told her to stay on her strong medication in order to "stay ahead" of her disease. Of course, I have no idea in what context this brilliant statement was made or what would happen if the disease "got ahead", but I'm wondering in what direction it is chasing her.

Helen is obviously impressed by such remarks. Do you really believe that those stupid little pills are keeping her alive? I admire Helen because she is still alive and very good company despite her occasionally over-drugged condition and her childlike eagerness to please her superiors (practically anyone qualifies in her opinion). I believe she is a whole and worthwhile human being despite the fact that she makes her home (for reasons of her own) in such a controlled environment as a convalescent hospital; but it seems that I'm the only one who believes that.

I sincerely hope that you (and others who think that they know what's "good" for everybody) can control the environment enough to keep earthquakes, pollution, fire, floods, or enemy missiles from inflicting harm to those who are alive and under your care. If you can't, shouldn't you encourage your fellow humans to fend for themselves as much as possible, rather than foster their dependence on "crutches"?

Sincerely, Rosemarie

This letter was not very well received. For the next few days Rosemarie was observed with baleful looks as she visited her friends.

On June 9, 1977, she received the following reply:

In reference to your letter of June 4 regarding Mrs. Helen Edsel.

Mrs. Edsel and her physician are, properly, the only persons who decide what her medications should be. For a person to take the course of treatment prescribed by their physician is not "nonsense". Unless, of course, you happen to hold a medical degree, it would be most unwise of you to attempt to prescribe to Mrs. Edsel.

It would be highly unethical of me to discuss Mrs. Edsel's medical condition with you and so she shall not. I will, though, address a few remarks to you, Ms. Rosemarie. For you to continue urging Mrs. Edsel (or any other patient) to go counter to her physician's orders is most improper.

We encourage our residents to develop themselves to their fullest extent. We do not encourage them to do foolish or dangerous things (i.e., refusing medication) nor to behave in a fashion antagonistic to their social and physical needs. Further, we do not appreciate your taking Mrs. Edsel out without observing the rules (with which you are well acquainted. Our residents may go out as they please, but must sign out. Our staff was quite worried over Mrs. Edsel's disappearance and I, for one, do not appreciate your part in this episode.

In the future, Ms. Rosemarie, you will be more than welcome at The Butterfly <u>if and only if</u> you observe the rules which we have set up to safeguard our patients.

Ms Matthews, Administrator (acting)

Rosemarie was very upset after reading this letter. She had never encouraged Helen to go counter her physician's orders. What she had encouraged Helen to do was to ask the nurse about the increased dosage. Neither had she labeled the course of treatment as "nonsense"; she had used that term to describe the words "staying ahead of the disease." Further, the "episode" of disappearance was nothing more than their forgetting to sign out before leaving. Knowing that this procedure was a necessary measure for insurance purposes, both had been conscientious about it in the past and were most apologetic upon their return this time. This had been the only time that they neglected to follow the rules that Rosemarie was supposed to have been so familiar with.

In actuality, she had never been given a set of rules. It was assumed that she was familiar with them because she had never broken any of them before.

Since Governor Black was indirectly responsible for the dilemma that Rosemarie currently found herself in, she decided to let him know that things can go wrong. On June 15 she wrote:

Dear Governor Black,

I have been a volunteer "cheerer-upper" in The Butterfly convalescent hospital, and I now find myself in a somewhat uncomfortable situation. I am NOT herewith asking for help, but merely wish to make you aware that even the best intentions can go awry. I have received the enclosed letter, and my response is as follows:

Dear Ms Matthews,

Alright, you win! Please advise me of the Rules in writing. After all, I wouldn't even participate in a game of Checkers or Monopoly without knowing the ground rules. I have one question, however: what is the OBJECT of the game in which we're participating, and what is its NAME?

With respect, Rosemarie

Rosemarie wasn't sure just what she was hoping to accomplish, but she sensed that it was time to protect her interests. She had acted in good faith as a good citizen, yet her intentions were completely misunderstood. She had not done anything wrong, yet she was being accused of not following rules that she had never seen. The people in charge (that is, the people in the State Capitol) and, if necessary, the people in Washington, D.C., would have to deal with this situation. The civil rights of citizens were at stake! This wasn't Nazi Germany! And this wasn't the Gulag Archipelago, either! This was Fairness, Cauliflower, a small city protected by the Constitution of the United States! Rosemarie was outraged at the injustice of a bunch of young people (the Director of Nurses and the Acting Administrator were both thirty-ish, and the smart-alecky aides were even younger) dictating in matters of personal health to women twice or three times their age.

The battle lines were drawn! Rosemarie declared war on The Butterfly and what it represented: a place to die in. Battlefields were also places to die in, but even there dying was no longer fashionable. The world had just come out of Vietnam! Life had become precious again! Convalescent Hospitals were places to get well in, or at least they should be if words and titles meant anything! This was a righteous war!

Biding her time, Rosemarie kept on visiting the patients. They noticed that she was not her cheerful self anymore. The staff was openly watching her, and that made her overly cautious in dealing with the patients. It was no longer easy for her to give someone a big hug, laugh at a joke, or sing a song, but she made every effort to be at ease among them. Nearly every day she returned to The Butterfly to let the patients know she cared.

On June 31, Rosemarie received a reply from the Department of Health:

Licensing and Certification Division
2800 Cleveland Avenue, Suite 9
Saint Rose, Cauliflower

Dear Ms Rosemarie

Your letter to Governor Black, dated June 15, 1977, regarding the facility administrator, has been forwarded to me for response.

I am forwarding your complaint to our Saint Rose District Office for review and investigation

You will hear directly from the District Office regarding the investigation. For further information and assistance in this matter please work directly with that office.

Sincerely,
Charlene Harrington, PhD

Rosemarie noticed that someone else signed the letter. Coincidentally, a TV news report of that time had mentioned the very name at the bottom of the letter. Apparently, it belonged to a lady who had been released from duty with the Licensing and Certification Division because of her dissatisfactions with that body.

Rosemarie felt that the time was right for making waves about the patients in convalescent hospitals. The country had already run the gamut of civil rights causes: Blacks, anti-war activists, women, and a variety of sub-cultures had made their causes known via the media. Somehow, she would find the means to keep this cause alive even if she failed to keep some of the patients alive. She would have to inure her heart to lost friendships in the pursuit of better conditions for all, but she was willing to take that chance. Her heart had endured great losses before, and it could endure them now.

She hoped that the ACLU would take an interest in her problems, so on July 5, she wrote them:

To the ACLU

Enclosed is a copy of a letter I wrote to the acting administrator and the director of nurses at The Butterfly convalescent hospital after enduring verbal abuse from the staff for volunteer work that did not coincide with their routine care of the patients.
I am not herewith asking for help but merely wish to inform your agency of the situation.

Sincerely, Rosemarie
cc: The Butterfly

It was at this point that the staff began to take Rosemarie seriously as an agent of change. They knew they could not just make her go away with intimidating remarks. Another discussion in the administrator's office brought out the fact that Rosemarie actually LIKED the patients and wanted to get back to the relaxed atmosphere of the previous year. Their surveillance of her every move in the hospital rooms and corridors had made her nearly paranoid about the possibility of someone dying while she was in the room. They had made her feel that she was the troublemaker and "problem-creator" who would surely get blamed if somebody died.

There had to be some way to protect herself against a lawsuit. Since she had never seen the written House Rules, she asked for a copy. Rosemarie received another letter from the acting administrator.

Dear Ms Rosemarie,

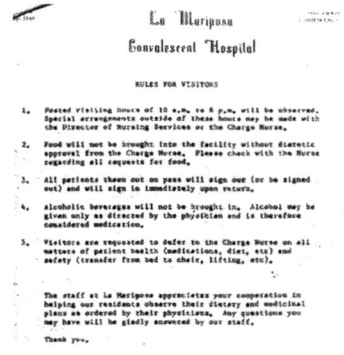

Per our conversation yesterday, enclosed please find a copy of the "Rules for Visitors". As I told you, these rules apply to all visitors to The Butterfly. As we discussed, if you wish to continue as a visitor to The Butterfly, you will have to abide by the same rules as any other visitor. I cannot and will not make an exception. If I do not hear from you, in writing, regarding your willingness to abide by these rules, I will have to assume that you will not observe the rules and will instruct the staff accordingly.

Thank you for your cooperation.
Ms Matthews

In response to this letter, Rosemarie wrote a letter and sent copies to the ACLU, the U.S. Public Health Service, the AMA, the Cauliflower Department of Health, and three personal physicians of patients at The Butterfly,

Dear Ms Matthews,

I am most certainly willing to abide by these rules. They seem to be reasonable. According to Rule 5, I would appreciate a request from the Charge Nurse (in writing) when she feels it would be beneficial and safe to let me visit. I cannot otherwise take the responsibility (due to possible legal ramifications) of being present on the premises, since my visits, talks, contact and communication with the patients MAY endanger their health and safety. How could I possibly know how I affect the patients? I only know how they affect me.

I herewith defer to the Charge Nurse on the matter of patient health and safety.

Sincerely, Rosemarie

It was Rosemarie's intention to demonstrate to people in power that rules which include "etc." leave far too much to the imagination and interpretation. Rosemarie had, indeed, been deferring to the professional staff all along, yet they had seen fit to make her feel as if she had broken some higher irrefutable law. She did not have the education and the certification they had; therefore, she was the one who had "created" a problem. She was the one who was assumed to be unwilling to abide by the rules. What she really was, was thoroughly confused. She wondered over and over: were these patients worthwhile U.S. Citizens or not? Had they done something wrong? Did they have the right to ask their doctors about their medication or not? Did they have the right to eat in state-inspected restaurants or not? Did they have the right to invite visitors to their place of residence or not?

When Rosemarie returned to The Butterfly the next day, she was met at the entrance by Ms Matthews, the acting administrator, who called her into the office to discuss the letters she had written to the State Health Department and to the ACLU. Rosemarie told her that the letters speak for themselves and that she came to visit the patients not the staff; furthermore, if the administrator wanted to boss her around, she could put Rosemarie on the payroll. Then she left the office and went down the hall toward the patients' rooms.

Visiting with the patients took a couple of hours. When she left, Ms Matthews handed her a letter dated July 7, 1977, which said,

Dear Ms Rosemarie,

Your refusal today to discuss the problem you are creating has left no alternative but that I request you to cease your visits to The Butterfly convalescent hospital.

As Rosemarie read this note, she couldn't help wondering whether she was actually guilty of creating a problem. Then she remembered that most of these patients had become ill long before she had appeared on the scene. She wondered what the problem actually was and what had put her at odds with two perfectly nice young professional women. What were they afraid of? Rosemarie really wanted to have someone DEFINE the problem, regardless of its creation or evolution, so she went home and typed this note,

Dear Ms Matthews,

Boy, I must be even more stupid that I thought! I've looked under the bed, in my drawers, and even in my purse, but I simply cannot find the problem you said I am creating. What does it look like? Is it bigger or smaller than a breadbox? Please give me a clue.

Don't you think you're giving me more credit than I deserve? I'm beginning to feel terribly important. Luckily, I know that I'm not; I'm only one of those disposable human bodies

Sincerely, Rosemarie

Rosemarie had become sarcastic. Since her childhood this had been one of those defense mechanisms that she couldn't or wouldn't control. Another week passed. Helen, Betty, and Rosemarie went out as usual. She also continued to visit her other friends who were in beds and wheelchairs. When she read a column by Jack Anderson concerning nursing homes, she wrote him,

Dear Mr. Anderson,

As a taxpayer and concerned human being, I volunteered my services in a convalescent hospital (chosen at random) last August. I became acquainted with many patients, and we established good rapport.

When a new administrator and a new director of nurses were hired, I was curtly asked to curtail my visits because I was "interfering with hospital procedures" (despite the fact that I had not caused so much harm as a broken fingernail). I had respected the PATIENTS' wishes and treated them as persons, reminding them always of my own vulnerability despite my age. I cheerfully encouraged them to use their own brains, legs, arms or whatever, in their "convalescence" (knowing that the automatic glandular system adjusts to the demands made on it and that the impression of my person would remain for a time within the imagination of the patient) I reminded them that they were in a hospital as patients, and that the staff was paid to serve them. I let them make me laugh, cry, and run errands.

I made them glad to be alive for the moment and let "the devil take tomorrow"; something may cancel it anyway!

To make a long story short, I soon realized that the patients were not patients at all but warm bodies not to be distracted from their mission: to die, and the slower the better. All this in the name of "caring for our elders" under the "safe" conditions and restrictions of modern medical care.

These patients are NOT being treated "as a piece of living meat" as you suggested in your column; they are being treated as a piece of dying meat, not worthy of decent food, pleasant surroundings, nor smiling faces and friendly debates to brighten their days. These pieces of dying meat were not worthy of the freedom to make a choice. Shame on all us "normals" for tolerating such treatment of any living, breathing American citizen who has not formally been charged with committing a crime. And shame on them for enduring (at taxpayers' expense) so much physical abuse in these "safe havens" in the hope of reward in "Heaven".

Most of the patients are on "guilt trips", afraid of making a mistake, or "flying" on drugs that teenagers would get arrested for, until one day an overdose or other shock to the system causes death "due to natural causes or old age".

And the world shrugs in resignation. We've done all we can by paying our taxes and minding our own business! Heavy charges? Can YOU prove otherwise?

Rosemarie

Naturally, the great Jack Anderson did not answer Rosemarie personally, but on June 6, 1978, he did write another column concerning this "National Disgrace". He mentioned the tens of thousands of America's most helpless citizens warehoused in institutions that have pleasant names but resemble concentration camps, where society quietly hides away its mental misfits until they die.
Rosemarie sent him a Thank You Note.

On July 20, 1977 Rosemarie wrote

Dear Ms Matthews,

Just to keep you informed that I do not take your treatment of my person lightly, I am sending you a copy of the letter I have written the following letter to the governor and the Licensing and Certification Division, Saint Rose, Cauliflower, after receiving your dismissal note:

I appreciate the response from the Health and Welfare Agency. Since my previous correspondence, I have encountered some verbal abuse from the staff, was threatened with police action, and was called to the administrator's office for a "chewing out". I always thought that our First Amendment freedom of speech included the right to remain silent, but it seems the administrator took exception to this. In my own defense I must state that I have not broken so much as a fingernail of any person in this institution. No one has died in my presence; each one has lived in my presence and was glad of it. I have carried on conversations, encouraged patients to make small wishes, reminded them that the sun still shines, and shown that a bright future awaits anyone who has the nerve to live. So why not live?

For this I was banished. As a volunteer, I must say, I am dismayed but not discouraged. The patients (even the so-called passive ones) keep telling me to be sure to come back every chance I get. THAT makes this whole ridiculous situation worthwhile. The only thing (?) I want to kill is time. Perhaps I should take up Tennis. I also included your letter and my previous response to show just how ridiculous this situation has become. I can't believe my husband's hard-earned tax-dollars are supporting this idiocy.

Sincerely,
Rosemarie

The day after she wrote the above letter, she received another letter from the Department of Health, stating that she would hear directly from the District Office in Saint Rose regarding their investigation.

Apparently, they had forgotten that they had already confirmed receipt of her "complaint" at an earlier date. She didn't even bother to answer this letter because she was beginning to be very disillusioned about America and disgusted with the bureaucracy.

On August 2, 1977, she received the following letter from the Saint Rose District Office:

Dear Ms Rosemarie,

In response to your letter dated July 20, 1977, I wish to inform you that since the arrival of your letter, we have been in constant communication with Ms. Matthews, Administrator (acting) of the facility. Ms. Matthews has written several letters to this office describing various incidents that you were involved in. She alleges that you have brought food such as doughnuts to patients on diabetis (sic) and low sodium diets.

She also alleges that you encourage patients to refuse medications, and that you have taken patients out on pass to lunch or dinner and have encouraged them to break their diets by telling them to eat whatever they please and telling them they are mistreated by the staff.

If Ms Matthews is correct in her allegations, then I would agree that you are causing a disruption in the patients' treatment program. Ms Matthews has sent us copies of the letters where she has tried to speak with you but that you have refused to listen to her.

Ms Matthews has made some very serious allegations concerning your conduct while a visitor to The Butterfly. On the other hand, Ms Matthews has sent to you a copy of the facility's "Rules for Visitors" and on July 28, 1977, you answered Ms Matthews letter in which you have stated that you are willing to abide by the rules.

I would suggest that you abide by the rules for visitors and have a serious talk with Ms Matthews concerning your alleged conduct. We are pleased to know that you take an active interest in patients confined to facilities such as this and we in no way want to attempt to stop you from performing a much-needed service. We do encourage you to continue serving patients, however, we ask that you abide by the rules and in no way discourage patients to deviate from their diets nor encourage them to refuse their medications. Some items of food or drink regardless of how much they may be desired by patients can be detrimental to their health and can also disrupt their treatment programs.

We certainly hope that you and Ms Matthews can work out a favorable solution to this issue where everyone will benefit by it. If we can be of any further assistance to you, please feel free to communicate with us.

Sincerely, Al Apple

When Rosemarie got to the part about Ms Matthews writing several letters describing various incidents that she had been involved in, she got so angry, she thought she was going to have a stroke. Rosemarie had had the courtesy to keep the hospital staff informed of every letter she had written, but Ms Matthews was free to write libelous allegations behind her back! After reading through the entire letter, Rosemarie composed the following letter:

Dear Mr. Apple,

Thank you for your thoughtful reply. Since neither Ms Matthews nor I can prove or disprove the charges, I have no further comment on them. I suppose all these allegations and insinuations shouldn't make any difference to me, anyway; after all, "sticks (hypodermics, included) and stones (pills, included) may break my bones, but words will never hurt me!" Or will they?

I can see now that my "services" are not really needed; if they are, by whom? My husband will dutifully keep on paying his taxes, I will be a dutiful wife and mother, and all of us may look forward to occupying a bed in a convalescent hospital some day, (if we live that long) where we will be treated. HOW will they treat us? Where does treatment stop and mistreatment begin? I wonder!

With this, I leave my future as a visitor to State Health Facilities up to you and the professionals. What's health without freedom to enjoy it, anyhow? And what have all the "freedom fighters" of the past died for?

Rosemarie

Rosemarie had written letters to the staff at The Butterfly, to Governor Black, to the Department of Health, and sent copies to the ACLU, the AMA, several physicians, and a few legislators. She frequently reviewed the gradually accumulating correspondence concerning The Butterfly. In a quiet moment, she sent another letter to Mr. Apple of the Saint Rose District Office of the Cauliflower Department of Health:

Dear Mr. Apple,

I just reread (calmly) your letter of August 2, 1977. I simply cannot believe that our American system is so entrenched in its own rules and regulations that the human persons supporting this system have given up their own logical thinking processes.

You speak of disrupting the patients' treatment program; does not the patient's death disrupt that program, also?

You speak of Ms Matthews' letters. She has tried to speak to me: True! I have refused to listen: False! I have listened very carefully and attentively, but I have refused to make verbal promises. You suggest I have a serious talk with Ms Matthews concerning MY conduct; whatever for? I know how I conducted myself at all times. I need no approval from her. I know she has the legal right to keep me out of the convalescent hospital; in fact, she has the power (here's hoping she won't exercise it) to do away with me completely!

Concerning the diabetic and low sodium diets you mentioned: the patients are not necessarily ingesting the food prescribed for them by their physicians, no matter what the paperwork implies.

And above all, if I were REALLY capable of reaching these withdrawn, passive, and often "hopelessly" ill members of society enough to encourage or discourage them in ANYTHING, I missed my calling! I should be a professional.

Sincerely, Rosemarie

Another letter went to the Honorable Grey Black, Governor of Cauliflower,

Dear Governor Black,

Are you truly satisfied with the end results of our system of convalescent care in publicly financed institutions? As taxpayer and volunteer, I am not! I can protest the treatment I have received at The Butterfly, but those who are patients or those who are victims (six feet under) cannot protest. Must I risk **my** lifestyle in order to bring a little life into a hospital room of two or three "little old ladies"?

Believe me, they are perfectly capable of laughing at my lame jokes, and they can make me laugh at theirs. Not many can see the advantage of a wheel chair over legs, but I can. When I meet someone without legs, I tell her that I appreciate her ability to move around without them. When I meet someone confined to convalescent hospital, I appreciate (with obvious understatement) the fact that it beats being confined to a grave.

Such comments often start lively discussions with the desirable (I assume) result of improved circulation in the body of the patient as well as my own. With those patients who are unable to discuss anything, I simply offer my hand and my presence in friendship and understanding. Often, a hand, limp from abuse or disuse, flutters toward mine in a gesture of returned affection. What possible harm could that do? These people have nothing to lose, but they have much to give. A large segment of society has jobs because of their presence in that hospital bed, and I appreciate that.

I would dearly love to continue to try reaching these members of the human race, but unless I can be reasonably sure of my own legal rights, I will not reach out again. My services are available; but how can I serve without risk?

Sincerely, Rosemarie

Since Governor Black did not answer this letter, Rosemarie wrote him another one in September:

Dear Governor Black,

Thank you for NOT replying to my letter of August 15. Your seeming lack of concern for law-abiding "grass-roots" citizens speaks volumes.

With deep sadness, Rosemarie

Rosemarie was becoming convinced that America was no longer the land of enchantment she had found in 1950. Now there was death all around her, and people were treating her as if she were an intruder. She tried to keep her spirits up by reading magazines and newspapers to look for signs of encouragement. She found an article written by U. S. Senator Hubert Humphrey that prompted a letter:

August 1, 1977

Dear Senator Humphrey,

"You Can't Quit" what? (Reader's Digest, Aug. 1977). I have been forced to quit so many times, it's not even funny. Usually my quitting has something to do with making the choice of the lesser of two evils, as in the situation I find myself in at the moment.

Basically, my philosophy agrees with that expressed in your article (except that I have not personally met "The Good Lord," so I'm not sure what you mean by that). In order to share the time I have and do something I thought was worthwhile, I started visiting patients in a convalescent hospital to extend my hand in friendship. After all, are they not living proof of the concern we tax-payers have for them. We feed them, care for them, cry for them and die for them. I wanted them to feel my personal respect and good will for them. After six months of nearly daily visits, many have become friends among themselves and with me. The staff became increasingly suspicious of me and attempted to "Get Rid" of me unceremoniously. My "never-say-die" attitude and the encouragement of the patients themselves have brought the situation to the following conclusion: I can no longer visit the patients on the premises due to the threat of possible legal ramifications which I can ill afford. I am a wife of a hard-working man and a mother of four teenagers who have not done anything to deserve having a mother in jail on a manslaughter charge. In this country it is far easier to commit a crime and be assured of one's rights, than to commit an act of friendship. I am ready, willing and able to do either, but I have my own reasons for acting as I do, as does every other living being on Earth. I do not have to believe in miracles; I am living proof that they happen, and so are you!

Enclosed please find copies of the correspondence which has passed between me and the staff at the convalescent hospital (randomly selected). Perhaps your experiences have given you a special insight into the problems of patients, alive, but not free to "be a part of a family and friends, a job, neighborhood, community and country."

Sincerely, Rosemarie

Rosemarie was not surprised that the good Senator did not reply to this letter. She had not actually asked for anything.

Rosemarie continued her visits, but the staff made them more and more uncomfortable for her. She eventually restricted her services to taking Betty and Helen out AFTER they had signed themselves out. The incident that brought about Rosemarie's final decision to stop entering The Butterfly happened on a Sunday afternoon.

Rosemarie and her husband were partying with a group of friends from the Elks when someone asked her how she was doing. She mentioned that she had been spending a lot of time volunteering at The Butterfly and that she was having some problems there. Suddenly she remembered that she had promised a patient she would bring a loaf of French bread to be shared at Sunday dinner with her room-mates. Rosemarie excused herself and drove to a bakery in town, bought a loaf of sliced French bread, and took it to The Butterfly.

A nurse standing near her medications cart recognized Rosemarie and told her that she had orders not to let her into the ward. Rosemarie told her that she really couldn't stop her, so the said, "Well, the police can stop you." Calmly, Rosemarie said, "That's right, their number is 422-1234" and squeezed past the cart which the nurse moved toward her in a menacing manner. Rosemarie looked the nurse in the eye and said, "Go ahead and push me against the wall; my husband and several friends know where I am." The nurse let go of the cart. Rosemarie took the French bread to Mae, Betty, and Kate, who were looking forward to sharing it at dinner. Rosemarie visited for a few more minutes and then excused herself because her husband was waiting for her to return to the party. Betty walked her to the lobby.

Both suddenly noticed two police cars with their lights flashing just outside of the entrance. Rosemarie had an idea why they were there but didn't tell Betty. She just said good-bye and walked out.

Outside, a policeman stepped in front of Rosemarie. She asked whether they had come for her. He said, "If you're Rosemarie Tong, we've been called about you." She asked him what she was being charged with. Another policeman stepped out of the other vehicle, and Rosemarie noticed a plainclothes woman sitting in the car. One policeman answered that she wasn't being charged with anything, but that they had been called because she was trespassing on private property. Rosemarie said that she didn't consider this hospital private property since it was largely financed with tax-dollars in the form of Medicare. He said that he didn't know about that, but that the people who run the place had called them because they felt that she was trespassing. Rosemarie argued that the people who LIVE there had invited her and that she was a tax-payer and that she had a right as a citizen of this country to be there.

The policemen could tell that she was not exactly wrong. Finally, one of them said, "Hey, lady, we're just trying to do our job."

This, of course, was the wrong thing to say to a woman who was born in Germany in 1937. All her life, she had heard about people who were just doing their job. All the years she had been in America she had had to endure comments about how the Germans had killed the Jews.

All her life she had felt guilty about having been a citizen of a nation that had put millions to death. Something snapped in Rosemarie.

She looked at the policemen and sadly said, "I know that. But before I leave, I just want to tell you that this is exactly the excuse that all of Hitler's men used as they marched the Jews to their graves, 'we're just doing our jobs'." The faces of the policemen flashed. Rosemarie wished them a nice day and left.

Back at the party Rosemarie told her husband what had happened. They stayed at the party for a little while longer and then drove over to the police station. She asked the receptionist whether they had anything in their records about a Rosemarie Tong. She remembered a call but couldn't find any record of the incident. A few days later, Rosemarie went back again to see whether any written report had been made: nothing. She took this to mean that she had not broken the law; otherwise, there would surely have been a warrant for her arrest.

This incident ended her visits, but she couldn't stop thinking about the issue. When she read a column concerning nursing homes by Vic Favor, the Cauliflower State Assemblyman from her District, she wrote him,

Dear Mr. Favor,

As a volunteer (private visitor, not affiliated with any group other than the human race), I gained many insights into the daily life in a convalescent hospital, and I would appreciate sharing my experiences with you. I was a volunteer at The Butterfly for more than one year, and I still take two of the patients out to lunch several times a week. I have been requested to stay away from the premises, but I have several letters which may surprise you. I would like to meet with you at your convenience. Please allow me an appointment to discuss some of the aspects of the care of the residents of this particular hospital which, I'm sure, is representative of convalescent hospitals in general. "The problems in nursing homes", as you called the events of the day, are often as easy to solve as fulfilling a patient's wish for a really good cup of coffee.

Since Mr. Favor did not think the issue important enough (perhaps he did not think Rosemarie important enough) to reply to her request for an appointment, she wrote to Evelyn Older, the Attorney General of Cauliflower about her concerns.

Dear Attorney General Older,

Because of my experiences during the past twenty months or so as a visitor in a local convalescent hospital, I have good reason to feel that the State of Cauliflower is not getting its money's worth from such facilities.

What I would like to know is--how would I, as taxpayer and citizen, in behalf of the State of Cauliflower, go about bringing suit against the operators of such facilities. Before I go any further, I would like to make it clear to you that I have no personal grudge to avenge. Actually, if the families of the patients, and the patients themselves are satisfied, I should also be satisfied; however, I am not!

If you would like to discover why I'm not satisfied, I am willing to be interviewed, put on the witness stand, or otherwise cooperative.

Sincerely, Rosemarie Tong

On the same day, May 23, 1978, she wrote another letter to Governor Black:

I must be terribly stupid, but I simply do not understand why, AT TAXPAYER EXPENSE, a convicted murderer (Sirhan B. Sirhan) gets three well-balanced meals a day, a comfortable bed, a Color TV, and other creature comforts right here in Sunshine County, when only a few miles away, a "terminally ill" patient, Calvin, who's probably never harmed anyone, gets food that's not fit for human consumption, enough medication to choke a horse, no TV, no smiling faces to brighten his day, and hardly any comfort at all.

Please, Governor Black, have someone (ANYONE!) explain this to me. Who allows such inequities to occur? How much longer must we allow this to continue? How can I protect my children from falling victim to such a system? Shall I teach them that they are better off in the long run by killing someone and going to prison than by being "good" and going to a doctor in case they get "sick and tired of it all?"

As mother of four teenagers, I need some answers.

Sincerely, Rosemarie Tong

The stress and strain of fighting a losing battle must have started to get to Rosemarie because when she received three replies with official letterheads within one week, she did not read them carefully enough and mistook them as just so much more bureaucratic red tape. They seemed too much like double-talk. These three letters, on rereading, did offer hope, but she was too emotionally involved to appreciate their significance at the time. She replied facetiously to the two letters from the Department of Health and the one from the Department of Justice:

June 8,

Governor Black has asked me to respond to your recent letter concerning patient care in health facilities. We are forwarding your letter to our Saint Rose District Office. A member of that staff will contact you, direct, to obtain specific information regarding your concerns.

Thank you for bringing these matters to our attention.

June 15,

We have received a copy of your May 23 letter to Governor Black. In order for us to investigate the situation which you describe, it is necessary for you to identify the facility. It would be helpful if you would identify the patient.

June 21,

This is in response to your recent letter which alluded to local convalescent hospitals but failed to mention any specific complaint. If you wish to disclose information for our consideration, please feel free to write to this office with any details you care to provide. This office maintains a record of all complaints received, and where the situation warrants it, an investigation is made. You may be sure that your complaint is of value to us.

The last letter was from the Department of Justice, and the other two from the Department of Health. Rosemarie was going crazy and began lashing out left, right and center. There was simply too much information and not enough moral support for her personal battle against death. A political campaign was also beginning to bring mail which spurred her on to write this letter to nearly a dozen candidates for public office:

Dear Candidate,

I just read the article in the Daily Republic which described some of your opinions on various subjects. No mention was made about your opinion on the subject which interests me the most: publicly funded and licensed convalescent hospitals.

Do you like (or approve of) what's going on in convalescent hospitals at taxpayer expense?

She did get a couple of replies, but the respondents just wanted to know what WAS "going on" in these places.

Rosemarie felt that they should go look for themselves. By this time, she realized that she no longer had an objective point of view. She didn't know WHAT was going on in those places and didn't trust her own judgment anymore. She was angry, hurt, outraged. Reading obituary after obituary in the newspaper and remembering a nurse's written assurance that she would not hesitate to protect the health and safety of the convalescent hospital's residents in every way possible,

Rosemary wrote to Ms Matthews, the Administrator:

Since our conversation last August, I have indeed stayed away from The Butterfly. The obituaries of the following friends of mine have appeared in the local newspaper since that time: Clara W., Anna R., Vivian C., Virginia L., Rachel L., Elsie M., Mae S., Betty R., and Eva G.

You assured me that you would not hesitate to protect the health and safety of your residents in every way possible. I stayed away from my friends because you threatened me with a lawsuit and convinced me that my absence would benefit their health and safety. What happened?

Sincerely, Rosemarie Tong

Rosemarie was beginning to crack under the stress. Again, on July 21, 1978, she reached out to the ACLU:

On July 3, 1977, I mailed a letter to you (the ACLU) with the following text:

The following is a copy of a letter I wrote to the acting administrator and director of nurses at The Butterfly after enduring verbal abuse from the staff for volunteer work which did not coincide with their routine care of the patients. I am not herewith asking for help but merely wish to inform your agency:

Dear Ms Rumple and Ms Matthews,

Due to my recent experiences at The Butterfly, I feel constrained to ask these questions: Do you (personally) consider the human beings under your care to be living breathing American Citizens with perceptions and responses of their own OR dying bodies being maintained under "safe" conditions until death do them part?

Do you perceive your own bodies to be less vulnerable than those of your patients to natural or man-made disasters just because of the difference in shape, blood-count, title and income, or number of years already lived? All it takes is one big earthquake or nuclear blast in your hospital, and we're all dead at the same time (I live only a few blocks away)

You need not answer these questions since your behavior will speak for itself.

Rosemarie Tong

More than a year has passed since that time. I have amassed the enclosed documents during this interval. As you (the ACLU) can tell from the correspondence, I cannot depend on assistance from tax-supported public servants. Perhaps YOU could inform me against whom I could possibly initiate a CLASS ACTION SUIT in behalf of all those who have paid taxes for many years while they were in good health and contributing to the greatness of this country in the belief that they would receive the reward one day.

> Are the "rewards" of a bed, a wheelchair, a few scraps of food, and daily sense-distorting doses of drugs, really what these living ancestors deserve? Just in case the thought occurs to you that I have enjoyed all the letter-writing of the past year, and that the experiences as a volunteer gave me something to do with my time, I should like to point out that I could have been earning a fair amount of money in a paid position instead (or perhaps improving my tennis game).

Sincerely, Rosemarie Tong

Rosemarie didn't hear anything from the ACLU until 1982, at which time they sent her a direct-mail solicitation for a contribution. She wrote them they had a lot of nerve asking for money when they had never even bothered to answer her plea when she needed their moral support the most.

In late June 1978, however, Rosemarie was very pleased to receive the most positive responses up to that time. Vic Favor, the Assemblyman from her District, had apparently taken her latest letter seriously, and the Chief of the Health Care Section of the Licensing and Certification Division of the Department of Health responded to the issue. The wheels of government were beginning to move. Vic Favor's letter read:

> *Dear Ms Tong,*
>
> *Your letter to me came several days ago, and quickly thereafter so did a response from the Department of Health. I would encourage you to take Mr. Smitt up on his suggestion to file a complaint with the Saint Rose district office. I do not doubt that reality falls short of specifications in this as well as many fields. I know of only two ways to mitigate that problem. One is to spend more money for better performance, which I support in this case but which the*

voters have just made much more difficult generally. The other is to keep the pressure on.

Let us know what you do, and thank you for writing.

Sincerely, Vic Favor

Mr. Smitt's letter stated,

Dear Ms Tong,

Don Haupt has asked that I respond to your recent letter in which you expressed concern regarding the food served to patients in convalescent hospitals. Cauliflower Administration Code, Title 22 Division 5, Chapter 3, contains regulations pertaining to skilled nursing facilities. Section 72301 lists dietary services as one of the services to be provided by these facilities. Section 72303 requires that the food be of the "quality and quantity to meet the patient's needs in accordance with physician's orders". This same section also requires adherence to patient preferences, three meals a day, between meal nourishments as allowed by the prescribed diet and that food is prepared in an attractive manner so as to retain nutritive value. The prescribed diet tray may vary from a regular diet, to any alteration necessary to conform to the physician's therapeutic plan, to a pureed or liquid diet, if ordered by the physician and if that consistency of food is the only type the patient can tolerate.

Inspection of long-term care facilities takes place at a minimum of twice a year to ensure that facilities adhere to the standards as set forth in these regulations. At the time of inspection it can be ascertained that the food is served in a timely and sanitary manner and in accordance with physician's orders. While inspectors cannot be present to assure that the food of each meal is consumed, Section 72311(c) states, "licensed nursing personnel ensure that patients are served the diets as prescribed by attending physicians, and that patients are provided with necessary and acceptable equipment for eating and that prompt assistance in eating is given when needed." Section 72311(d) requires that any marked or sudden change in weight shall be reported promptly to the attending physician".

Personal visits to individual patients are made during inspection and allow for patients' complaints regarding food service.

If you have a complaint regarding a specific facility or the diet of a particular patient is receiving, you may contact the district office.

Sincerely, Bill Smitt, Chief

Rosemarie followed Mr. Favor's and Mr. Smitt's suggestion and wrote a letter to the Chief, Licensing and Certification Division of the Department of Health:

Dear Mr. Smitt,

I really appreciate your thoughtful letter explaining the regulations pertaining to dietary services in skilled nursing facilities.

Perhaps you have gotten the idea from my previous correspondence that I have some kind of personal grudge against a particular facility. While I did not appreciate the treatment I got from the staff at the facility I visited for nearly a year, I bear no personal enmity against anyone in particular because I can't be sure whether they were concerned with losing their jobs or their patients. I realized from the start that my presence would represent a threat to either. I might have acted in the same way if I were in the responsible position of hospital administrator or director of nurses.

My concern does not deal with any "hurt feelings" I may have suffered, but with the fact that living human beings are residing in public facilities at public expense without the benefit of the kind of food, therapy, friendships, and freedoms of choice that most other human beings in this country take for granted. Believe me, when a 97-year-old mother of three financially secure sons (all three owning beautiful homes) is on Medicare and is expected to eat a nearly raw baked potato without butter and a little bit of stringy meat for a Sunday dinner in a room with two other patients whose condition is not exactly appetizing, I take positive action when she asks me to purchase a few doughnuts for her. I figure if her environment and the loving concern of her family haven't killed her, neither would a couple of doughnuts.

I could go on and on about the things I have witnessed, but I have no wish to bore you. All I can say is that my husband and I are tired of footing the bill for such goings-on, and my guess, in view of the result of the recent election (the passing of Proposition 13), is that many other tax-payers feel the same.

Rosemary also wrote another letter to Vic Favor:

Thank you for your letter. I doubt that it is necessary to spend more money since $900 monthly per patient should certainly suffice! My husband supports a family of six on not much more, and I personally know several patients who could get along quite well in an apartment on $900 a month if all kinds of middlemen didn't take their cut first. For example, a friend of mine, confined to The Butterfly (laughingly called "skilled nursing facility") but quite capable of tending to her own affairs such as eating in restaurants, sleeping, walking, talking, shopping, playing Bingo, taking care of her personal toilet, all UNASSISTED, wanted to move into a more private environment. We checked with the Parkside Manor on Table Avenue, Fairness, Cauliflower, a private apartment complex for pensioners. This facility serves three nutritious meals a day, has carpeted rooms with private baths, and many other amenities. The total cost would be $460 a month; there was a vacancy, and my friend qualified as far as her medical condition was concerned. We immediately went to the Social Security Office to find out about the financial arrangements. It seemed only logical that the government would gladly reduce its cost of maintaining my friend's EXISTENCE by nearly 50% and at the same time make my friend's LIFESTYLE more comfortable. (At least, she wouldn't have to eat her meals in the presence of two other patients, one of whom invariably uses the bedpan at mealtimes). My friend was quite depressed, but I was not surprised to discover that there was no possibility of reducing the $900 to $460, since the move would make my friend ineligible for Medicare and MediCal payments. Her Social

Security and SSI checks alone would not be sufficient to finance her private room at Parkside Manor. I realize that my friend is only one of perhaps thousands of physically and mentally capable human beings who are confined in "skilled nursing facilities" for financial rather than medical reasons. I also know that this lady and many others would know how to spend $900 monthly if they were given the money directly instead of receiving the MINIMAL SERVICES this money buys. I wouldn't even mind paying MORE taxes if the people who receive the money, ranging from janitors to shareholders in these facilities, ACTUALLY rendered the services they get paid for. Your second suggestion to keep the pressure on is well taken, but I'm getting awfully tired! Besides, just what kind of pressure should I apply? I've already considered picketing, setting off a bomb, screaming from a rooftop, and other more violent acts, but that would only get ME attention, and the patients still wouldn't get good food, good therapy, good companionship, and good twentieth century medical services. How much longer must I hold my finger in the dam without receiving some kind of compensation

Sincerely, Rosemarie Tong

Apparently, Vic Favor had recognized the seriousness of the situation and passed Rosemarie's letter, along with the following note, on to Henry O. Bennett, Area Director of the Social Security Administration in Berkeley, Cauliflower.

Dear Mr. Bennett,

Enclosed is a letter from a constituent who seems to make a compelling case for a new category of recipients, who now, obviously are considered in as much need as people requiring assistance with their day-to-day living functions.

I would be most appreciative if you could explore this issue and its possible solutions.

Thank you.
Sincerely, Vic Favor

Wow! A new category of recipients for Social Security benefits! An Assemblyman taking Rosemarie serious enough to get someone official to explore the issues she had raised! She was moved, and she could hardly wait to hear what this Mr. Bennett had to say. She wrote Vic Favor a Thank You note and kept an eye on the media for developments.

On Wednesday, August 23, 1978, the Sacramento Wasp carried an article, "Error Haunts Nursing Homes". It stated that Cauliflower's nursing home industry, after what appears to have been a major error in lobbying strategy, suddenly may be faced with increased penalties for law violations involving their patients. Well, fancy that! It seems that both the Assembly and the Senate agreed on legislation that would tie appropriations of MediCal for patient care to penalties for violations. The bills in question are Agnos' AB 1644 and Senator Beverly's SB1886, both of which have the Governor's commitment that he would not sign the appropriations unless the penalties are written into the bills.

In November 1978, Rosemarie finally received the long-awaited response from Henry O. Bennett of the Social Security Office in Berkeley. It explains the various benefits a person may apply for, and it made some specific suggestions about Helen. Rosemarie answered Mr. Bennett's letter with the following,

Dear Mr. Bennett,

I received a copy of your recent response to our correspondence concerning my interest in patients in convalescent hospitals from Mr. Favor's office. Thank you very much for this thoughtful and informative reply.

Two recent events at The Butterfly have made me wonder just exactly what the purpose of convalescent hospitals is. Two patients, the friend I had previously mentioned, as well as another lady I know, have bruises on their heads. One has stitches on top of her head. She told me that she had lost her balance and hit her head on something hard but she didn't tell me what. The other has an awful-looking bruise over the entire area of her left eye. The eyeball itself is still intact, but the eyelid and surrounding tissue is black and blue. She told me she just lost her balance and went down, hitting the floor headfirst. Considering the condition and medication of these two patients, I have no reason to assume anything. It is entirely possible and highly probable that there was NO foul play.

However, since these two are representative of many patients in skilled nursing facilities, and most of these patients easily trip over their own feet and lose their balance, I do not understand why the floors in these facilities are so hard that a simple fall can result in a major injury. Why is there not soft carpeting or at least softer cushioned flooring of the easy-to-clean type?

As I asked before: What exactly are we trying to achieve? Is it the purpose of these "skilled nursing facilities" to keep these human persons bedridden or securely fastened in their wheelchairs, or is it to encourage these people (who, I'm sure, have spent their youth and health contributing to the development of this country) to try walking again, talking again, and living again? In short, are they dying or living?

In response to this letter, Rosemarie heard again form the Saint Rose District Office. This time a Health Facilities Evaluator wrote her regarding The Butterfly,

Your letter of November 20, 1978 to Mr. Bennett of the Social Security Administration was directed to this office for appropriate action.

Your letter does not make a direct complaint against the staff or facility; therefore, it is not possible for this department to take any specific action, however, I did visit The Butterfly on December 19, 1978 to discuss the incidents you mentioned and also make a determination if patients were needlessly restrained.

The incidents you describe appeared to have been unavoidable and the facility gives evidence of making every effort to prevent injury to the patients.

Marijuana Vogel

Rosemarie replied,

Okay, I'll take your word for it; I'm tired of worrying about sick people, anyway!

It would appear that the case was about to be closed, but Rosemary's mission was not completely accomplished yet. Since her husband is a retired military man, they receive a newsletter for retired personnel. In the Nov.-Dec. 1978 issue she found an article related to the issue of Nursing Homes. On December 27 she took the time out of their Christmas holidays to write a letter to the Director of the Veterans Administration:

I just read the VA News Brief in the "USAF News for Retired Personnel" about the new Nursing Home at the Memphis VA Medical Center.

I would surely like to know just who these 120 fortunate people are that will get to exist in this expensive palace.

My goodness, $4.9 million for 120 people figures out to $40,833.oo per person, and even at today's real estate prices, that much money could build a private residence for each person. A private residence would, in the long run, be much more comfortable and lucrative for these people because a private residence can be shared with friends, relatives, pets, hobbies, or hired help. It can be leased, rented, remodeled, sublet, or sold, while a room (even one in a palace, with or without a balcony) is merely a place to EXIST indefinitely.

Would YOU like to become a resident in such a place?

Please don't bother to respond to this letter if you only want to tell me that these people will be "cared for" and/or nursed back to health by a loving staff. I've visited too many nursing homes that already exist to be taken in by such sentimental demagoguery. A concentration camp is still a concentration camp, no matter whether it is in Germany, Russia, or Memphis, Tennessee.

Another thing I would like to know: just who is supposed to keep on financing such encapsulating of human bodies? (See attached newsletter)

Rosemarie sent copies of this letter to President J.C., Senator Edward K. and Congressman Claude P.

The President and the Senator ignored Rosemary's barb, but Congressman P. replied:

In your recent letter you criticized the spending of $4.9 million by the Veteran's Administration for the construction of a nursing home in Memphis that will accommodate 120 patients. The Committee has not developed any body of information on the motivation for, or need for, construction of a nursing home in Memphis. From the beginning of its operation, the Aging Committee has been promoting home health care and home chore care. Our investigations indicated that it is not only more humane, but also less expensive, to maintain all but the most severely disabled in their own homes.

In the 95th Congress members of the Aging Committee appeared before the Ways and Means Committee to testify on the need to amend the Medicare law to expand coverage for home health services. This bill (H.R. 13097) was reported by the Committee, and approved by the House, but time ran out before it could be passed by the Senate. We will renew our efforts to expand home health (care) and home chore services in the 96th Congress. Enclosed is a press release which expresses my views on this subject

It is interesting to note that both Mr. Henry O. Bennett of the Social Security Administration and Congressman Claude Pepper stress the benefits of people being in their own homes. In addition, they both mention chore services—a program which provides through local welfare departments house-cleaning help for people who qualify. (See attached press release)

Rosemarie sent Congressman Pepper a short note, thanking him. In February 1979, she received a reply from the Veteran's Administration. It was written by John Byrd, Director of the VA Medical Center in Memphis, Tennessee.

Dear Ms Tong,

Your letter to the Administrator of the Veterans' Administration has been referred to our medical center for reply.

Extended care facilities at this medical center are vitally needed for the treatment of veterans in our area. Within ten (10) years, the largest group of American War Veterans, those from World War II, will be reaching the age of 65. Most of them will be reaching the age of retirement, fixed incomes, increased chronic illness, and a need for different kinds of health and support services.

Despite all the anxieties about the environment, people are living longer today. Elderly people with chronic diseases are frail and fragile, and they need a longer time to recover. They also need support services. These are people who need something not as intense as hospitalization, but not so little that they can live independently.

We cannot begin to compare a dollar amount against the medical treatment of a veteran. The Veterans Administration's motto is "To care for him who shall have borne the battle, and for his widow, and his orphan". We shall continue at this medical center to give the best medical care possible to our veteran population.

Sincerely, John Eagle

Being married to a veteran, Rosemarie was, of course, impressed with the Veterans Administration's motto. The arrival of his letter, accompanied by a rousing rendition of the Stars and Stripes Forever and the American Flag waving gently in the breeze, caused palpitations in Rosemarie's heart. Gratefully, she wrote him,
Your letter warmed the cockles of my heart!

Actually, she thought then (1979) and thinks now, that citizens BETTER compare a dollar amount against the medical treatment of a veteran. It seems that some graduates of medical schools expect to make their education expenses back within months of the commencement exercises. The lifeblood of the Body Politick has been jeopardized from Watts to Vietnam, through smack, crack and pot, by hook and by crook. The national health depends on the integrity of the system.

Meanwhile nothing had changed at The Butterfly. Rosemarie was still taking her friend, Helen, out to lunch at fairly regular intervals. She kept Rosemarie informed of the daily events. One day, she talked about Betty's accident. Betty had apparently fallen onto the hard floor some time during the weekend and received a considerable bump on the head. When she (Helen) had inquired of the nurses about a doctor being called (because of possibility of permanent damage to her already frail person) she received no answer. On Monday, Helen telephoned Betty's doctor herself and was told that his office had received NO notification of the incident. Helen then told the secretary, "Well, as of now, you've been notified!" Rather than just get upset about such information, Rosemarie wrote the Governor again and sent copies to Betty's doctor, the Cauliflower Department of Health, and the administrator of The Butterfly (who had in the meanwhile changed names: now it was a Mr. Br....).

Less than a week later, Rosemarie received a reply from the Licensing & Certification Division of the Department of Health:

Dear Ms Tong,

I have discussed your letter with Mr. Apple from our Saint Rose District Office and forwarded a copy of your letter to him. He shall contact you with the results of their investigation.

Thank you for bringing this to our attention.
signed Chief, Health Care Section

Shortly thereafter, Rosemarie received a long letter from the Saint Rose District Office. The Health Facilities Evaluator had made an inspection (she should have called Rosemarie to accompany her to The Butterfly but didn't) and found everything in order, especially Betty's medical records. Nothing was mentioned about whether Betty was satisfied with the way things were. Helen and Rosemarie stayed in contact until one day Helen mentioned that she was scheduled for surgery the following day. Rosemarie was amazed to hear that. Helen said that was going to have her hemorrhoids taken care of. With relief Rosemarie thought that this was not very serious. Since they were eating lunch at the time, she jokingly retorted, "If you don't tell me about your hemorrhoids, I won't tell you about mine". The two then changed the subject and spent the rest of the afternoon shopping. Rosemarie couldn't believe her ears when she called the hospital a few days later. Helen had had open heart surgery! Even though Rosemarie had been a very close friend of hers for two years, there had been no mention about open heart surgery. Several family members and the staff knew Rosemarie's address, but they had not notified her! Rosemarie went to visit her at the Inter-community Hospital. Helen was barely coherent but recognized Rosemarie. A few days later she was transferred to a convalescent hospital in the State Capitol. When Rosemarie visited her several weeks later, she looked awful. Whatever the operation was supposed to accomplish was not yet evident. Later Rosemarie heard rumors through the grape-vine about a young doctor who had come to Fairness, performed a few surgeries at Medicare expense, and was drummed out of town by the legitimate medical community.

As 1979 wore on, and her desire to affect the conditions in convalescent hospitals was realized, Rosemarie began to make plans to enter UCBezerkly and resume her studies which had been badly neglected over the previous two years. Her simple interest in taking college classes at Solano had been transformed into a burning desire to major in English so that she could tell the world what she had learned at The Butterfly!

Weekends Rosemarie caught up on reading the newspapers. One by one the people she had met at The Butterfly were featured in the obituaries. She fought long battles with depression but doggedly continued to believe that she had made a difference. TV shows were featuring older actors. The Gray Panthers had formed an interest group and become politically active. Now and then a convalescent hospital or nursing home made the news for violations. Magazines, devoted entirely to older citizens, began to be published. A Senior Center was built in Fairness, and many other cities and towns planned similar facilities. The wall had been cracked.

A recent newspaper article, "Huge penalty against nursing homes" (Craig Marine, The Examiner, Oct. 17, 1986) proves that the state is no longer afraid to move against the violators of the laws of common decency. However, the most heartening news came to Rosemarie in a Sacramento Wasp article (Dec. 26, 1985), "Nursing home trial: A claim that neglect was murder". The article describes a young prosecuting attorney, who at his own expense, emotional and financial, is pressing charges.

He argues, "This is not simply a situation involving negligence. How many warnings does somebody have to receive before their conduct moves up the ladder from negligence to, finally, knowledge? My interest has stemmed from my feelings about the wrongs that were committed. There's little doubt about what was taking place at that institution. They were mistreating patients and killing patients."

The motive? Money. The prosecutors charge that the way Medicaid funds are disbursed on a per-patient basis, rather than for actual care rendered, encourages cost-cutting and patient neglect. The case is being watched with keen interest--and some degree of alarm--by the nursing home industry and by those who seek to reform that industry.

Conclusion:

After submitting that essay to the professor, I had finally achieved a calm place in my heart. I had spread the news about convalescent hospitals and now it was up to the system to adjust itself. I was free to pursue my interests in other avenues. My three daughters had graduated from high school and our son was about to be a sophomore. My husband and my counselor at Solano College encouraged me to think about a four-year college. I chose UC Berkeley, but first…another step back.

MOTHER OF TEENS

My crisis of 1976 and the frenzied letter-writing that followed, somewhat revolved around my role as mother. I had taken many of the scare messages in the media far too seriously and wanted to protect my family against the unfeeling system. When I regained my composure, I became a more balanced person, but my family remained my main focus.

Through my contact with the elderly folks in the convalescent hospital, I gained a true respect for survival and experience. With that, I gained more respect for my own life with all its ups and downs. My children had turned into teenagers, and my involvement with them had to take a new direction. My control of their lives had to evolve into support. I found several ways to achieve that.

One by one, they had obtained their driver's licenses. As expected, this in itself is traumatic. Vivi, for example, drove our huge station wagon over one of those cement curbs in a parking lot and tore up the underside of the car. Lisa was rear-ended at a downtown traffic light. Kathy called the police to report a stolen car. She had driven the car to Solano College but returned home in a friend's car. When I noticed that the car was not in the driveway, she thought it had been stolen. Sheepishly, she discovered it later exactly where she had left it. Lisa rear-ended someone at a stop light.

John's adventure with his first car was a real pip!

"Ma'm, do you own a bronze Toyota?" a man's voice on the telephone at two in the morning certainly got my heart to skip several beats.

"Yes." I tried to remain calm but kicked Lee awake.

"I'm police officer so-and-so, and we have an abandoned Toyota here. Do you have a key?"

"Oh my God! Love, something bad happened to John. His car has been abandoned. Let's go!" I couldn't get dressed fast enough. It was a Saturday night, and my mind reeled with thoughts of John in a ditch somewhere.

Lee took the phone and got the location from the cop. We jumped into our car and flew across town. As we approached the designated area, we noticed two young guys sauntering along the darkened street.

"Get in the car." John and his friend George squirmed into the back seat. "Well, what do you have to say for yourself?" I demanded. Lee was quiet, but the muscles in his jaw were twitching.

"We egged a house, and when they called the cops, we hid in the bushes. Then we decided to walk home," John explained very matter-of-factly.

"Let me hear how in the world you got stupid enough to egg a house. You haven't even been drinking. Did you take something I can't smell???" I was pretty aggravated and didn't pull any punches.

"No, we were just driving along and these guys cut us off," John offered.

"Yeah, we got mad, so I told John, 'Let's buy some eggs and get even with them.'" George chimed in.

"How did you find their house?" I wondered.

"We knew these guys from school. We weren't out to hurt anybody."

I thought, these are good kids after all. A couple of pranks gone wrong. "How did the police get involved?"

John said, "I guess their folks must have called 'em."

I could sense Lee softening. "Let's just see what the police has to say."

We arrived to a small group waiting by our Toyota. Apparently, the boys admitted cutting off John and his friend, but they thought they had gotten away and went to bed without telling anything to their parents. Suddenly, their younger sister started screaming because their house was being bombarded with eggs. That's when the cops were called.

I tried to find out how we could straighten out this mess and make up for the damages. The parents of the boys, however, were far too angry with Lee and me to listen. The mother yelled something about how badly we had raised our son, and that something needs to be done about the wild kids in town.

I stayed calm. "Seeing that you have all the answers, you should run for Congress," I finally got my word in edgewise.

"Easy, lady," one of the cops looked at me.

"If I had gotten hold of your kid, I would have hit him so hard he'd have blood coming out of ears!" The boys' father tried to intimidate me.

I jumped in his face, "Listen, I survived World War II in Germany, and you can't scare me with talk about blood running out of ears!" We were nose to nose.

"Okay, that's enough!" The cops finally got strong. "Let's figure out what needs to be done and go home to get a good night's sleep."

"Do you want to make a claim. We have homeowner's insurance," Lee, the logical one.

"No, we've already hosed down the house, and if the boys come to help clean up the rest of the mess (eggshells on the ground) we'll call it a night." Bloody ears had calmed down enough to talk civilly to Lee.

For the following month John was on foot.

Life was definitely never dull with teenagers around the house. Most of the time, there was plenty of laughter, music and excitement.

"Guess what, Mom," Kathy and Lisa rushed through the door. "We're going to be in the Rose Parade!"

The high school band director had received an invitation to march in the Rose Parade. As members of the Band Boosters we had a great deal of work ahead to raise the money for the highly prized event. Finally, we were ready. Kathy would march the French Horn, and Lisa was chosen to carry one of the tall flags in the very front row.

For years we had watched every Rose Parade on TV, and now my own daughters were to participate. I could barely contain my pride. I notified all the relatives, and they promised to watch TV on New Year's Day. My own parents had previously planned a trip to Germany, so they sent regrets along with an invitation to use their home in Southern California as a place to stay.

Another special event took place that summer. I had somehow been cajoled into establishing a local "Junior Music Makers." A group of adults, including my neighbor Gisela and me, regularly gathered to perform short musical selections for each other. One of the members suggested, "Since you have three girls that play so much music, why don't you start a club just for musical teens?"

Indeed, why not? Vivi, Kathy and Lisa agreed. They recruited several of their high school friends and we met regularly to perform solos for each other. I was truly happy in my little home.

GRAMMA GOES TO COLLEGE

So what now? Despite my painful experience at Solano, I went back to enroll in more classes. I continued to get good grades but noticed that my attitude had changed. I no longer idolized college professors; consequently, I articulated my dissent whenever it occurred. My counselor suggested that I seriously consider a four-year college as soon as possible. He apparently saw something of value in me that needed a larger platform.

"Love, what do you think of my going to UC Berkeley?"

Lee was cautious. "Why that one?"

"Well, it's close, and it has a good academic reputation. Besides, I used to admire the Free Speech Movement in the sixties. I know that we can't afford it, but my counselor said he'd try to get me some financial aid."

"Remember, we talked about this before. If you get a degree from a university, you'll be able to get a good job and help the kids later," Lee, the logical one, mused. "You've always been supportive when I was in the Air Force and attending college classes. You helped me get a degree, and now it's my turn to help you." What a guy!

"Okay, I'll fill out some applications, and we'll see what happens." My heart pounded as I thought about my dream of a university education coming true.

My application for a financial Cal grant was denied. Apparently, we had been too efficient in our financial dealings. We owned a home and had practically no debts, so I didn't qualify for grants. Lee decided that we didn't need to take out a loan. We would cover costs as they came up.

"Look, I got the Regent's Scholarship!" I yelled as I ripped open the envelope. "My counselor told me that he'd recommend me for it, but I didn't think that it would actually happen!" I was ecstatic. First I thought that it involved money, but I soon discovered that, again, money was based on need. All I would get was a hundred dollar honorarium and a certificate. Boo hoo.

The next day another envelope arrived. As a benefit of the Regents' Scholarship, I was offered a room in Stern Hall, a women's dorm on campus. Naturally, I would have to pay the full fees, but the room was reserved for me. All I needed to do was let them know within a certain deadline. I couldn't believe my eyes. A private room on campus! What will they think of next?

Lee and I had been concerned about whether I would commute or try to get a room in Berkeley during the week. Suddenly, here it was. We decided to accept it.

"Sure, Mom, I think it's great!" Kathy was still living at home and enthusiastic when I told her about my plan to go to UCB. She and her new husband Ted were also expecting their first child. They would soon be moving out.

"Don't worry, Dad and I can get along during the week without you. Ha Ha," John chimed in. He was in high school and really didn't need me to fuss over him constantly. I was reassured. Native American sons, I understand, would be raised by their mothers until they were a certain age, and then they had to go with their fathers to be trained in hunting, etc. That thought freed me from guilt about leaving my home during the week.

Lisa and Viv were also impressed. They had already moved to places of their own and no longer needed my daily contact.

With all the arrangements made, my wardrobe ready and a special bank account, I set forth to meet the first day of school. Boy, was I nervous!

For one thing, in order to get the classes I wanted, I had to participate in the scramble. It's not a simple matter signing up but a matter of going to the class at scheduled times and hoping that there is still enough room. Those students who are accepted into a class get a special little slip and then go register. This can be quite a nerve-wrecking process.

For another, all the other first-year students are also nervous, making the tension palpable.

Then there all the details of meals, books, long lines and unfamiliar buildings to manage. Within a couple of days, I was accustomed to the melee, and my schedule was organized.

This hubbub was certainly different from the social life I had left at home. Lee and I had been participating more in Elks Lodge events. In fact, I had recently attended a very fancy wine and cheese tasting party at the Elks. Now I was simply one of thousands of first-year students at UCB.

During my first week at Stern hall, I met a few of my fellow students in the A-wing, but I was not particularly interested in socializing with them. They were, after all, the age of my own children. I was there to study and earn a degree, but I was pleasant.

One evening, two girls knocked on my door and invited me to join them down the hall. They explained that a bunch of girls were planning a wine and cheese tasting party and they would like to have me come. Inwardly, I realized that I would probably be asked to buy the wine, but I accepted the friendly offer. I walked down the hall with them and joined a room full of girls. There must have been at least twenty girls crammed into a small room.

"Come in. Come in, Marianne. We're glad you could come," one friendly voice welcomed me.

Introductions all around were followed by inviting me to the planned party.

"Do you think you could possibly bring a couple of bottles of wine?" Here it was. I was over twenty-one, and they weren't. I looked around at their innocent young faces and thought of my own daughters. How did their mothers feel about their daughters in college?

"Will this wine and cheese tasting party be just for us, or will there be boys invited?" I wondered.

"No, it's just for us girls to get acquainted," one of the girls explained.

"Well, since your parents trusted you to come to Berkeley, I could probably bring a couple of bottles of wine," I was still hesitant but wanted to hear more.

One of the girls in a back row asked another, "Who's going to bring the pot?"

Before I could stop my big mouth I asked, "Oh, are we going to have a fondue?"

The entire room stopped chattering and focused on me. Finally, a loud voice declared, "Oh my God! The generation gap!"

"Girls, I think I'll beg off on this party. I usually go home on weekends, anyway. Thanks for the invitation." I smiled and left. Over the next three years, those same girls and I became friends and shared many a bagel and hot cocoa, or even a pizza or two; however, we never did have that fondue.

One afternoon in late October, I got an urgent phone call.

"Love, Kathy is in labor. Do you want me to come get you?" I had promised Kathy that I'd be with her since her husband was out of state in basic training.

"Yes, I'm done with my classes today. I'll be waiting for you."

Kathy was already in the hospital when I got there. We walked the halls for a little while. A first child can sometimes take a long time, but Kathy was getting more and more urgent.

"Mom, I'd better get back to bed. Oh and by the way, I want you to take pictures," she added.

I was so excited, I could barely handle the camera. Suddenly her water broke. What a gush! I had no idea that my little Kathy could produce such a flood. Not long after that we wheeled her into the delivery room, and her little son Teddy was born. For a moment I became a tree that felt a branch emerge from its trunk. There was no pain; just a great feeling of completeness. Then the feeling passed, and I was able to focus the camera on Kathy again. She was doing fine and smiling about her little son.

The following day, Lee took me back to college. One of my classes that day was Chinese 1A. I had been doing very well in that class, so the teacher often called on me. She asked me a very well practiced question, and I was expected to give a very well practiced answer. I explained, "Sorry, my mind has been completely wiped clean. Last night I watched the birth of my grandson."

The professor just smiled and left me alone the rest of the hour.

Not all professors were that considerate. In the English department I met considerable resistance. Some simply couldn't understand that an attractive forty-two-year-old was actually at UCBerkeley for an education, and I didn't feel it necessary to prove my happy marriage and family life to anyone.

One incident with the professor of The Augustan Age was particularly devastating. I was doing all the assigned reading and attending all the classes. I worked diligently on all the assignments and turned in my papers on time. One assignment called for responses to David Hume and John Dryden. The question was what would Hume say about Dryden, and what would Dryden say about Hume. I wrote a paper that I was sure would earn at least a B. I knew that the professor did not employ a reader and read all the student papers himself. A D- naturally drew me into the professor's office.

After debating the merits of the essay for a half hour, and becoming more and more frustrated, I asked, "Well, what **do** you want?"

Sitting behind his desk with a peculiar expression on his face, he scanned me from head to toe and said, "Well, if you don't know **that**, you'll have a difficult time passing my class." I was stunned. It was too late to withdraw without a penalty, so I remained in the class. Despite my very best efforts on subsequent assignments, I received an F for the course.

Proving sexual harassment proved to be futile. I had no evidence and my attempts to get another professor to evaluate my essays were met with stone faces. I struggled for a couple of weeks and went to an Ombudsman, but nothing was done. In fact, I was eventually notified by a black officer of campus security that my name had been submitted as a potential trouble-maker. The irony of this situation was not lost on either of us. We were both living the American dream of equality under the law, but the professors could or would not see that.

One late afternoon that American dream seemed on the verge of disaster. I walked into the day room in the dorm and noticed that most of the students were clustered around the TV. I thought, "Boy, that must be an interesting episode of their favorite soap opera."

One of the girls turned to me, "Marianne, have you heard? The president wants eighteen-year-olds to register for the draft."

Of course, I was aware that the world situation had taken an unpleasant turn with the Ayatollah Khomeini and the hostages, but I didn't expect a draft. My son was eighteen.

Glued to the TV, some of the girls were crying about their brothers and boyfriends. The atmosphere in the day room became more and more somber. Suddenly I felt a compelling urge to cry. My grandfather, my father, my stepfather, and my husband had risked their lives in uniform. For what? Now the world wanted my son too!

I ran to my room and threw myself on the bed. I cried so much that my pillow was soaked, and I was afraid that I would get a stroke. I thought about calling Lee to come get me, but then I realized that I would upset him. I didn't want him driving on the freeway that way. Then I thought about calling my oldest daughter Vivienne, who was living in San Francisco. She would remain calm.

"Mom, please don't cry. I'll be over in about an hour."

"Th-th-thanks, Viv. I really need some company as soon as possible."

More crying. What can I do, what can I do? My mind was racing, and the tears were flowing. I thought, "I ought to offer myself instead of my son." A tiny little smile crept into my heart.

In my mind's eye, the picture of my son being slain in battle was suddenly replaced by a picture of myself in a recruiting office. The look on the imaginary sergeant's face made my smile grow. I felt invigorated. "That's what I'll do," I thought. "Maybe I can shame my generation into taking action. We're the ones who have brought the world to the current state, so we're the ones who have to straighten it up."

I jumped into the shower and fixed my tear-streamed face. I started humming a little song. My heart was healed again. I now had a new direction.

"Boy, Mom, you really scared me. What happened? You look okay now." Viv wondered at my transformation as she walked into my room.

"Let's go have a bite to eat, and I'll tell you all about it. I really appreciate your coming. This gives me some time to think about my idea." I gave Viv a big hug, grabbed my purse, we and walked into the evening air.

"Listen, Vivi, have you heard that the President has reinstated the draft registration for eighteen and nineteen-year-olds?"

"Not really. Why did that upset you? We were a military family for a long time." Viv was still puzzled.

"All I could think of was that the sacrifice so many of us have made for my son to have a chance at freedom was all for nothing. I almost stroked out at the idea that John might be forced into something he didn't believe in. If he wanted to volunteer, I wouldn't stand in his way;

however, if our country needs people so badly that they have to take boys against their will, I'll offer my own services."

"Mom, what are you talking about? You're too old to join," Vivienne didn't buy my rambling.

"Look, Viv, if all they want is a warm body to fill a uniform, I qualify. If all they want is someone to shoot an enemy, I qualify. If all they want is someone who knows how to survive under stress, I qualify. In other words, what exactly do they want? If I can't pass the basic training, well, then I'll have to concede."

"Have you talked about this to Dad?"

"He has told me many times that my faithful service to him for the past twenty-five years deserved his faithful support of whatever I felt I had to do. I haven't approached him with my newest idea, but I'll call him later tonight. I'm sure he'll support me."

For another hour or so we enjoyed a pizza and talked some more. Viv remained a little doubtful, but she expressed her faith in my good judgment before we called it a night.

Feeling determined and knowing my next step, I called Lee. Would he think I had gone over the edge?

"Love, what will you do if they accept me?" I asked, almost afraid to hear his answer.

"Love, I'm retired from the Air Force, and I'm not stuck to the job I have now. If you are accepted, I'll move with you just like you did when I was in the service. You just follow your heart and do what you think is best. I'm with you." What a guy!

My opportunity to take action came just a week later. The annual Career Fair was taking place in the Pauley Ballroom on campus. As I sauntered in, I noticed a very tall U.S. Marine captain trying to talk a young male student into signing up. I stopped to listen. There was great talk of the many choices a young recruit could have in the Marines. This would be a wonderful chance for a college graduate.

After the young man left, I approached the captain. "I'd like to offer my services," I was very friendly.

The captain looked at me. "Well, what could you do?"

"I speak languages, and I'm physically fit. What I can do depends on what needs to be done."

The captain looked dubious. I went on, "I understand that the country is in great need of more people in the armed services. Why don't you let me fill out an application, and then we'll see how things go."

"Ma'm, I'm going to have to ask you how old you are," he seemed a little embarrassed for such a personal question.

"What do you mean," I asked. "There are parts of me that haven't even been developed yet. My body is constantly replenishing itself. Do you want to know how old my fingernails, hair or skin are?"

"Ma'm, you know what I mean. I mean when were you born?"

"Oh! you want to know what it says on my birth certificate. Do you really think an enemy is interested in that?"

He didn't like the way this argument was going. He apologized. "Sorry Ma'm, I'm not the one who makes the rules. There are age restrictions on enlistments."

"Look, you're just a captain in the Marine Corps. I know that you don't make the rules, but I do know who does make the rules. If you won't let me fill out an application, I want you to tell me that in writing."

He scribbled a quick note: The Marine Corps has missed out on a great lady. She should have come to us about seven years ago.

I smiled all the way back to my dorm room. This note was not much ammunition in my battle, but it was ammunition nevertheless.

I typed out a letter regarding my not being allowed to fill out an application. Copies of the letter and the note went to my congressman and U.S. Senators as well as Van Amberg, a local TV anchorman.

The next morning I got a phone call. "We'd like to interview you as part of the aftermath of the President's proposal to reinstitute the draft."

That afternoon, I was sitting in the courtyard at Stern Hall being interviewed by Ken Maddy. A cameraman was busy filming us as I stated my case. Ken wondered, "Would you actually serve if you were allowed in the service?"

"Of course. My husband and I are used to military life. If I get any encouragement from other Americans of my generation, I'll go forward with my protest."

Ken told me that I'd be on the evening news that night. Lee came to pick me up, so we could all watch the TV News at home. A whole minute was devoted to the "Anti-draft" protests. Among the interviews, my segment was labeled, "Grandma wants to become a Marine." My family cheered me on the screen.

I never heard from any individual or group regarding the age limitations in enlistments. Fine. If people would rather send their kids into battle than take care of the enemy themselves, then I'm okay with that. I had done all I could.

A YEAR OF CELEBRATIONS

It started out just like any other year. We had the holidays behind us, and each one of us had a routine. Lee was working in the Post Office, and John was going to school. Kathy's husband Ted had been transferred with the Air Force to Germany, so Kathy and her little son Teddy moved there with him. Lisa and her husband Les had moved into a mobile home with their little daughter Leilani. Vivienne had moved to Mountain View with her fiancé, Bob. I was continuing to struggle through classes at UC Berkeley.

"Mom, Bob and I are getting married on the 22nd of May." Viv called me all excited.

I was happy for them, but asked, "Why May? That's Finals week here at Cal. Can't you make it in June? Where are you going to have the wedding?"

"Oh, we'll have it in Fairfield, but you won't have to do anything. Bob and I will take care of things."

"Can't you have it in June or July? That way I could play the proper mother of the bride." I was trying to be very diplomatic.

"No, Bob wants it in May."

"Alright, we'll make it somehow. Have you already found the church and the place for the reception? How about the invitations?" I wondered whether Viv had really thought it through.

"Mom, we're just starting, but if you could help, that would be great. We'd like to have a wedding with all the trimmings. White gown, tuxedoes, cake, everything."

"Okay, Vivi, let's do it right. I'll help as much as I can."

From my experience with Lisa's wedding two years before, I knew how much planning and work had to go into a wedding. That occasion had turned into quite a production.

At that time, I was not going to school and had plenty of time to devote to an August wedding. I even made Lisa's bridal gown and the bridesmaid dresses. Despite her pregnancy, Kathy wanted to be a

271

bridesmaid, so we chose a lovely flowing pattern that looked good on all the girls and fit Kathy too. We had the reception at the Elks Lodge with lots of help from friends and relatives.

Lee and I had not been invited to Kathy and Ted's wedding. They simply went to Tahoe and returned to inform us that they were married. I really didn't want Viv's wedding to be that cut and dried.

I decided that I would take "Time-out" from my studies to participate properly in Viv's wedding as the mother of the bride. Perhaps I could take only two classes for the Spring quarter and then return with a full load in the Fall. But no. Bureaucrats, being what they are, did not allow that. I had to withdraw completely and then reapply. Okay. Fine.

So I was home that spring, sewing lovely lavender bridesmaid dresses. Viv came home several times and together we made all the arrangements. I loved playing a significant role in the wedding, and Viv was very appreciative. The only thing that was not perfect about the wedding was the photography. Even though the young lady professed herself to be a professional photographer, she delivered a disappointing product and even lost the negatives.

The highlight of the wedding was Bob singing to Viv as she walked down the aisle with her father.

"Guess what Mom." Whenever any of the kids approached me with that greeting, I was ready for the worst. Lisa said, "I'm going to have another baby." This was good news, not bad.

"Wonderful. When are you due?" I could hardly stop smiling. My family was growing, and I loved being a mother and grandma. I was tempted to give up the whole school thing and devote my time to my family.

"Not till October, and I want you to keep going to school." Lisa could read my mind. She knew how much getting a degree meant to me.

"Yes, I'm all set to go back in August, but I'll be there for you if you need me."

I was more convinced than ever that I needed to finish school. World events were still shaky, and my children and grandchildren would need a set of healthy and informed parents to depend on if things got rough in this country. The way I saw it, things would indeed get rough within my lifetime. There was too much controversy in the media regarding our dependence on oil-producing countries, the war on drugs, contamination of our food supply and a variety of other topics. If I didn't stay level-headed, my family might get confused and buy into the chaos.

So I planned out the rest of the year: my classes in August, our annual birthday party in September, a new baby in October, our twenty-fifth anniversary in November, and our annual Christmas Eve at Gramma's house in December. Somewhere in there, I had to find the time to visit my folks in Southern California and Lee's family in Fresno.

Thank goodness our family didn't waste much time on squabbling. We all knew what we wanted and how to get it. Then we went and did it.

We were visiting Viv and Bob one Friday evening in October when Lisa called.

"Mom, I've gone into labor, and I think I'm going to have the baby tonight." It was time, and everything had gone according to schedule. I thought.

"Is Les going to take you to the hospital?"

"Mom, Les isn't home. He's gone with some guys to Chico," she sounded somewhat embarrassed.

"What in the world is he doing in Chico, when you're nine months pregnant?" I wasn't very pleased with the things I was thinking.

"They like to party there." Okay, enough said.

"Lisa, it will take about two hours for us to get back to Fairfield. How close are your contractions?" I wondered.

"Oh, they just started about an hour ago, and they're still pretty far apart. I'm pretty sure I still have quite a few hours before the baby is born."

"We're leaving in a few minutes. Dad will take care of Leilani, and I will go with you to the hospital if Les isn't back yet," I assured Lisa.

"Thanks, Mom."

At the hospital in Vallejo, Lisa and I settled into a routine. She was in considerable pain, and I was considerably disturbed. I didn't want to show Lisa how annoyed I was with her young husband. I wondered how I could make things better and remembered that I had my textbooks with me. One of my assignments was to read Wordsworth poetry.

"Would you mind if I read some poetry while we're waiting? I have to read this by Monday morning." I explained.

Lisa thought that might be a good idea. She wanted to hear my voice, and if I read, she wouldn't have to answer me.

When the nurse came to check on Lisa, she was amazed. Lisa was all nice and calm, and the birth process was on track.

Soon we were in the delivery room, and I watched my cute little granddaughter Kaala come into the world. Lisa and I were very proud of our accomplishment.

When her husband Les returned, I didn't really have to say anything. He knew, and I had other fish to fry.

I went back to my classes. The single room in the dorm had been assigned to another older woman, so I had to share a double dorm room with a young coed. This meant, of course, that I had to use the common showers down the hall. I didn't mind. I still had a home of my own in Fairfield, and Lee came to pick me up on Friday afternoons.

Plans for our Silver Anniversary were coming along. Lee and I wanted to make up for the wedding we didn't have. I ordered invitations, a cake, live music, catering, and decorations. I bought a beautiful long dress and looked forward to the day. My dad promised to take good pictures, and lots of other relatives and friends planned to attend. My mother was particularly sweet during that time. Without rehashing the difficulties we had endured twenty-five years earlier, we were aware that we now had this opportunity for drawing a little closer.

It turned out to be a wonderful party. I took the memories back to UC Berkeley with me. Whenever I was particularly upset about something I heard or saw, I remembered my lovely family and celebrations to calm me down. There were many occasions to upset me.

One such situation arose in a linguistics class. I was surrounded by about 150 potential doctors, dentists, lawyers and other young professionals. They were taking copious notes while the professor was espousing his opinions. I was probably the oldest person in the large crowd.

Suddenly, I heard the professor explain in all sincerity that older people had a more difficult time learning languages because their hearing deteriorated with age.

"What's this?" I thought to myself. "What kind of nonsense is he telling these young people? What if they actually believe this? Won't that influence the way they treat older people in their professions?"

I had already learned that challenging a professor during a lecture was not productive, so I remained quiet. I did, however, make an appointment with the professor to discuss my concerns. After all, I was living proof that an older person's hearing was keen enough to hear him make such statements. Also, why did the university accept my money for English and Chinese classes despite the belief that older persons weren't able to learn new languages? I wanted to discuss this with the professor. He listened to me, stood by his opinion and never did work my concerns into his lectures.

My challenge, no matter that is was done privately and unobtrusively, earned me another F. I had to retake the class with another professor to earn a better grade and protect my GPA.

Another incident left an impression. While explaining a piece of literature, one English professor made an analogy to the current administration in the White House, Ronald Reagan. Suddenly, he exclaimed, "I hate that swine!"

I was stunned. Such an outburst must certainly have some impact on the young students sitting all around me. I resolved to send a note to the professor regarding the possibility that some young hot shot might take him seriously and try to get rid of the president. I vividly remembered the assassination of President Kennedy and the attempt on President Ford's life. Events like that are not good for the country.

After the next class, the professor asked me to stay. He wanted to discuss the note I had written him. I explained my concern that professors sometimes forget just how much their words influence young people. I had no particular political interests in either party and was neither conservative nor liberal, but I was worried about this country. Our freedoms make us vulnerable, and another assassination would not do anyone any good. This professor understood my concern and did not retaliate. He explained that he had been tear-gassed during a campus protest by state troopers under Governor Reagan. We parted on a friendly basis. Only a few months later, President Reagan was shot.

Somehow I passed the rest of my classes and worked my way toward a diploma. By December 1982 I had earned enough credits to participate in the June 1983 commencement exercises.

In the meantime, I had become a grandmother for the fourth time.

Kathy and Ted were stationed in Germany. The thought that my father and his wife lived only about an hour's drive away gave me some comfort. Still I missed them all, especially my little Teddy. When Kathy wrote to tell me that she was pregnant, I almost went to Germany; however, I had become afraid to fly.

In September 1982, Janine was born, but I would have to wait till February 1983 to meet her.

"Kathy's plane will be landing soon." A large crowd had gathered at the San Francisco international airport. Ted's grandmothers and parents as well as Kathy's sisters and two little nieces were impatiently checking the monitor.

"I can't wait. I'm so nervous." I wondered what my cute little Teddy would be like. How would the little cousins get along?

"There they are, there they are," someone yelled as Ted emerged from the gangway tunnel. Hugs, tears, kisses, pictures. Then we all piled into the cars.

The three sisters rode together. They had always been close and now there was a whole hour on the freeway for chatting.

When Kathy and Viv walked into our living room, they headed straight for the piano and played duets for about an hour. It was as if they had never been apart. Their body language and rhythm told the rest of us that they had a special bond. Tears kept coming to my eyes. How much happiness could I take?

And so we had another occasion to celebrate. "Let's have a great big Baptism party for all four grandchildren," I asked Lee.

"See whether that's what Lisa and Kathy want before you make all kinds of plans," he cautioned.

"Great idea, Mom, we'll contact the church."

The party took place in our half-finished addition to the house.

WHAT NOW, MY LOVE?

Sitting on one's laurels can become quite uncomfortable. After raising my children, graduating from UCBerkeley, and taking care of my house, I found myself with time, time and more time. I didn't want to volunteer in convalescent hospitals anymore, so I kept busy with handicrafts and gardening.

Kathy and Ted had been transferred to Plattsburgh Air Force Base in New York, taking two of my four precious grandbabies with them.

Lisa and Les rented the house next door to us, so I had sweet Leilani and cuddly Kaala close by, but I didn't want to impose on them too much.

John was still living at home, but he and Lee had jobs, so they weren't home during the day.

Viv and Bob lived and worked in San Jose, so we didn't see them very much either.

In other words, the empty nest syndrome threatened to creep into my world.

"So, Marianne, what are you planning now that you have your degree," asked Bob P, our insurance agent during a visit in June.

"Oh, I'm planning to redecorate our home and perhaps write a book. Who knows. I'm open to suggestion."

Bob was also a member of the Solano County Board of Education, "We need substitutes. This year a lot of substitute teachers no longer qualify because they haven't taken the CBEST (California Basic Education Skills Test). We'll probably lose a lot of our subs because they won't pass. Why don't you take the test? We'll put you on the sub list if you pass it."

"Ha, ha Bob, me a teacher! But I read in the paper that the deadline for applying for the test passed yesterday. I guess I'll have to wait till next year," I said with relief. I was far too afraid to speak in front of crowds to be a teacher. "Bob, I would be too nervous. I've heard how students treat substitutes."

"Would you consider taking the test if I can get you in this year? We really do need subs, and I'm sure you'd be fine."

"You know me, Bob, I'm always ready to jump in where angels fear to tread."

He asked to use the phone, and when he was done, he handed me a note and said, "It's all set. Next Wednesday, show up at this time and place at UCDavis. When you get the results, take them to the school district office and ask for an application. Good Luck!"

"Wow!" I thought, "Just like that I have a new direction to go in."

"Love, Bob P. was here. You'd never guess in a million years what he wanted," I told Lee as we were having dinner.

"Well, don't keep me guessing. What are you up to now, Love?" he wanted to know.

"He wants me to be a substitute teacher in Solano County school districts, and I'm seriously considering it. I will have to take the CBEST and pass it and fill out a bunch of applications."

"He has faith in you, and so do I. Go for it."

"Mom, you don't want to be a sub! You have no idea how kids in school treat a sub!" John offered when I told him my new plan.

"Well, I've been treated pretty badly and survived. I think I'll be okay. Besides, I'm used to being in classrooms," I was trying to convince myself rather than John.

"Okay, Mom, just don't let them get you down."

The test was a three hour ordeal in a huge auditorium. This was the first year that all California teachers had to take and pass this test, and it seemed that they were all taking the test with me. The three parts of the test were math, reading and writing. I felt that I had done fairly well, but it was difficult to gauge.

Toward the end of summer vacation the results arrived. I had passed! In fact, in two sections I had achieved a superior rating!

"Why am I so nervous? My heart is pounding like crazy. I'm just going to fill out an application," my mind raced. "What if they actually hire me?"

They did. My first assignment was in a high school German class. My native language, and I had taken some college courses in German at UCB. Besides, German is an Elective, and only students who really want to learn are in this class. I breezed through a very pleasant day.

"Love, it was great! I'd love to be a real teacher and have my own classroom one day." Even though I was exhausted, I had enjoyed my experience. A new dream began.

"Wouldn't you have to go back to college and take more courses?"

"I'm talking about the future, Love," I said. "There is no credential program near here, anyway, and I don't want to leave you or my home. If they ever offer a teaching credential within driving range, I'll consider it. In the meantime, I'm okay with substituting."

"Okay, let's keep that for the future then. Just enjoy yourself." What a guy!

"I'm never going back!" I yelled as I stormed into the house. "What a bunch of brats!"

"Now what?" Lee wondered.

Not all my experiences as a sub were as pleasant as that first day at Armijo High School. Middle schools were particularly challenging. I had certain ideas how a class should behave, and the students had other ideas, such as throwing paper wads, talking out of turn, and walking around without permission. Never mind such shenanigans as a girl bringing out a razor and starting to shave her leg or a boy calling me a f...ing b...ch. All these distractions had to be dealt with at the expense of the time I should have spent with the well-behaved students.

"Love, you know, if you want to quit, I'm with you. You don't have to endure abuse from anyone."

"I know, but I really like teaching. It's just that a few bad kids can ruin a whole day. They draw all the attention, and I'm not experienced enough to prevent that," I explained. "I was just venting about quitting. I'll stick with it and see whether I can learn how to control a class. I'm not going to let a few brats destroy my dream of becoming a teacher."

My dream had become a solid goal, and I was heading in the right direction. I had plenty to do to chase away the "empty nest syndrome" and thus remained a happy homemaker. Our children would not have to worry about "poor old Mom" sitting alone at home. They certainly took advantage of the freedom I gave them.

Chapman College offered a Teaching Credential Program a couple of years later, Despite the expensive units, I was one of the first to sign up. I had not given up my dream of becoming a teacher and getting my own classroom.

It was not easy for a person my age to get a teaching job, but eventually I was hired as a Special Education teacher. I taught for thirteen years in three different school districts (each time getting a little closer to our home) before I retired in 2004.

GRAMMA'S SUMMER SCHOOL

"Wow, that's quite a lunch! You ought to make 'em pay for it." My son, a mail carrier, had just stopped by to say hello to his nephew and three nieces when he made a special delivery in the neighborhood.

"John, they don't have any money, and I'm not going to charge my own daughters for my grandchildren's lunches," I dismissed him at first impulse, but I was intrigued. "John, what if I pay the kids and then charge them for all the things I do for them?"

John looked up in surprise. "Mom, I was just kidding. Don't take everything I say so seriously."

The seed had been planted. By 1988, I had become a substitute school teacher as well as the grandmother of three granddaughters and three grandsons. Our four children were married and living within easy driving range. Most of the grandparents I know have out-of-town or even out-of-state grandchildren. Lee and I considered ourselves very blessed. We were eager to support our family in any way possible. One of the greatest pleasures of my life was the "Gramma School" I conducted during school vacations. Starting in the summer of 1985 my four oldest grandchildren usually arrived early in the morning three or four days a week. Our daughters were grateful for the "day care," and I was grateful for the opportunity to influence my grandchildren. The thought of charging for this precious family experience never entered my mind.

"John, you gave me a good idea. I'm sure I can figure out a simple system; after all, I'm a trained teacher. In the classroom that kind of thing is called a Token Economy," I explained.

John started to roll his eyes, "Mom..."

"Sit down and have some enchiladas with us," I interrupted. "I'll let you know what kind of plan I come up with. For now just enjoy your lunch with the kids."

Leilani had been listening. At ten, she was the oldest at the table. "Gramma, are you really going to charge us for food?"

"Yes, but I'll also pay you for the work you do for me," I assured her.

Now Teddy my nine-year-old grandson got interested. "You're going to pay us, Gramma?"

Even seven-year-old Kaala and six-year-old Janine had stopped eating and were listening to the discussion.

Suddenly, I realized that the whole idea had already taken on a life of its own. The rest would be simple implementation: a checkbook would be perfect for keeping track deposits and withdrawals.

After John left to go back to his mail route, the kids and I cleaned up the kitchen and then got back into our routine.

Our day of "Gramma School" typically started with the Pledge of Allegiance and usually consisted of German language arts and math before the first recess. Depending on the weather, recess could be spent in the swimming pool or by the basketball hoop. Sometimes we walked to the neighborhood park to feed the ducks; sometimes we stayed indoors and played a board game. There were plenty of free-time activities to choose from. Between recess and lunch the time was structured for music. There were simple music theory worksheets as well as piano practice on my brand-new grand piano.

Lunch preparation was my responsibility, but a special assistant was selected each day. The assistant set the table and made sure that each person's cup was in the correct place while the others worked on simple paper and pencil tasks. The decorative plastic cups had been labeled with their names and social security numbers to make memorizing that important information easier.

"Gramma, when are we going to start getting paid?" Leilani and Teddy were still excited about my conversation with John.

"I'll think about it and probably have it worked out by tomorrow. That's **my** homework for tonight. Okay?" Actually, I had already envisioned the checkbook idea and only needed to work out the details.

"Y-a-a-ay!" Teddy was always enthusiastic about new ideas. Now he was hugging his sister and two cousins. "Gramma says we're going to get paid tomorrow!" he yelled as he danced around.

"Easy does it! Teddy," I tried to stem the tide, but there was no holding back. "I tell you what: why don't we design the checks on the computer and print them right now?" I offered.

Now all four of them were jumping around. I walked over to my little IBM PCjr with all four hovering around me. Together we designed the checks, printed them and cut them apart. We were still working on them when Grandpa returned from work. He got off at three o'clock and joined the late afternoon fun.

"Guess what Gramps! Gramma is going to pay us for working here," Teddy was the bearer of this surprise.

"You're what?!" Lee wanted to know with a puzzled look on his face. "How much money is this joke going to cost me?"

"Don't be a grumpy grampy," Leilani soothed him. "We're just going to have pretend checkbooks."

Lee looked quizzically at me, "Tell me about it."

"Okay," I knew whenever he prompted me like that he was ready to listen without raising all kinds of objections. "Here is what I'm going to do."

I laid out my plan:
We would use a checkbook as an accounting tool

- Simple materials
    o Checks designed and printed on my home computer
    o Registers unused ones from our bank account
- I'll write a weekly deposit in the register
    o current legal minimum wage for each hour spent in our house
    o plus any bonuses earned for effort above and beyond
- The kids will write checks to me for expenses
    o current prices for lunches
    o transportation costs for outings
    o fair market price for piano lessons
    o fines for infractions of house rules (i.e., sibling fights, bad language)

Lee nodded, "Sounds like you're just making more work for yourself."

"Love, having the kids here is a lot of work, anyway. Having a system to clearly show them how much their work and my work is worth can only be a good thing. Just imagine how much they will learn from dealing with everyday actual dollar-and-cent experiences. Teddy and

Leilani are old enough to learn about the relationship between work and money. Once Janine and Kaala know how to add and subtract decimal numbers, I'll prepare checkbooks for them, too."

"It's just that I got nervous when Teddy declared that you were going to pay them for their work," Lee assured me. "It sounds like a good idea to me. Can I charge them when I fix a toy or do something else for them?"

"Sure, they are so excited about getting checkbooks, they're ready to write checks to anyone that asks for money," I smiled as I remembered their enthusiasm.

And so, in one day, an idea was born. I put up a time chart where each child posted the hours to the nearest half hour. By the time the parents came to pick up the kids we had checkbook covers, registers and the first ten checks ready. My daughters were just as skeptical as Lee had been, but after my explanation they thought it was brilliant.

"We'll see," I cautioned them. "It's all in the consistent practice. If we can keep the system working for two weeks, we'll get into the habit, and it will be easy to continue. If I let even one lunch slide without making them write checks, they won't take it seriously anymore."

Both Lisa and Kathy wanted to know the same thing Lee had asked, "Can we make them write checks to us, too?"

"I don't see why not. It would probably be a good idea, though, to make sure that it has something to do with coming to Gramma School at my house; otherwise, they'll get confused. Remember, this has nothing to do with getting an allowance or whatever system you have worked out with them. This is an accounting system for Gramma School."

Throughout that summer Teddy and Leilani diligently kept track of their many expenses. Since we had a variety of activities, the check-writing became an automatic behavior during the last half hour of our day. Kaala and Janine worked hard on their math skills because they wanted checkbooks too.

"Grandma, will you still have Gramma School next year?" Kaala asked one day.

"God willing and the creek doesn't rise, Lover, I'll be here waiting for you," I replied.

"Then I'll get a checkbook too, won't I?" Janine walked up with a hopeful expression on her face.

"You bet, Sweetheart," I smiled. "You're getting better and better in your math, so you'll be ready to keep your checkbook register straight. Next year, you and Kaala will get your checkbooks."

Both the little girls happily skipped away. There was a nice cool doughboy swimming pool in our backyard, and it was a hot day. Soon the joyful sounds of children splashing each other made my heart glad. How blessed I was! All four had already copied their pages out of a German children's book and practiced their piano pieces for the upcoming recital.

Oh, those recitals! Here was another idea that evolved over the years. It started in 1982 as a simple desire to pull my family together for an annual party. We chose September because Lee and two of our four children were born in that month. Our September Party would be a family reunion as well as a good opportunity to celebrate their birthdays. By 1985, the year I started my little Gramma School, our parties had become a family tradition.

I told the kids that I decided to show at the next party what they had learned that summer. "Grandma, I'm going to be too nervous," Kaala was shaking her head.

"Sweetheart, you've played those pieces a million times," I exaggerated. "You'll be fine. Your mommy and daddy will be so proud."

Before our first recital, we were gathering in our school room while the audience was getting anxious in the living room. No one knew what to expect.

To the delight of everyone, the performances proceeded without a hitch. Our efforts were met with a great round of applause. Then we enjoyed a good meal and some party games before calling it a day.

Each year the family looked forward to our September parties. The preparations for our recitals became the focus of our summer work. Two of Leilani's cousins, Puanani and Cheala, had also joined us for two days a week, expanding my little group to six. The only boy, Teddy, held up admirably against the girls. He could outtalk and outplay all five of them. We learned to include an emcee and poetry in the recitals. We even planned printed programs.

The 1988 Recital was particularly exciting. The audience sat expectantly in the living room.

Suddenly, the stereo blasted a rendition of "When the Saints come Marching In," and our little group marched out carrying the music instruments I had accumulated over the years. To keep the kids focused on their "public performance," I had them walk around in a circle and sing another song together. Then the solo performances began. The parents were enchanted with their dressed-up children as they approached the piano one-by-one and seriously played their pieces. Each performer also recited a poem to a well-deserved round of applause.

"That was fun, Grandma, can we do this again for Christmas?" Leilani wondered.

"Then we'll have to learn some Christmas carols, but will we have time?" I asked.

"Yeah, yeah! We'll come back during the Thanksgiving break and there's some time during the Christmas break. Sometimes we could even come on weekends to practice," Teddy was being very generous with my time.

"Okay, I'll work it out with your parents. Let's plan to perform a nice Christmas recital before opening the presents on Christmas Eve."

"A-w-w-w," suddenly a Christmas recital didn't seem to be such a good idea. "Why can't we open our presents first?" Four disappointed faces crowded around me.

"Look, I don't know yet. It's only September. Let me work out the details with your parents. If there's any more whining, you'll have to write me a $50 fine from your checkbook."

"Never mind, Grandma," Teddy protected his new-found wealth. By the end of that summer we were very proud of the nearly $500 he and Leilani had earned. The checkbook register had made their hard work and consequent earnings real.

"Really, Grammy, I'm sure whatever you plan will be fine," Leilani chimed in. "Don't be so impatient, Teddy. We'll still get lots of presents, even if we have to open them a little later," she turned to her cousin.

Apparently, my idea of teaching accountability through the checkbooks had achieved the desired results. Both Teddy and Leilani had learned that their behavior directly influenced their rewards. With that system in place, I didn't have to use any other consequences, such as "Time-out" or "Yelling" or "Spanking" or "Telling your Mother." I simply reminded an offender to "Write me a check for a fine."

As time went on, the system became self-sustaining. By the summer of 1989, Kaala and Janine had both earned their checkbooks with their math skills. When their mothers came to pick them up, the girls proudly displayed the registers as if they were Olympic Gold Medals.

One afternoon, Leilani aggravated me with a negative attitude. After she had balked at a task, I said, "Okay, then write me a $50 fine."

She retorted, "Who cares? It's not real money, anyway!"

I was momentarily stunned but calmly asked her, "What makes you think so?"

"My dad said that these stupid checkbooks are just pretend anyway!"

"Oh, is that so?" My mind was racing. "You mean when I take you bowling and you write me a check, that's not real? Or when I feed you a great lunch of Tacos and you pay me with a check, that's not real? Or do you mean that all the work you do here is not real?"

She said, "We're just playing. It's like "Ducky Bucks" or some other stupid thing in school. It's not real money that we can spend in a store."

"Leilani," I sat down and took her seriously. "Listen to me. I know exactly what you mean. This is the same problem some adults have. They think their credits cards are not real either, so they just go to a store and buy anything they want. You are right. This is not real. It's a system to keep track of the time you spend here and the things you do. It's also a system to keep track of the things I do for you."

"Yeah, I understand that, Grandma," Leilani had calmed down, "but what's the good of getting more and more dollars then? What are we going to do with the leftover

money when we don't have Gramma School anymore?"

Secretly, I was thrilled at this evidence of critical thinking. Outwardly, I needed to find an answer to her excellent question.

On the spur of the moment, I answered, "Leilani, on the day you graduate from High School, I'll turn all the leftover dollars in your checkbook into cash dollars you can spend in any store."

"Grandma, where are you going to get all that money?" she almost screamed out with wide open eyes.

"Leilani, when you make me proud by graduating from High School, I'll somehow get the money even if I have to sell my house." Of course, I translated "sell" to "second mortgage" in my mind. I had been generous enough with my grandkids that they trusted me to have enough money to cover my promises.

"Teddy, come here! You won't believe this!" Leilani yelled.

"I'm busy playing Legos. Leave me alone." Teddy was being lazy.

"It has to do with money and it's important. Come on everybody. Grandma just promised something." They all came running.

I had made it a habit to keep making promises to a minimum. Usually, I thought very carefully before promising anything. I wanted the kids to trust me.

Once they were all gathered around me, I explained my plan to them, "When you graduate from High School, you can write me a check to cash in all the money you still have in your checkbook. Then I will give you the actual American dollars that you can spend anywhere in town."

"Are you serious?" Teddy was skeptical.

"Teddy, I just told Leilani that it is a great accomplishment to graduate from High School. I would give you a graduation present anyway. This way, I can just look in your checkbook to see how much I should give you. Don't you think that's a good idea?"

"Man, I'm never going to pay for my lunch or piano lessons anymore. I'll just save my money!" Teddy was always thinking.

"That's not the way it works, Teddy. You'll still have to pay your expenses around here. You can't save all your money. Some of it will have to be spent," I explained. "But notice that your balance keeps going up and up. By the time you and Leilani graduate in 1997, you might have $5000 or more."

"Wow!" Both Leilani and Teddy were breathless.

"Gramma, what about Kaala and me?" Janine piped up.

"Of course, Sweetheart! This goes for you two too."

"You said yoo-too-too, Gramma. That's funny," Kaala repeated. "Tell me again what you're going to do. I don't understand it."

"Kaala, right now you are only in the third grade. You know that you will be going to school a long time. If you keep going to school and getting good grades, you will graduate from High School in 1999, and

Janine will graduate in 2000. On the day you graduate, I will look at your register and see how much money you have in your checkbook. Whatever you have, whether it is $100 or $1000, you can write me a check, and I will give you the real American money for it.

"Dang! Did you know that, Leilani?" wide-eyed Kaala asked her sister.

"Gramma just explained it to me. I didn't know that's what she had in mind when she first gave us those checkbooks." Leilani was still somewhat skeptical.

"To be honest, I didn't know I had this in mind at first either, but sometimes good ideas just happen." I explained. "Now it's time to get back to work. Please get out your math folders."

All four gladly went to their cubbies to get their folders out and start working.

THE EVOLUTION OF
THE CHECKBOOK

Over the years it was simple for the first four grandchildren to keep track of their accounts. We continued our summer school every year until Leilani and Teddy were in high school. They didn't come quite as frequently as before, but they kept adding to their balances.

As five more grandchildren joined the family, we had to adjust our system. Leilani's brothers, Keoki was born in 1986 and Kimo in 1988. John's children, Eric was born in 1990 and Kelli in 1993. Vivi's daughter Leah was born in 1996. For several years, I continued Gramma's Summer School with Keoki, Kimo, Eric and Kelli, but it had become much more sporadic. Also, John's family moved to Sacramento, making our contact too infrequent for the checkbook idea. Leah lived out of town and never had the chance to participate.

I had to think of some other way to be fair to the younger five grandchildren. Since much of the outcome for the oldest four depended on their success in high school, I made an adjusted deal with the younger five.

I explained my new plan to them:

- Every high school semester A = adds $200 to the checkbook
- Every high school semester B = adds $50 to the checkbook
- Every high school semester C = adds nothing
- Every high school semester D = subtracts $50 from the check-book
- Every high school semester F = subtracts $200 from the checkbook

The boys agreed that this would be fair, since they couldn't come over as much as the other grandchildren.

"This means I will want to see your high school transcript, you know," I told them as seriously as I could.

"Yes, Gramma, we know!" They rolled their eyes in unison.

At Leilani's graduation, Lee and I happily handed her a check for nearly $5000. She assured all the others that Gramma kept her promise.

"You'd all better do well in school and graduate," she admonished her brothers. She already knew that Teddy, Kaala and Janine would do well. They also earned their cash pay-out because they had acquired a life-long interest in learning. Leilani knew that her little brothers were a different story.

Despite some bumps in the road, each one graduated on time. Keoki, Kimo and Eric received their money "No strings attached."

"Here you are, you've earned it!" I said handed each one the money. I fondly remembered their sincere efforts in playing the piano, learning German and especially "being haive" (as Teddy used to call behaving).

At this writing, Kelli and Leah are still attending school, but there is little doubt that they will achieve their goals, too.

LOOKING BACK

Writing this book has given me a chance to get a clear vision of my personal history. Throughout the years I evolved from a little girl who couldn't write the cursive ***a***'s on a slate into an educated grandmother who uses a computer to publish her own book. I can see that many people contributed to my exciting life and encouraged me along the way. I appreciate them for that.

It seems that one story leads to another, and one memory leads to another. My mind's eye recalls a number of other stories that have not yet taken shape: our grandson Teddy's illness and death, my husband's fascinating Chinese family history, my stepfather's revenge on me, and my teaching career in Special Education. Who knows? Perhaps in time I'll write those stories, too.

·

CPSIA information can be obtained at www.ICGtesting.com
Printed in the USA
BVOW03*2351150114

342032BV00003B/19/P